BREAKING BREAD

The Filmic Foodscape of Postwar Italy

Food for Thought
Food for Pleasure
Food for Change

Series Editors
Jayeeta (Jo) Sharma (Toronto)
H. Rosi Song (Durham)
Robert Davidson (Toronto)

Editorial Advisory Board
Cristiana Bastos (Lisbon)
Shyon Baumann (Toronto)
Daniel Bender (Toronto)
Andrea Borghini (Milan)
Miranda Brown (Michigan)
Sidney Cheung (Hong Kong)
Simone Cinotto (Gastronomic Sciences)
Tracey Deutsch (Minnesota)
Jean Duruz (South Australia)
Rebecca Earle (Warwick)
Beth Forrest (Culinary Institute of
    America)
Michael Innis-Jiménez (Alabama)
Alice Julier (Chatham)
Lindsay Kelley (New South Wales)
Zeynep Kiliç (Alaska)
Mustafa Koç (Toronto Metropolitan)
Charles Levkoe (Lakehead)
Ken Macdonald (Toronto)
Raúl Matta (Göttingen)
Massimo Montinari (Bologna)
Fabio Parasecoli (New York)
Jeffrey Pilcher (Toronto)
Elaine Power (Queen's)
Signe Rousseau (Cape Town)
Kyla D. Tompkins (Pomona)

Breaking Bread

The Filmic Foodscape of Postwar Italy

NIKI KIVIAT

UNIVERSITY OF TORONTO PRESS
Toronto Buffalo London

ISBN 978-1-4875-6464-3 (cloth)   ISBN 978-1-4875-6466-7 (EPUB)
                                   ISBN 978-1-4875-6465-0 (PDF)

Library and Archives Canada Cataloguing in Publication

Title: Breaking bread : the filmic foodscape of postwar Italy / Niki Kiviat.
Names: Kiviat, Niki, author
Series: Culinaria (University of Toronto Press)
Description: Series statement: Culinaria | Includes bibliographical
   references and index.
Identifiers: Canadiana (print) 20250243245 | Canadiana (ebook)
   20250243296 | ISBN 9781487564643 (cloth) | ISBN 9781487564650 (PDF) |
   ISBN 9781487564667 (EPUB)
Subjects: LCSH: Motion pictures – Italy – History – 20th century. |
   LCSH: Food in motion pictures.
Classification: LCC PN1993.5.I88 K58 2025 | DDC 791.430945 – dc23

Cover design: Will Brown
Cover image: Unsplash.com / Natallia Nagorniak

We wish to acknowledge the land on which the University of Toronto Press
operates. This land is the traditional territory of the Wendat, the Anishnaabeg,
the Haudenosaunee, the Métis, and the Mississaugas of the Credit First Nation.

This book has been published with the assistance of Greenwich Country
Day School.

University of Toronto Press acknowledges the financial support of the
Government of Canada, the Canada Council for the Arts, and the Ontario Arts
Council, an agency of the Government of Ontario, for its publishing activities.

For Phoebe

Contents

Illustrations

Table

Acknowledgments

In my twenties, I was obsessed with the following: the complicated histories of Italy, foreign films, and experimenting in the kitchen. How exciting that these diverse interests came to form the cornerstones of this project. I thank Barbara Faedda and Elizabeth Leake for pushing me to embark upon and persevere through such a labyrinth. I would also like to thank Nelson Moe, Daniele De Feo, Ara Merjian, Claudia Bernardi, and Francesca Calamita for cultivating my interest in Italian food studies, inspiring new avenues and arguments of this manuscript, and seeing the light behind early drafts. Carlo Arrigoni, Irene Bulla, Jo Ann Cavallo, Massimiliano Delfino, Jenny Rhodes, and Julia Sirmons powered through my big ideas, too. This project has been strengthened in so many ways because of all of you.

In 2018, I was honoured with the Austin Oldrini Travel Fellowship, with which I was able to conduct research at the Mario Gromo Bibliomediateca in Turin. Thank you to Fabio Pezzetti for guiding my library research, and special thanks to Carla Ceresa for assisting me in the archives. These findings are most clearly shown in my chapter on Totò.

Six years later, the final iterations of this project were undertaken with great support from Academia Barilla in Parma and the Cineteca di Bologna. While this return trip to Italy lasted only five days, these last stages somehow felt effortless. Enormous thanks to Dr. Giancarlo Gonizzi for curating an impressive list of historical and primary sources, especially my access to every issue of *La Cucina Italiana* since its reprisal in 1952. An equally as hearty thank you to Davide Badini, Roberto Chiesi, Anna Fiaccarini, Emiliano Lecce, and Luca Miu for compiling newspaper articles on all the films and cast in question; the chapter on Sophia Loren in particular benefited from these new interviews and commentaries.

I am so thankful for those outside the world of Italian studies, and outside the Academy altogether, who dedicated a tremendous amount of time to read first drafts of my work, as well as write and conference with me over the years. Many thanks to Drs. Eleonora Sartoni, Erica Drennan, and Almu Marín-Cobos for their friendship and insightful comments throughout the entire project; it was an honour to write alongside you all.

In the formation of this monograph, I am especially indebted to Drs. Chase Gregory and Christina Lopez for their immense support, across state lines. I am grateful to Drs. Isabella Bertoletti, Erica Moretti, Francesca Calamita, and Claudia Sbuttoni for welcoming me into their seminars as a guest lecturer; Chapters 2 and 3 were honed in part by the thought-work behind those talks. And though our collaborations are on outside projects, I also want to thank Drs. Eilis Kierans and Serena J. Rivera for joining me in unpacking the messy nexus of food studies, our conversations evolving into beautiful volumes of their own.

I thank Kate Kent, Stephanie Berland, Dr. Nicole Bouranis, Carter Rogers, Keli Young, Amanda Yepez, Heather Dow, and Taylor Stern for their endless support and the joys of friendship. I also want to thank Heather and Carter especially for taking the time to proofread my work very diligently and astutely.

The COVID-19 pandemic threw the entire world for a loop – and that's putting it lightly. For more than two years, everything was in flux: masks, zooms, social distancing, the pursuit of new hobbies and projects. Fear and devastation loomed outside, but this book would be nothing without that time and isolation: the quiet and space within which I reformulated old research into the pages before you today.

Over those two years, a lot happened – that's also putting it lightly. Ben, Suzy, and I left the bustle of Brooklyn for life outside the city, not unlike Adua and her friends in Chapter 3. I am indebted to you both for your support and warmth, especially when life got tumultuous: new house, new surroundings, new stressors, new lifestyle. But oh so much joy. I love you both to the moon and beyond.

With our move, I bid farewell to my time in the Academy, joining the faculty at Greenwich Country Day School. This book would not have been completed without the unbelievable support of the administration: Adam Rohdie, Jackie Jenkins, Dr. Chris Winters, Dr. Andrew Ruoss, and Lauren Waller. My life in Connecticut has been made all the brighter by my new friends and colleagues: Dr. Trevor Aleo, Mary Alindato, Dr. Anna Cruz, Kosanna Poon, TJ Ramirez, Dr. Ben Schwartz, Josh Swift, and the entire World Languages Department. I am especially grateful to Trevor and Anna, who helped me to make sense of Marco Ferreri's "non-sense." I also thank Dr. Nate Haag and Ez Homonoff for joining Trevor and me in our weekly writing group in the home-stretch of this project.

Finally, I would like to thank my mom and dad, Mary and John, for always pushing me to be my best. I would like to thank my stepparents, Steve and Sue, for their kind, attentive ears, and a constant willingness to help. I'm forever moved, shocked even, by the celebratory pride, genuine curiosity, and countless hours of babysitting that the Kiviats and the Birnbaums have showered me with – thank you all for believing in me.

People say that publishing a book is like having a baby – something else that put my life and work into perspective. In certain ways that statement is true: the adrenaline, the screen-time in the wee hours, the tears of frustration and exhaustion. But at the end of your labours lies a beautiful, live creature of which you are forever proud. Phoebe, this work is dedicated to you: You are the greatest masterpiece of my life.

BREAKING BREAD

The Filmic Foodscape of Postwar Italy

Introducing the Filmic Foodscape
of the *Boom*

The following is an examination of Italy's postwar filmic foodscape: a gastronomic *mise en scène* as a way of investigating moments of continuity with prewar traditions, but also denoting drastic breaks with the familiar. The historical premise for such work is the *boom economico*, or the Economic Miracle, which categorizes the decades following the Second World War. These are the years in which Western Europe revitalized its infrastructure and experienced demonstrable fiscal growth, thanks in part to the funds disbursed through the European Recovery Program (ERP), better known as the Marshall Plan. By way of the Plan, named after US Secretary of State George C. Marshall, the United States offered financial assistance to sixteen European nations, contingent on their rejection of Communism. Western Europe's rejection of Soviet politics would admit them entry into America's "irresistible empire."

Tied to these countries' receipt of billions of dollars of Reconstruction funds was the importation of the American way of life: a hegemony of soft power, built on the allure of big-brand goods.[1] The propaganda was rich: Imagine summers of the postwar era, complete with baseball, hamburgers and hot dogs, and Coca-Cola![2] People imagined that by subscribing to American capitalism, especially the "middling cuisine" of the working and salaried middle classes, the hunger, poverty, and destruction rampant across Europe could vanish.[3]

This book, in turn, focuses on the case of Italy, zooming in on its cinema as a veritable response to such historic changes: depictions of the hypnotic allure of, as well as the militant resistance against, American-style consumption. On Italian soil, the sparkle and innovations of the suburban American home went toe-to-toe with the rationalism and science behind Soviet advancements. As a visual of such a clash, one might consider the Moscow World Fair of 1959, the site of the Kitchen Debate between US Vice President Richard Nixon and Soviet Premier Nikita Khrushchev. Historian Victoria de Grazia offers the following portrait:

> The Soviets had shown the latest advances in space exploration, including full-size models of the three Sputniks, advances in agricultural technology, peaceful uses of atomic energy, and their latest-model automobiles. Only as an afterthought did they add a couple of "way of life" touches, a fashion show and a kitchen. By contrast, the U.S. exhibit was entirely dedicated to the American way of life. The 50,000-square-foot main exhibition hall, enveloped by a fan-shaped aluminum roof, was divided into two areas: "the house of culture," with a diorama of American life; and a "house of items," chock-full of consumer goods. Between one exhibition and another, the fair included three kitchens, the one set up by General Foods and General Mills to prepare ready-made cakes, frozen, and other convenience foods; Whirlpool's Miracle Kitchen; and the color-coordinated kitchen that was the center of the three-bedroom ranch house, jokingly called "Splitnik" to call attention to the walkway that enabled visitors to cut across the interior.[4]

The "Splitnik" illustrated in figure I.1 – the interior of the "house of items" literally cut through to allow for visitors' exploration and awestruck reactions – is a metaphor for the identity crises of the postwar West, with Italy geographically and psychologically caught in the middle. Its filmic foodscape is thus situated amid clashing value systems, socioeconomic stratification, and the debate between the conveniences and mesmerizing novelties of American consumption on the one hand, and the traditions and austerity – *la cucina povera* – of Italy's own eating habits on the other. Like the construction of the American home on enemy Russian soil, Italian films in this period captured massive cranes, gargantuan housing projects climbing towards the sky, planes and helicopters, and the Fiat 500. As new homes were constructed, there was a kitchen revolution: Italy's foodscape rebuilt. This book, thus, presents a filmic trajectory of such continuities and changes: the grappling with recent hunger, and how that hunger morphs on screen from a physical into a spiritual desire.

Continuities and Breaks with Italy's Eating Traditions

Overall, simplicity and rusticity perhaps best define Italians' relationship with food in recent history. Historians underscore Italy's austerity, dating back to price controls and rationing under Fascism, as well as sharecropping systems which determined the country's agricultural output.

Figure I.1. Nikita Khrushchev (second from left) pointing his finger at Richard Nixon (second from right). The two leaders are standing beside the model kitchen display part of America's exhibition at the Moscow World Fair of 1959: the site of their contentious Kitchen Debate. Photo by Howard Sochurek – The LIFE Picture Collection/Getty Images.

Carol Helstosky emphasizes how Italy's food choices derived from contests of power; food was a resource that had to be managed in order to preserve the order and productivity of a nation.[5] Under Fascism, the government called for propagandistic "battles," working to diminish Italy's export markets and discourage consumers from buying foreign goods, thereby seeking to increase the domestic production of foodstuffs, such as wheat.[6] Thus, across the Fascists' twenty-year regime and later, the war, as they navigated tight rations and the increasing monopoly of the black market, Italians learned to "make do": to survive on whatever resources were available. Food rationing called for a wide array of substitutes – chicory, barley coffee, chestnut meal, synthetic oils[7] – and leftovers became the subject of entire cookbooks.[8]

The consequences of "making do" were twofold. The need to stretch and substitute ingredients sparked great culinary creativity, inspiring housewives to convert rations into healthy, simple, yet pleasurable meals.[9] Authors of cookbooks and other domestic literature promoted the healthfulness and simplicity of the Italian diet, judging it superior to the heavier diets of Northern Europe, and they encouraged housewives to make versatile recipes such as *minestra*: "simple and inexpensive, it was defined by one author as 'a dish that keeps the population healthy and strong and demonstrates our fairly simple way of life.'"[10] Thus, Italians consumed a rather limited diet of cheap ingredients capable of sustaining farmers and manual labourers, adapting their food choices to government interventions and suggestions by the media and propaganda campaigns.

In addition, in the absence of food, there was a heightened emphasis on conviviality and family values: a feeling of togetherness that existed independently of how much (or how little) food was on the table. There was a positive spin put on material deprivation. Thus, these foods and rhythms of eating became so habitual, so ingrained in the culture, that after Fascism, Italians continued to uphold and even treasure the simplicity of their diet. Between the years 1948 and 1958, the Italian diet changed, but largely in terms of the quantity and the availability of novel foodstuffs. As consumers' disposable incomes increased, the Italian plate expanded calorically, allowing for more meat as well as exotic and pre-prepared products, such as tropical fruits and cake mixes. Economist Carmela D'Apice notes that, between 1951 and the end of the decade, consumption of bread products declined from 21.1 to 15.3 per cent, whereas meat consumption increased from 17.6 to 21.5 per cent; end-of-decade findings also revealed that 5.1 per cent of total food expenditures were on sugar, cocoa, and sweets – a criterion absent from 1951 data altogether.[11] Historian Emanuela Scarpellini echoes D'Apice's findings, but she adds that "traditional" hallmarks of Italian cuisine were still upheld:

> What increased, even exploded, was the consumption of food for the "rich," once too expensive and limited to the elite. In comparison with the 1930s, all dairy products (milk, cheese, and eggs) doubled. Wine consumption increased, and beer even more, but what increased most of all were three symbolic products: beef, sugar, and coffee. The average housewife of 1970 finally enjoyed a choice of food that was rich and varied. The miserable ingredients of the past were put aside, although this did not mean she rejected some of the characteristic foods of traditional Italian cooking; in fact, she consumed 173 kilograms of wheat and 47 kilograms of tomatoes a year.[12]

Isolating the symbolic value that Scarpellini assigned to beef, historian Rachel Laudan reads America's development of the hamburger as a symbol of its growing hegemony – how, from Japan to Brazil to Mexico, elites decided that their countries must modernize their cuisine along Western lines or fall behind economically and politically.[13] Was Italy to follow suit? Indeed, consumption of meat rose in this period, and the average caloric intake had doubled since the war, but people still ate rather conservatively, preferring a diet largely based on pasta, vegetables, legumes, and bread.

There was splashy advertising for new appliances and pre-prepared products, but the menus presented in domestic literature remained largely the same, continuing to instruct women on shopping and cooking economically. One magazine in 1959 promoted a contest, challenging women to prepare a meal for a family of five for under 1,000 lire; the winning entry, totalling 810 lire, consisted of grated carrots, semolina *gnocchi*, meatballs, spinach, and baked apples, served with bread and wine.[14] Hunger was decidedly a thing of the past as the nation encountered abundance for the first time. Nevertheless, Italians' consumption habits changed little, as families purchased and ate the same ingredients as before, and the media, too, perpetuated the prowess and allure of austerity.

America's Soft Power in Italy: "Some Quirk Which We Can't Locate"

The Marshall Plan has historically been hailed by Americans as the impetus for Europe's Economic Miracle, but to what extent was it "miraculous" for Italy? This section considers the boosts to Italian infrastructure brought about by the Plan, but of greater interest is America's expanding hegemony: the tentacles of soft power extended across the recovering continent, as depicted in Italian media. The Oxford Dictionary defines "miraculous" as that which "brings welcome consequences." Yet, given Italy's legacy of austerity and conservatism, not only was reception of the Plan mixed, but it revealed deeper issues in the national psyche. With the disbursement of ERP funds began a trend of US goods and funds, and of American-born marketing innovations, without ever addressing the true nucleus of the problem: the fatigue and lack of confidence pervading Italy's first years as a Republic in the wake of two decades of Fascist interventions and, subsequently, world war. The time had come, apparently, for Italy to "buy" happiness,[15] yet the Marshall Plan could not undo the traumas underlying the nation's instability.[16]

Reckoning with its legacy of Fascism and having weathered the clashes of Allied and Nazi forces, Italy was one of the greatest recipients of ERP funds, receiving a total of approximately $1,204 million from the Plan's inception in 1948 to 1952.[17] Yet, almost immediately, the Plan was met with caution. In September 1947, just three months after Marshall's announcement of the Plan in his Commencement address at Harvard, James Dunn, US ambassador to Italy, warned, "While the Marshall Plan is still a light of hope in the dismal road Italy walks, it is a dim and distant one for the weary traveler."[18] ERP funds were to be used for the rebuilding of infrastructure, and in this regard, Italy's revitalization was partly successful: 90 per cent of funds were invested in public works projects.[19] The *Cassa per il Mezzogiorno*, proposed in 1950, was a foremost initiative of the Italian South. Modelled on the Tennessee Water Authority, part of America's New Deal, the *Cassa* oversaw agrarian reforms: the redevelopment of irrigation and drainage systems and aqueducts.[20] Amid trends of increased industrialization and urbanization, however, *Cassa* improvements were, at best, obsolete and unbalanced, as only 12 per cent of ERP funds were distributed to the South – compared to the 65 per cent directed to the North, over half of which (33 per cent) went to Piedmont alone.[21] At worst, these reforms were irrelevant, patching up a nation that required a more profound reckoning.

Pushing instead for a "politics of productivity," the Marshall Plan did not necessarily intend to create a consumers' Europe.[22] Despite the millions of dollars and cans and boxes of goods donated through the ERP and, before that, the United Nations Relief and Rehabilitation Administration (UNRRA), there was uncertainty about what such goods were and how they were to be used. In 1947, Sue Sadow, technical food specialist for the Italian UNRRA mission, developed and distributed a volume of 121 pages and 115 recipes, describing what the goods were and how they were to be used and conserved, suggesting ways to prepare preserved fish, dried legumes, and powdered "soup": Composed of a flour made from dried peas or different kinds of beans, this became the base for various dishes, even tagliatelle and pizza.[23] The instructions made these foods alien, unrecognizable to the Italian palette.

In addition, the makeup of Italian homes and towns was not on par with America's expectations, either. With the refrigerator alone, the American home appeared light-years ahead of Italy's hardware. Jonathan Rees outlines the history of Frigidaire's rollouts from the 1930s to the 1970s:

> … A model from 1970 appeared to differ greatly from a model produced forty years earlier. Frigidaire, for example, introduced the first sealed rotary compressor in 1933, matching color exteriors for its entire appliance line in 1954, modular appliances in 1956, and frost-proof freezer systems

for refrigerators in 1958. The 1960s saw a huge variety of new features for refrigerators: automatic icemakers, icemakers inside refrigerator doors, adjustable shelves (in the doors and in the cabinet), vegetable crispers, meat keepers, covered butter and cheese compartments, charcoal filters to soak up food odors, just to name a few.[24]

While American families were toying with these new features, the rest of the Western world could not keep up. By 1957, over 90 per cent of American homes had refrigerators; Italy, France, and West Germany all hovered just over 10 per cent.[25] In November 1958, of 25,000 Italian families surveyed by Doxa, an average of 84 per cent of homes did not have a television, refrigerator, or washing machine: 81 per cent in the North, and 88.4 per cent in the South, Sicily, and Sardinia; in cities with populations over 100,000, only 25 per cent of homes had refrigerators.[26] A 1960 study by economists Giorgio Fuà and Sylos Labini reported even more drastic results: 42 per cent of homes across Italy did not have private toilets; 69 per cent did not have baths; 85 per cent had no gas; and 47 per cent had no running water.[27] How, then, could Italy function in America's world of big brands and supermarketing?

In the supermarket space, one sees the persistence of old consumption and purchasing habits despite the introduction of groundbreaking novelties; these incongruities defined eating during the Economic Miracle. Several historians report on the advent of the supermarket in 1957. Scarpellini records the Italians' fascination with the novel pre-packaged and frozen products adorning the supermarket's fluorescent-lit aisles and filling shopping carts. Her commentary below reflects the contrasts of the "Splitnik" kitchen – a euphoria of American consumer novelties mixed with conservative values of austerity and practicality:

According to the newspapers there were "God's gifts from all over the world": sharks' fins, swallows' nests, Neapolitan mozzarella, all kinds of boxes and tins, meat in clear film wrapping, an entire department dedicated to quick-frozen food (thank goodness for the fridge!), not to mention "normal" food at bargain prices. The customers were ecstatic. An elderly lady stopped a manager to enthuse: "My relatives in America have for years told me of these wonderful stores … I have prayed over the years that I might see one and shop in it before I must pass on … believe me, this is the answer to all my prayers," while another lectured: "Just remember this next time you vote, they don't have any of these in Russia." It was just like having America in Italy. One's first visit to the supermarket was unforgettable.[28]

Table I.1. Refrigeration adoption rates around the world in 1957

Country	Adoption Rate (%)
United States	90
Canada	84
Australia	70
Sweden	50
New Zealand	26
Denmark	25
West Germany	14
France	12
Italy	11

Data source: "Refrigerator a Luxury in British Homes," *Times of London*, 25 September 1957.

However, Italy's reception of the new shopping space was not universally positive. When Nelson Rockefeller and his proxy, Richard Boogaart, introduced Supermarkets Italiani SpA to Milan in 1958, the city was already home to 14,000 outlets that sold some kind of food – those groceries designed in tandem with the rhythms of Italian consumption and with what kitchens could, and could not, sustain. Despite seizing full control of the production, refrigeration, packaging, and shipping sectors, and therefore offering products at one low price, unburdened by a lengthy, costly chain of distribution, the supermarket was jettisoned for the neighbourhood grocery. Italy's infrastructure of narrow stone streets and dense concentration in urban areas was not suited to the mammoth supermarkets and wide-ranging parking lots of, for example, suburban California. Second, Italy's shopping habits – intimate connections and friendships with the neighbourhood *fruttivendolo*, butcher, etc.; a credit system; shopping at specialty shops for daily necessities instead of shopping *en masse* – did not align with the anonymity and independence of the supermarket experience. With supermarket expenditures comprising only 2 per cent of Italy's food shopping in 1971, a disappointed Boogaart poignantly remarked, "If I were a psychoanalyst, I would say that they [Italians] had some kind of quirk which we can't locate ..."[29]

The introduction of goods and ideas representative of the American way of life thus prompted three different paths for Italy's economic recovery: accept and embed these goods into Italian culture, thereby accepting America's political values delivered with their consumer durables and innovations; reject the goods, and thus keep American capitalism at bay; or follow a third path, neither Marxist nor capitalist, which reframes these goods within a different space and time.[30] This book, in turn, is at once historical and psychological, a negotiation of changing times and arenas across the exploration of *consumption, Italian-style*: the longing for foods and praxes of the past, as Italy moves forth in its postwar future. What changes in these decades is the *desire* surrounding food, as hunger transformed from a physical, visceral feeling to an emotional, spiritual craving. Now that food was readily available, the desire to survive was thus fulfilled; Italians no longer had to "make do" with limited quantities and substitute ingredients. Instead, they had to "make do" with excess, negotiating their alimentary abundance with a nostalgia for economically harder, yet gastronomically simpler, times. They sought to extract the tastes, imaginative creativity, conviviality, and memories of years past. Thus began a circling back towards what was.

My work sits, thus, at a complicated nexus: the worlds of anthropology, economics, gender studies, history, biochemistry, and cultural and literary studies colliding on one plate. In special focus are two pillars, food and film, which at once undergo and reveal some transformation in Italy in the decades following the Second World War; these lenses guide an exploration of narratives of austerity and radical gluttony. It is argued that Italy's eating habits changed relatively little, but as these films posit, the transition from hunger to excess – and from starvation to supermarkets – is not only apparent, but enormous. This book reveals the evolution – both the progression and devolution – of the filmic foodscape. The anxieties surrounding food begin as a lighthearted, comedic nostalgia, but later transition to fatalistic panic.

The kitchen is a place of traditional culinary practices and ingredients, from which sensations of home and conviviality are continually generated; yet, as the arena in which food is stored, prepared, and often consumed, the kitchen is where the changes to the postwar foodscape are most visible. In my analysis of films released from 1954 to 1973, the kitchen is treated as a site of both recognizability and *unrecognizability*, terms that require some expansion. The foremost point of recognizability is the food itself; as one watches these films, her visual register acknowledges and accepts that pizza is pizza and cherries are cherries. Unrecognizability, meanwhile, represents the changes surrounding those foods, and the consumer functioning within a space that is hereby alien. It is the feeling that someone does not understand, belong among, or recognize the people, objects, and rituals that are part of that changing arena; alternatively, they might not be recognized themselves. In the readings that follow, these directors, actors, and writers grapple with such unrecognizability by way of the stomach: the organ with which to digest food and, moreover, to process the changes that that gastronomy represents. This friction manifests first as nostalgia and hilariously taboo acts not yet in tandem with changing socioeconomic expectations. It then progresses more darkly into panic, lamentation, and, ultimately, a state of nihilism, where, by 1973, traces of gastronomic tradition and of sense appear all but lost.

Hungers from Neorealism to Marco Ferreri

This book begins in 1954, the year Steno's *Un americano a Roma* is released. Steno's work, intended as parodic, at once exhibits America's benevolence towards and subversion of Italy through consumption. Italy's reception of America is presented as frenzy, even lunacy. The beginning of the film acts like a newsreel, guiding us through Italy's history both before and after any contact with America. It opens with a montage of classical Roman monuments, as "Yankee Doodle" plays in the background. A voiceover then announces that the dream of going to America began with Christopher Columbus, but since 1492, Italy's fever for America has only risen. Chief among the fevered is Steno's protagonist, Nando Mericoni (Alberto Sordi). A Roman working-class youth, clad in blue jeans and a T-shirt, speaking a gibberish that is believed to be "Kansas City American," and surrounded by American memorabilia, Mericoni is so obsessed with America that he is ultimately institutionalized, prescribed electroshock therapy to abate his lunacy. Though entranced, he fails to understand America: His manifestations of the culture are absurd and distasteful, right down to his dinner plate. In the most popular scene of the film, Mericoni comes home late from watching Westerns at the local theatre, only to find that his *mamma* left him a plate of macaroni and a straw-adorned bottle of wine: stereotypically traditional Italian cuisine. His one-sided conversation with the macaroni, and simultaneous concoction of "American" foods, deserves full transcription:

> I don't eat macaroni! I am *American*! Red wine … I don't drink red wine! Americans eat jelly. *This* is American food! The Americans don't drink red wine … they drink milk, so they don't get drunk! You guys ever see a drunk American? I've never seen one. Americans are strong. You can't fight against the Americans! They eat jelly! Macaroni, I'll destroy you! You're like a worm, macaroni. Yogurt, jelly, mustard … this is American food! A little milk … This is the stuff the Americans eat! Healthy, substantial stuff [*eats the jelly, mustard and milk "sandwich", but he looks repulsed, and spits it out*]. How nasty! [*exchanges it for the plate of macaroni.*] Macaroni, you provoked me and now I'll destroy you. I'll eat you! Worm, I'll eat you![31]

Figure I.2. Three scenes from the 1954 film *Un americano a Roma*, directed by Steno.

At first glance, this scene is absurd. Who would dare eat a jelly, mustard, and milk sandwich? The concoction makes little gastronomic sense, yet it is what Mericoni perceives as an emblem of power: the foods of sober, strong, healthy Americans, invincible against the Italian "worms." In turn, over the course of his monologue, he is grappling with his own position as a young Italian "seeking refuge in the American dream."[32] However, through his indigestion of the sandwich, Mericoni – the physical body and the *italianità* he represents – struggles to tolerate the influx of American exports redefining his Italian identity; the unlikely ingredients of the sandwich form the bases of his madness by soft power. This scene is but our first dive into Italy's postwar filmic foodscape, rife with confusion and shock to one's senses.

The 1950s also signal the end of neorealism, a landmark period in Italian cinema. With the use of non-professional actors, recycled film stock, and on-location shooting, neorealist cinema of the 1940s illustrated societal downfalls: the loss of community and of morals amid high unemployment, homelessness, and, as this book underscores, hunger. *Un americano a Roma* and neorealist films do not look alike. Nevertheless, despite the growing quantity of food in the decades following the Second World War, and despite the stark formal differences between neorealism and later cinematic periods, there remained an unease communicated through food.

For example, in *Ladri di biciclette* (1948), through the employment of non-actors and seemingly banal objects, from bicycles to Rita Hayworth posters, director Vittorio De Sica and screenwriter Cesare Zavattini constructed an ethical code with which to seek truth in the face of Fascism and the war's vast traumas. Ostensibly, *Ladri* is about Antonio and Bruno, a man and his young son, who track down Antonio's stolen bicycle. Through the glaring loss of this singular object, De Sica and Zavattini reveal deeply troubling, more macrocosmic changes in society, such as the loss of solidarity in a time of desperate unemployment and its chain of repercussions: starvation, eviction, heightened crime, and worse yet, death. Surrounding the missing bicycle are feelings of panic and anxiety, as the two protagonists ultimately question how they will procure their next meal.

Meanwhile, in the films discussed in this book, unlike the material scarcities of neorealism, food is not only present but grows to excess. Yet, the anxieties around eating continue, which I assess through points of recognizability and unrecognizability: The viewer recognizes Mericoni's blue jeans and Westerns, but she fails to understand his gibberish and is repulsed by his American sandwich. Not only has the amount of recognizable food increased, but more profoundly, the characters in question and their creators must reckon with the myriad socioeconomic and political changes that enable such an increase in food, leaving people hungering for a status quo – for an arena of familiarity in which to consume these foods.

This book, thus, accentuates the element of panic that ensues when one ventures beyond one's comfort zone and ultimately realizes that she does not belong. Unrecognizability is a connective tissue which links neorealism to later works. Neorealism, built on the glaring absence and the feverish pursuit of food, as well as the lack of community and solidarity, underscores moments of intrusion: of permeating spaces where people are not welcome. In Roberto Rossellini's *Roma, città aperta* (1945), Pina (Anna Magnani) oversees the storming of a bakery, with police looking on stoically; in breaking into the bakery, Pina and the other women of the neighbourhood violate someone else's property. And returning to *Ladri*, Antonio and Bruno's sense of doom is most poignant as they spend their last lire on cheese sandwiches. In this scene, Bruno and Antonio, too, receive messages that they do not belong in this site of food. The viewer is made to feel uncomfortable as the camera cuts to a wealthy boy across the room, sneering menacingly at Bruno, looking down on the gas attendant and his unemployed father. In addition, the diegetic song of "Tammuriata Nera" infiltrates the scene, where a neighbourhood band sings of Italy's Black babies, born to Italian mothers who

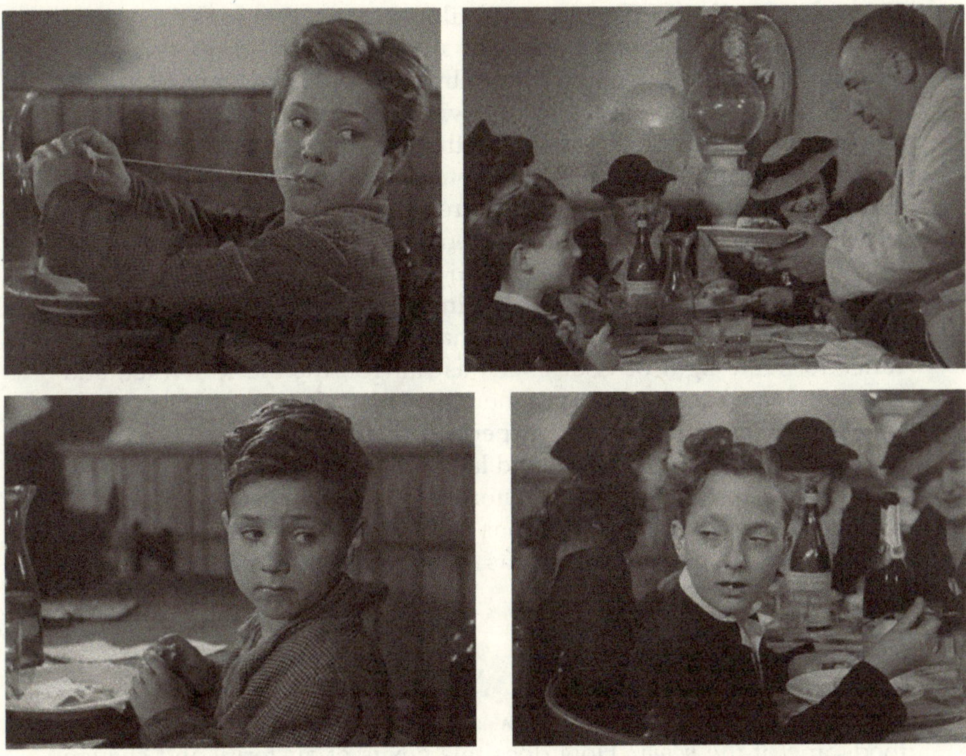

Figure I.3. A series of exchanges between Bruno and a wealthy boy at the *trattoria*, from the 1948 film *Ladri di biciclette*, directed by Vittorio De Sica

were impregnated, forcibly or voluntarily, by Black American GIs, presented as striking outliers within a predominately white society.[33] These intrusions – into a bakery, a woman's body, and the white nation – are hereby presented as a long-lasting legacy. In turn, this book follows suit, exposing characters eating, cooking, fornicating, and defecating outside their usual zones of comfort and recognizability.

Italian film criticism sees the 1950s as an anomalous era, comprising films that do not belong alongside neorealism. The "rosy" films of the 1950s and the comedies of the 1960s were, perhaps, a platform for little more than rising comedic stars and beautiful, buxom, iconic figures. This era is generally dismissed by film scholars as meaningless fluff. Sandro Zambetti offers biting criticism: "The fifties represent the worst period in the history of the Italian cinema – with the exception of Fascism. It was a period of so-called pink neorealism, of '*Love, Bread and …*,' and

'*Poor but Beautiful*,' of flat composite films put together for a fast profit. The Italian cinema was pervaded by mystifying optimism, escapism, and happy misery ... Not too many films deserve to be remembered."[34] However, based on the interactions with food in these films, I encourage a much more serious reading of these works, as these instances of hunger, consumption, and preparation reflect just the beginning of the changing foodscape beyond the theatre. Despite the motifs of sameness and continuity illustrated in the aforementioned historicizations of the material culture of the *boom* years, and despite film scholars dismissing the 1950s as a "rosy" and even meaningless time in Italian cinema, the films in question are exhibitions of major transformation. While these films do make light of issues such as hunger, the black market, and grave poverty, the characters in the films I consider not only recognize that their society has indeed experienced great shifts, but they also seek – hilariously, seductively, and later, savagely and nihilistically – to return to what they conceive as "normalcy." But the new normal is not what once was, so their interactions with foods – foods recognizable or easily imagined despite such shifts – illustrate acts of panic parallel to 1940s neorealism.

The Organization of This Book

With neorealism in the rear-view mirror, what comprises the filmic foodscape of the *boom*? How does this nexus of austerity and change transpire on screen? This book is divided into five chapters, or, rather, two halves: first, continuity and desire, and second, rupture and violent rejection. These halves represent continuities and breaks, respectively, as I follow the transformation of Italy's "rosy" cinema into dark, nihilist auteurism.

At the centre of the first half are two stars: Totò (Chapter 1) and Sophia Loren (Chapter 2). During the *dopoguerra* and through the beginnings of the *boom*, Totò and Loren, representatives of a humble, impoverished Naples, rise to an apex of Italian – and, in Loren's case, global – stardom. The films discussed in these chapters reflect this tumultuous history: the changes rocking the nation to its core. In the work of Totò, the visceral hunger that he experiences matches that of the very recent past, and in particular, that of the South; his portrayal of physical hunger in *Miseria e nobiltà* (1954) is continuous with the material deprivations that viewers themselves recently felt. When food became readily available, however, a new hunger emerged: a hunger for what was, as Totò upholds the dietary routines to which he was long accustomed. When Totò and Peppino, preparing for their trip to "faraway" Milan in

Totò, Peppino e … la malafemmina (1956), fill their bags with several kilos of the foods of their native South, they are clinging to the foods of their roots, of their past – as if a return to the "old world" of Naples were unfathomable.

Meanwhile, through her interactions with foods in some of her early films, as well as in her 1971 cookbook, Sophia Loren embodies the multivalence of hunger. As Cesira in *La ciociara* (1960), Loren portrayed a mother struggling against *la carestia* of occupied Italy; hunger is once again a physical sensation. But as Sofia in *L'oro di Napoli* (1954), and as Sophia Loren, the budding culinary icon, she not only satisfies the stomach but also adds a sexual dimension to hunger. Loren softened both the hunger pangs and the blows of the changing sociopolitical arena, leaving her viewers to desire simultaneously her body and the food she prepared, ultimately inviting us to eat with her. In the process, Loren crafted a stardom at the nexus of Italy's various cultural networks, one which exuded a sense of harmoniousness between the polarized entities of the Marxists and Christian Democrats, North and South, and one which suggested a balance between the sexes at a pivotal moment for women's emancipation. The viewers' points of recognizability are, thus, Loren's body and the foods that she procured and prepared amid the unrecognizable turbulence of changing sociopolitical protocols and expectations.

The iconicity of Totò and Sophia Loren positioned the two stars at the epicentre of this changing national narrative, as their characters contend with war, starvation, and the repercussions of organized crime and the black market; their very stardom, their massive symbolic capital, was founded on the trials and tribulations of Italian society. These are two figures on which the Italian public grounded and envisioned itself, because the struggles that characters and spectators faced appeared to be the same. Despite the hierarchical distance that separates spectators and stars, Totò and Loren were framed as one with their audiences. These performers constructed sites of recognizability and an overarching sense of belonging, the foundations of which are the commonalities of hunger and food. Indeed, little is more convivial than food, and its absence is universally regarded as painful. Both stars, thus, capitalized on these modes of community.

But Totò's and Loren's respective relationships with food are more complicated; it is not merely a question of hunger or consumption that defines their performances. They both channelled the desire for food, but they interacted with the aforementioned consumption history in different ways. Totò, the star persona of actor Antonio de Curtis, translated the newfound alimentary excess into his bodily demeanour, turning the once-excruciating pursuit of food into comedy. By 1958, as the *commedia all'italiana* movement took off, viewers were long accustomed to de Curtis's *maschera* (stage persona): the comportment of a clown, a collection of bewildered looks and excessive gesticulations, and the *furbizie* of a stooge, hilariously parodying the hunger that once was. Totò's buffoonery placated the new distaste and consumers' wariness surrounding food. In Chapter 2, Loren, too, applies her bodily features to the food. However, she sexualized and capitalized on the struggles not only to survive but also to fit within Italy's Catholic heteropatriarchy, among Italy's women: housewives barraged by the messages of mass media, as well as mothers, those in the workforce – or, ultimately like herself, both. Her voluptuousness aesthetically softened the poverty, hunger pangs, and illegality of the black market prominent throughout her early work directed by Vittorio De Sica. By 1971, she became an author herself, inviting readers of her cookbook to partake in the conviviality, family values (love, harmony, togetherness), and nostalgia; everyone was welcome at her table.

On the other hand, as stars, Loren and de Curtis were situated at the very top of Italy's socioeconomic pyramid. Accordingly, they offer an inaccurate representation of how these changes – especially rapid industrialization – impacted the working class and even the lumpenproletariat, devoid of class altogether. Meanwhile, other filmmakers exhibited those who longed not only for the wholesome community that characterizes the work of Totò but also for recognizability at all: for a moment that precedes industrialization, exploitation, and the cultural markers that construct and marginalize the Other.

Loren – who wrote of lavish dinner parties, sojourned in Hollywood, and recalled with delight her first lobster cocktail with Cary Grant[35] – is hardly the exemplar for the suburban stay-at-home mom, and certainly for those women who remained at what feminist Andrea Dworkin defined as the "social bottom."[36] Chapter 3, of which prostitutes are the focus, follows women who attempt to exit sex work to pursue livelihoods in food production and vending. This chapter at once laments women's engagement in domestic tasks without compensation and *gravitates towards* such "honest work." Yet, in *Adua e le compagne* (1960, dir. Antonio Pietrangeli), the four prostitutes' continued registration with the police bars them from establishing a restaurant in their own names, thereby forcing them into a reframed pimp-prostitute dynamic. And Mamma Roma, in Pier Paolo Pasolini's eponymous film (1962), emulates the lifestyle of the Roman bourgeoisie, but does so from the margins of Fascistic *borgate* housing. She fails to recognize the surveillant police state in which she still lives. She and her son, Ettore, struggle to connect to each other and to a world inscribed with the codes of patriarchal neo-capitalism, imposing grave consequences on the estranged family.

Indeed, in the films discussed in the second half of this book, the outcome of the analysis is decidedly darker and more pessimistic. The lightheartedness at the core of Totò's and Loren's work transitions to exploitation, defeatism, and nihilism. As the filmography advances towards worldwide protests, the global energy crisis of 1973, and the terrorist acts of the Years of Lead, once-simple times grow increasingly turbulent. In turn, the eating in these latter films becomes frenetic, savage, and grotesque – representative of a panic not unlike neorealist dealings with food, although food is now very much available. The hunger and consumption presented in the work of filmmaker and poet Pier Paolo Pasolini – first in *Mamma Roma* and on larger display in Chapter 4 – are centred on these very inequities.

Using the cinema and narrative theories of Pasolini, Chapter 4 explores the connections between continuity, rupture, and "revolution." In this book, revolution is defined two ways. It is, in the Marxist sense, the proletariat contending with exploitative forces. It is also the turning of a wheel, emblematic of a progression in a cycle back to naturality and austerity. In *La ricotta* (1963), Stracci, an extra in Orson Welles's diegetic rendition of *The Passion of Christ*, struggles to procure not only his next meal but recognition of any kind, because his existence is repeatedly overshadowed by the demands of the star and of film production at large. Literally crucified by indigestion, Stracci has no other way of "making revolution"; he does not die because he eats too much cheese, but because, until his very public death, he is invisible to the capitalist forces of the film industry. As the film poignantly concludes, Stracci has to die in order to be recognized. While Stracci does not lead a political revolution, his death, nevertheless, marks a turn – a revolution – in Pasolini's oeuvre.

In his 1966 film *Uccellacci e uccellini*, Pasolini reveals further contentions within 1960s society, ultimately lamenting the death of Communist leader Palmiro Togliatti. *Uccellacci e uccellini* reflects the struggles of the proletariat to persevere as the Party enters grim, uncharted territory upon Togliatti's passing; a Marxist crow warns of such changing tides of power, but he is savagely consumed by none other than Totò, thereby marking the satiation of his hunger ten years prior. Through the employment of a violent food chain, along which hawks, sparrows, a talking crow, and Totò are situated, the need to survive is prioritized over brotherly love; the hawks eat the sparrows, and Totò eats the wise crow. Whether Totò gains any value from his consumption of the professorial bird is questionable. What happens next in this societal digestive cycle?

This book also suggests a turn towards the tenets of neorealism: deprivation, the absence of solidarity, but also the notions of survival and rebirth. Chapter 5, thus, takes leave of Pasolini and discusses the work of Marco Ferreri, a longtime apprentice of Cesare Zavattini; we enter the realm of neorealism, Ferreri-style. The hunger presented in Ferreri's *La grande abbuffata* (1973), shot during the height of what economist J.K. Galbraith names "the affluent society," is very different from that in *Miseria e nobiltà* and, before that, neorealist films. Nevertheless, death at the hands of food continues to be the central theme connecting these film periods. In neorealism, the objective was to eat to survive and, thus, escape death. In *La grande abbuffata*, meanwhile, four wealthy protagonists – played by comedic stars Marcello Mastroianni, Ugo Tognazzi, Michel Piccoli, and Philippe Noiret – gather for the ultimate "gastronomic seminar": a weekend during which they commit suicide by consumption. Overwhelmed by an excess of food, the protagonists lose their ability to distinguish between smells, appearances, and tastes, and eating has become an automated fixture of the day's routine. Ferreri's response to the loss of sense is the loss of life. The director orchestrates a feast of total destruction: the stripping of all symbols, of all cultural markers, of his protagonists' consciousness, as a way of abandoning a world so deeply, unrecognizably different from the traditions and virtues of decades past. This undoing of symbols and, ultimately, of lives is reminiscent of neorealism, which exhibits the simplest mode of existence – where "we just are." Indeed, at the end of this world is a reawakening: an almost paschal rebirth that Ferreri's work shares with neorealism. The children of 1940s neorealism persevere, as does the schoolteacher Andréa of *La grande abbuffata*; the four men bequeath the world to her, leaving her to perpetuate not only the rich traditions and rituals of previous generations but also a world of anxieties, unsure of what the future holds; the feeling of unrecognizability continues.

In sum, what follows is a procession through Italy's postwar foodscape, across continuities and ruptures, as considered through filmic tropes of recognizability and unrecognizability. These characters satisfy the fundamental need to eat, occasionally exaggerating such moments of procurement and consumption, within spaces and moments of significant change. The following images of hunger, conviviality, predation, and overeating reveal the continuities of eating, as well as just how little has remained the same.

Chapter One

Totò and the Continuity of Hunger

Introduction: The Rise of Italian Comedy and of Totò

The year is 1958: the unofficial start to the *boom economico*, and the year the comedic masterpiece *I soliti ignoti* was released. In this film, director Mario Monicelli introduces his viewers to a group of fumbling, inept men: Tiberio, a camera-less photographer (Marcello Mastroianni); Peppe, a washed-up, hopelessly romantic boxer (Vittorio Gassman); a young womanizer (Renato Salvatori) who falls in love with the sister of Ferribote, a hot-headed and overly jealous Sicilian; and Capannelle, an old, toothless man simply on the hunt for food. They organize what promises to be the ultimate assignment – breaking into a luxury apartment and conducting a major jewel heist – but they lack both the self-control and strategic thinking to be even remotely successful. They fail to extract the keys for the neighbouring apartment because love-lost Peppe gets sidetracked. Once inside, in order to access the jewels next door, they attempt to drill a hole through a wall, only to hit a water pipe and flood the room. Drilling a second time, they realize belatedly that their hole destroyed the kitchen of the apartment they are in. With time running out and the jewels inaccessible, the men give up the heist. The kitchen being the one space open to the men, in the end, they settle for the sustenance and comfort of *pasta e fagioli*: a soup of pasta and beans. If nothing else, the men's hunger is satiated, and their failure is placated with a steaming bowl of comfort food. Pasta, it turns out, is the real gem in their grasp.

The chapter begins with this synopsis for two reasons. *I soliti ignoti* represents a pivotal moment in Italian film history: a decisive break from the "fluffy" comedies of Italy's past in its progression towards the *commedia all'italiana* of the 1960s. Indeed, comedy Italian-style came at the decline of melancholic neorealism. Neorealist cinema was seen as an appeal for outside aid, for the war's victors to witness and respond to the devastations ravaging Italy: grave poverty, high unemployment, and hunger and housing insecurities both during the Second World War and in the years immediately thereafter. These films experienced greater commercial success outside Italy (chiefly, in the United States), because viewers abroad did not have a direct connection to Italy's collective suffering; they were thus inclined to watch exhibitions of such conditions.[1] Italians, however, were not nearly as interested. To elaborate further on this phenomenon, let us take the example of Vittorio De Sica's *Ladri di biciclette/Bicycle Thieves* (1948). In this film, as discussed in the Introduction and exhibited in figure I.3, there is a scene in which the protagonists, Antonio and his son, Bruno, attempt to enjoy a small lunch, bought with the last of Antonio's money; with his bicycle stolen, Antonio has no way of reporting to or completing his job, so his employment is indefinitely suspended. The atmosphere of the *trattoria* in which they dine appears to be lively and convivial, but Antonio and Bruno, calculating their survival between bites, are made to feel unwelcome in such a jovial space. The camera pans between young Bruno, quietly eating a mozzarella sandwich, and a boy at a nearby table – well-dressed and having a lavish lunch with family – who sneers in Bruno's direction. This interaction is intended to make the protagonists, and, by extension, the Italian viewer, uncomfortable. The anxiety that this scene induces is reflective of viewers' own experiences in the postwar period; in turn, viewers sought refuge from, not repetition of, these painful sensations. The 1950s, then, became an era of international co-productions and "sword-and-sandal" films, such as *Hercules* (1958) and *Ben-Hur* (1959), and lighthearted, "rosy" domestic films, where beauty glossed over poverty; examples include Dino Risi's *Poveri ma belli/Poor but Beautiful* (1957) and *Belle ma povere/Beautiful but Poor* (1957). These latter films had the levity which was precisely the grounds for the farces of Antonio de Curtis, far better known by his screen persona, Totò.

Totò, in the minor role of Dante Cruciani in *I soliti ignoti*, plays a wizened, near-senile lock expert who teaches the would-be crooks how to open a safe, among other basic robbery skills. Totò's role is small yet powerful, catalysing the film's acclaim. By 1958, after years of popular theatrical and cinematic performances, "Totò" was a household name across Italy. The senility that Monicelli assigned to Totò – not to mention the near-cameo size of the role – is thus an interesting choice: Why reduce a mega-celebrity (who, in the film, was even given the name of Dante, a forefather of Italian culture) to a position of brief comic relief? Monicelli cast Totò as the old, senile teacher as a means of juxtaposition; Totò embodies tensions between continuity and change. For one, Totò was decidedly older and more experienced than Gassman and Mastroianni, who both proceeded to dominate the screens of the 1960s. Yet, as Gassman settled into his comic niche after sixteen years of dramatic roles, and as Mastroianni's career was just taking off, Totò's career had been heavily marked by changes. In particular, this chapter examines the development of Totò and his filmography as representative of a *gastronomic* crossroads.

Food, and the camaraderie surrounding a meal, are exhibited only in the closing sequence of *I soliti ignoti*. Yet, this film is a demonstration of how far Italy, in terms of history and its cinema, had come since the Second World War. From the launch of the Marshall Plan in 1948 to *I soliti ignoti* in 1958, Italy underwent remarkable transformations. The notion of hunger is generally considered among such changes. For the first time, the diet of Italians contended with abundance, as innovative, frozen, and pre-prepared products flooded the market, and there was simply more food available, both in terms of quantity and options. Viewers recognized in Totò the very gastronomic transformations imposed upon themselves: chiefly, the overcoming of hunger, as well as the influx of new, foreign products into the Italian market. However, unlike the urgency and desolation of hunger presented in neorealism, Totò's hunger coaxes a smile.

Totò: Clowning Around with Hunger

As the neorealist film movement waned and the golden age of Italian comedy was born, Totò utilized both food and his body to veer from the neorealist tradition of depicting a very real and painful hunger. By prompting the viewer to instead *laugh* at those very pangs, Totò's comedies promoted the continuity of hunger, as well as the austerity and the rusticity of Italy's eating. However, his work prioritized the conviviality, imagination, and nostalgia associated with the gastronomy of the past.[2] As food increased in availability, these emotions and expressions guided viewers' remembrance of hunger in a way that bypassed the darkness of neorealism. Totò's humorous interactions with food – both real and imagined – encouraged a "return to the whole": the evocation of wholesome memories and experiences in order to manoeuvre through life in a foreign place and, moreover, a foreign time.[3]

Although not the most traditional method of working through trauma, psychologists have defined humour as a way in which people confront adversities, mitigate negative circumstances, and see light through darkness. To quell the hunger of the *dopoguerra* and also to make sense of the massive changes impacting Italy in the 1950s, Totò offered a beacon of hope. Through bodily exaggerations and by calling attention to the absurd, Totò was the human embodiment of humour.

In so doing, Totò not only alleviated the tensions once associated with hunger but also encouraged a sense of togetherness and continuity, heightening the notion of conviviality in the Italian food tradition. He functioned as a kind of group therapy; viewers gathered at the movie theatre to watch a recognizable act through which they, as a collective, were able to acknowledge and process the trauma of hunger as it unfolded on the big screen, and also to recognize that, upon exiting the theatre, they would return to a world of consumer novelties. Thus, for their ninety minutes together, Totò invited spectators to reminisce – even laugh – over the hunger that once was, and reflect on the onslaught of changes that Italy underwent in this period: at once upholding continuity and suspending worries about what lay beyond the theatre. In his play on such gastronomic transformations, for the moment, viewers belonged simply to a world of laughter.

What follows, thus, is an exploration of de Curtis's creation of Totò, and how this figure embodies continuity: the connections not only with his audience but also between hungrier times and Italy's increasing affluence, as well as between sixteenth-century comic tradition and the *commedia all'italiana*. In so doing, this chapter considers Totò's strong attention to the body: not merely his heightened awareness of the body's presence and kinesthetics in performance, but also his marriage of corporeality and theatrical props. Food – and just as notably, the lack thereof – is Totò's prop *par excellence*. He converts the collective feeling of hunger, the sensation of nothingness in one's belly, into wholesome laughter; he thus accentuates conviviality, an *emotional* fullness, amid such changes in gastronomy. Through his work in the films *Miseria e nobiltà* (1954) and *Totò, Peppino e … la malafemmina* (1956), Totò renders a world where we can laugh at his – and greater Italy's – hunger: a very real experience just ten years prior, but now one rich with absurdly imaginative possibilities. Indeed, as the credits roll and the curtain goes down, the filmic escape comes to an end, snapping viewers back to reality; Totò's "therapy session" has ended. Just like the spaghetti of *Miseria e nobiltà* (1954), referenced later in this chapter, the world that Totò perpetuates is contained to the filmic imaginary.

The *maschera* of Totò and the Traditions of Hunger

The relationship that Totò fostered with his audience on the premise of hunger positions him on a long timeline of hungry comics. Totò reflected the highlights of Europe's Golden Age of literature and courtly performances, as well as the turbulence of Italy's rural South in the 1950s and 1960s.[4] He transported picaresque, extravagant, and crude episodes of consumption, crafted by the likes of François Rabelais and Miguel de Cervantes in the 1500s, to the twentieth century. With its roots in sixteenth-century Spain, the objective of the picaresque novel is, in short, to "get by": to survive whatever societal circumstances are thrown at characters. These stories detail the adventures of *pícaros* – social rogues, such as beggars, tricksters, and con-artists, generally born into poor families – who must outwit their superiors/masters to survive.[5] This description resonates greatly with Totò, who, too, engages in acts of charlatanism and trickery to achieve his objective – which in these films is, simply yet fundamentally, to eat. Totò's interactions with food recuperate the grotesque banquets in which Rabelais's giant characters, Gargantua and Pantagruel, partake, as well as the relationship between the idealism of Don Quijote, Cervantes's protagonist, and Spain's struggle against starvation.[6]

However, more than Don Quijote and Rabelais's giants, Arlecchino is the preexisting case in the European comic tradition to which Totò is most frequently compared. Arlecchino, or Harlequin, is a comic stock character of Italy's *commedia dell'arte*; he is a caricature of an everyday Italian who schemes to subvert the establishment in order to "get by." Historian Georgia Lawrence-Doyle offers the following brief character profile of Arlecchino, citing the work of Jean-François Marmontel:

> A rogueish clown and trickster (*zanni*), Arlecchino is the most enduring of the stock characters of *la commedia dell'arte*. Marmontel describes this figure as "… a mixture of ignorance, simplicity, wit, awkwardness and grace. He is not so much a fully-developed man as a great child with glimmerings of rationality and intelligence, whose mistakes and clumsy actions have a certain piquancy …"[7]

In terms of gastronomy, Maria Park Bobroff, though writing from the French perspective, names several instances in which Harlequin sinfully enjoys wine and *macarons*, and even manages to sexualize his girlfriend's casserole, licking his finger after penetrating the sauce.[8] Bobroff furthers Harlequin's deviation when he drinks from a sick maid's enema, mistaking it for broth; soap, meanwhile, is mistaken for cheese.[9] Totò shared Arlecchino's puppet-like movements, as well as the *furbizie*: the comedic stunts and petty crimes similar to those described by Bobroff, which he committed not out of gluttony, but for survival. Indeed, whereas Arlecchino played tricks to satiate a penchant for mindless eating, Totò's foremost objective was to procure food.

Figure 1.1. A depiction of the Arlecchino/Harlequin archetype, colourfully dressed as a clown. Courtesy of New York Public Library, Digital Collections.

Harlequin's confusions are repulsive and hilariously nonsensical, but his thoughtless consumption of inedible objects – both intended for cleaning – actually fouls the body. Totò's consumption practices, meanwhile, seek to restore the body and soul: to feed and replenish an active yet starving body, and also to give him – and his wider audiences – a means of stabilizing both the body and psyche in a period of national flux. This process is underscored by Totò's unique *maschera*: a "mask" accentuating his struggle for control and his theatrical excess, prompted by the collective feeling of hunger.

He surely shares the excessive buffoonery of Arlecchino, but Totò's own *maschera* is the subject of numerous books. The *maschera* speaks to the elastic versatility of Totò; de Curtis developed a character so intensely that, regardless of role, name, or job description, Totò remained Totò, thereby masking both the character profiled in any screenplay and de Curtis the actor.[10] In *Miseria e nobiltà*, in which Totò plays a nineteenth-century scribe by the name of Felice Sciosciammocca, the idea of Felice is all but forgotten, as Totò's essence consumes every scene. The *maschera* of Totò even outshines the deeply auteurist work of Pier Paolo Pasolini, which will be elaborated upon further in Chapter 4. How, then, did Totò monopolize any film in which he starred, and hence, how does hunger emerge as the master signifier of his narratives?

De Curtis studied, expanded upon, and recreated for contemporary audiences the preexisting work of Charlie Chaplin, Macario, and Gustavo De Marco, and in particular, the meticulous attention these greats paid to the body.[11] In this act of *autotradizione*, Totò is an intertextual figure, utilizing his body to accentuate the *physical* sensations of hunger, manifested by a growling stomach, headache, dizzy spells, and even hallucinatory visions, like a mirage in the desert.[12] Since Totò's comedy is one of hunger, de Curtis does not merely distort his physical features for comic effect, but he uses his body to demonstrate the hunger once collectively felt by Italians, the South in particular.[13] Indeed, words are inefficient in expressing hunger; spoken and written language inadequately conveys visceral bodily needs. It is instead through hyperbole of physical movements – walking, trotting, jumping, falling, and exaggerated facial expressions and hand gesticulations – that Totò communicates the sensations of hunger and its consequent weakness and delirium.[14] His bulging eyes and violently erratic gesticulations convey bewilderment: Where could he – or his fellow citizens – seek solace amid such changes? His gestures spoke particularly strongly to Neapolitan spectators, fostering the aforementioned sense of collectivity; the viewer, especially someone in the South, was attracted to Totò's kinesthesis because his movements were designed to extract those same feelings of recent hunger from within the viewer herself.[15]

Hunger, however, is not just physical. Totò communicates a multidimensional hunger, exhibiting an intense desire for more than just food: a desire for stability, harmony, and, ultimately, a sense of continuity between the disparate parties of a geographically and socioeconomically stratified country, upon which the next section elaborates. Totò remained Totò, without having to assume different roles, and was thus a means of constancy amid the waves of changes Italy underwent in the 1950s. Especially telling is a 1981 letter that director Elio Petri wrote to Franca Faldini, Totò's longtime partner both on and off screen. The letter not only effectively cements de Curtis as Totò, but it also hints at the social stakes of Totò's cinema. Petri wrote:

> Totò could impersonate any character, on stage, on screen, and we would get the impression that he was revealing the essence of a fake mask: of falsehood in society, not on stage or the screen; in other words, it is absurd to be poor, absurd to be rich, absurd to be a crook, in the way that one could be a security guard, white-collar worker, or a scientist. He does all this while miraculously being himself, with the levity of an anarchical Mandrake.[16]

Though I would not necessarily deem Totò anarchical, as Petri writes above, Totò embodied feelings of conservatism amid the macrocosmic changes of the postwar period: the governmental coalitions forming within and outside of Italy; the advancements of the West and the growing American hegemony; and the schisms dividing the industrial powerhouse cities of Milan, Turin, and Genoa from the South. Totò communicated a wistfulness for less complicated, less turbulent times. Several scholars underline the multiple and abstract dimensions of hunger that Totò expressed by way of a single look: the craving to fulfil one's bodily needs, such as food and sex, as well as a desire for prestige, security, and stability – almost as if Totò's clownlike behaviours were intended to mirror the atmosphere of precariousness in this period, underscoring the sense of chaos impacting every level of society.[17] Assuming the role of a human marionette, Totò is a metaphor for the loss of control and of normalcy. In turn, he suggested laughing at such madness. Totò's consistent *maschera* and food-centred sketches emotionally grounded spectators, even if the food is as much a hallucination as the promises of the *boom* itself.

An Interlude on Naples and *Jettatura*

A discussion which combines Totò, hunger and desire, and the imaginative quality of eating and storytelling would be incomplete without Naples. In my exploration of continuities and ruptures in Italy's filmic foodscape, Naples remains an important site. On one hand, as the backdrop for *Miseria e nobiltà* – both the film and Eduardo Scarpetta's 1887 play – as well as the home of the Caponi brothers in *Totò, Peppino e … la malafemmina*, Naples is presented as the geographical point of recognizability, the hub of the food and folkloric traditions that Totò practises and perpetuates across these works. On the other hand, historians frequently reference Naples, bustling city and regional capital of Campania, in their treatments of Italian stratification: moments of geographic, cultural, and socioeconomic rupture. Throughout the late eighteenth and early nineteenth centuries, Italy was the prism through which Enlightenment thinkers imagined the European South. In his 1826 *L'homme du midi et l'homme du nord, ou l'influence du climat*, a work emblematic of a phenomenon known as the Southern Question, Swiss philosopher Charles-Victor de Bonstetten establishes a set of binaries dividing North from South and, by extension, Italy from its neighbours north of the Alps:

MAN OF THE NORTH	MAN OF THE SOUTH
lives in a monotonous environment	lives in an abundant and varied environment
reason, reflection	imagination, feeling
industry	effortless subsistence off the earth

lives indoors	lives outdoors
fixed routines	no fixed routines
planning	no thought for future
banks	no banks
social opinion	egotism
can be educated/reformed	cannot be educated/reformed[18]

In this period, philosophers, writers, and travellers considered Naples to be an epicentre of the contrasts between nature and society, civilization and savagery, and past and present. According to Northerners (those in countries north of Italy, but also those in the northern Italian regions of Piedmont and Lombardy), the South was considered the "sick sister" of the Italian nation or, to quote Communist leader Antonio Gramsci, a "ball and chain."[19] Naples was even described as the "last stop" in Europe before Africa, thereby likening it to a city at the end of contemporary civilization: The farther south one travelled, the farther into filth and into the past one delved. In his travel logs from 1848 to 1852, British economist William Nassau Senior wrote that Neapolitan streets with "filthy carriages, full of filthy people, threaten every instant to crush you. Filthy pedestrians, whose contact is loathsome, elbow you at every turn; the air is full of dust and stink; horrible beggars swarm round."[20] Forty-five years earlier, Frenchman Augustin Creuzé de Lesser wrote, "Europe ends at Naples and ends there quite badly. Calabria, Sicily, all the rest belongs to Africa."[21] This language is indeed negative and extremist, and this exploitative, even racist treatment of the South deserves more commentary than I give here. Nonetheless, these descriptions of the South add contexts to Southern stardom. The next chapter, on Sophia Loren, expands upon subsistence off the earth and the sex appeal of her autochthony. Central to this chapter on Totò are, meanwhile, imagination and feeling, and how his exaggerated body and facial expressions uphold the gastronomic history and traditions of his native South.

Along with the imagination of Naples and Totò's connections to the *commedia dell'arte* and the picaresque of the fifteenth and sixteenth centuries, it is also necessary to mention *jettatura*: a literary custom, born of Naples's own Enlightenment movement, founded upon images of intense desire and fascination. *Jettatura*, although it avoids the dark, occult connotations of the Mediterranean "evil eye," presents disorienting images and ideas that fascinate the human eye, working off of one's subconscious desires and greed. To add some further context, in his findings published in *Magic: A Theory from the South* (1959), anthropologist Ernesto De Martino records the thoughts of Tomasso Campanella:

> The eye manifests many magical things, because when one man meets another, from pupil to pupil, the more powerful light of one man disorients and strikes the other, who cannot withstand this, and often the former transmits the passion that he has on his patient … One who looks at something with admiration arches his brows and wishes to open his eyes as wide as possible to take in the admired thing, in order to know it and enjoy it better. Through this widening of his eyes, he sends out spirits that are very greedy for the desired and admired thing.[22]

Jettatura is a phenomenon through which to explore how feelings of hunger transform from a visceral need for food into different dimensions of desire. In the following films, viewers encounter images of lavish banquets and heaping plates of spaghetti, and this chapter assesses how Totò amplified the notion of desire, converting those images into something multisensorial, leaving the viewer to imagine the aromas, the flavours, and the warmth of such dishes – in the words of eighteenth-century law instructor and literary scholar Nicola Valletta, to "give body to a shadow and create something from nothing, for the amusement of a learned brigade."[23] In other words, building upon the collective's recent exodus from physical hunger, these images bewitch Totò and, through his exaggerated expressions, they fascinate the viewer. The famous *spaghettata* in *Miseria e nobiltà* is, in the end, but an illusion, and Totò – and his viewers – are left hungering for more. Naples, home of this tradition of irrationalism, is a most fitting setting for the imagination and trickery that arise in the following pages.

Miseria e nobiltà: Imagining Hunger

Miseria e nobiltà, directed by Mario Mattoli in 1954, showcases Totò, food, and hunger, as well as theatrical co-presence: a oneness shared between performers and the audience. *Miseria e nobiltà* sits at the nexus of food and spectacle: a simultaneous focus on one's hungry stomach and on diegetic theatre, ballet, the families' elaborate game of "make believe," and the theatrical film product itself. With Totò at the helm, this film is perhaps the strongest example of Italy laughing at its longstanding tradition of hunger – the newfound satisfaction with which it was treated amid the tumults of the *boom*. This section further explores this exemplar, defining Mattoli's theatrical medium and underlining the development and solidification of Totò by way of theatre.

In so doing, this section assesses Totò's kinesthetic and performative responses when food is first absent but then becomes not only available, but abundant, through the Sciosciammoccas' evening of charlatanism.

Miseria e nobiltà is the third time Totò reprised his role of Don Felice Sciosciammocca, following *Un turco napoletano* (1953) and *Il medico dei pazzi* (1954), all of which were directed by Mattoli and adapted from nineteenth-century comic plays written by Eduardo Scarpetta. Totò is assumed by several film scholars to be perfect for the role of Felice, a "historic Pulcinella"[24] himself: yet another persona that embodies the provincialism of the South and is intensely focused on food.[25] Totò and Felice embody the same personality traits, including and especially Felice's namesake: happiness. Despite the hardships, hunger chiefly among them, devastating the South, happiness prevails on several levels. *Miseria e nobiltà* concludes with a happy ending in the plot, but, more specifically, the concluding line of the film has Totò breaking from character and, before a curtain call, appealing to the audience (the diegetic spectators of the play, but also the viewers of Mattoli's film), "It is enough for me to know that the audience is pleased."[26] Totò the actor, paid to put on a promising spectacle, depends on their good reception; the icon thrives when his spectators get the jokes, especially when they are told "live." The spectators' happiness derives from Totò's theatricality and his excessive physical responses to food, and lack thereof.

Indeed, Totò was developed over decades of theatrical revues, debuting on the silver screen in 1937. His deep-seated connection to the theatre impacted his cinema, as he treated a film set as if it were a live performance. Film scholar Masolino d'Amico mentions just some of Totò's quirks amid production:

> Totò continued to work in cinema as he did in theatre: He improvised, he refused to be dubbed; he reluctantly did retakes … and he needed the theatre employees to applaud; he observed theatre hours, insisting on shooting in the afternoons (you can't make people laugh in the morning, he used to say).[27]

Theatre is distinguishable from cinema for its co-presence. Plays are performed in real time, whereas films are but the final cut of a lengthy process, including repeated takes, editing, and dubbing. In addition, in cinema, the cast is among the audience only virtually, as actors' images are captured on a reel for widespread distribution. In plays, meanwhile, a curtain is raised, rendering the actors not only visible but tangible; in certain performances, audiences are even active participants, engaging directly with the actors. The divisions between star and spectators are reduced by the conventions of theatre. Acting in theatrical productions about hunger thus adds yet another dimension of universality to Totò's work, as he is theatrically co-present, but he also communicates a sensation widely and collectively experienced over the past decade. Although *Miseria e nobiltà* is, in fact, a film, Totò's co-presence with the audience – a move harking back to his revue days – is showcased perhaps most strongly in his collaborations with Mattoli.

The theatricality of the film is clear in its very conception; the screenplay was adapted from Scarpetta's 1887 play of the same name. Scarpetta's play, a glimpse into the socioeconomic changes affecting Naples at the turn of the twentieth century, centred on the life and loved ones of Felice Sciosciammocca, a character that Scarpetta invented at the tender age of seventeen.[28] Felice is a scribe whose career prospects are dwindling because of rising literacy rates, and whose family is thus forced to room with that of his friend Pasquale (Enzo Turco), an equally unfortunate photographer. With no incoming work, there is no pay, and thus, no means to buy food to feed their families. Just when total starvation appears inevitable, Ottavio (Giuseppe Porelli), a local marquis who wishes to marry a ballerina, presents Pasquale and the families with a proposal. In order to convince the ballerina's father, a chef, that she is marrying into an elite family, as well as to verify that she is an acceptable bride in the eyes of the nobles, Ottavio hires both families to play his relatives at a dinner held at the chef's house. With nagging hunger pangs and thoughts of nothing but food, the group enthusiastically agrees to engage in the fraudulent act, assuming fake names and donning costumes to uphold Ottavio's scheme. When the scheme fails, foiled by Felice's wives of past and present who come to reveal his true identity and thus unravel the plan, love nevertheless reigns supreme, as the play ends with several couplings: the ballerina and the marquis; Pasquale's daughter and the ballerina's brother; and Felice and his first wife, too, rekindle their relationship. The play ends on a happy note, as hungers for food and love are both satisfied.

In Mattoli's adaptation, he frames the film as a play, maintaining the theatrical qualities designed by Scarpetta. The film's opening mirrors the moments preceding a play; the viewer sees members of the audience settling into their seats, evaluating what parts of the set they can see despite the drawn curtains, and scanning the playbill for more information on the cast and performance they are about to watch: "the best comedy by Scarpetta."[29] The opening credits, in fact, assume the form of a playbill. The audience of the "play," and thus the audience of the film, immediately recognize the name of Totò, listed first as the "play's" lead actor; Sophia Loren, as Gemma the ballerina, is second. These two stars are thus the principal actors, although it is clear from even the earliest scenes of the film that *hunger* is the most palpable, recognizable presence. The sketches developed by Totò enrich Scarpetta's play, transporting the text to more contemporary circumstances, but almost all of these sketches concern food and hunger; hunger is the master signifier.

Mattoli's portrait of hunger requires an elaboration of food traditions particular to Naples. On one hand, Naples has been praised for its vibrant and varied gastronomy: a celebration of creativity in its use of local resources. In their fieldwork, anthropologists Elisabetta Moro and Marino Niola depict a gastronomically robust Naples, including a lengthy list and description of food, which reveals not only the variety in local produce and seafood but also the multiple ways in which these foods were prepared and served. They write:

> The promenade of Naples became a gastronomic passage. Here the Mediterranean diet was served for all budgets. Pizzas, spaghetti with shellfish, fried-algae *zeppole*, poached sea bream, fried anchovies. Sautéed vegetables, stuffed vegetables, and ones covered in Parmigiano-Reggiano cheese. At the hands of the Neapolitans, eggplants, peppers, broccoli florets, squash blossoms, zucchini, and artichokes abandoned their usual vegetable state to become delicacies – so good that they would make one close her eyes, because the pleasure principle, especially for a population this resistant to sin, hence becomes a way of life.[30]

Yet, on the other hand, despite the apparent richness of Naples's food scene, hunger remains a common denominator between the Naples of 1887 and of the *dopoguerra*. This legacy of hunger enabled social scientists to further stigmatize Southerners. At the start of the twentieth century, studies by social scientists Pietro Albertoni and Felice Rossi (1906) and anthropologist Alfredo Niceforo (1901, 1907) highlighted the connections between the southern Italian diet and trends of physical, intellectual, and moral underdevelopment. Niceforo's *Italiani del Nord e italiani del Sud* (1901) publicized a correlation between the lack of protein in the Neapolitan diet and a "deficit of energy and a tendency toward indolence,"[31] which would support the hypothesis that hunger was the motive for Totò's *furbizie*. Meanwhile, Albertoni and Rossi, describing the peasantry of Abruzzo, noted physical features that suggested malnutrition: "Gestures are without enthusiasm, the eye without expression, the mouth impassive and half-open, cheekbones protruding."[32] These studies are fraught with eugenic language. Antonio Gramsci, the pioneer of Italian Communism, wrote in his *Prison Notebooks* that, instead of acknowledging that the causes of this poverty were external – in short, that the North exploited the South – these studies reinforced that

> there remained only one explanation – the organic incapacity of the inhab- itants, their barbarity, their biological inferiority. These already wide- spread opinions (Neapolitan "vagabondry" is a legend which goes back a long way) were consolidated and actually theorized by the sociologists of positivism (Niceforo, Sergi, Ferri, Orano, etc.) … Thus a polemic arose between North and South on the subject of race, and about the superiority or inferiority of North and South.[33]

Thus, Totò's early work shares this complex backdrop of hunger, but the negative, racially charged portrayal of hunger stops here. Totò's exaggerated gestures and expressions – the way his body manoeuvred the hunger and austerity of Naples in both the 1880s and later decades – could not be more different from the portrait suggested by Albertoni and Rossi. His physicality is a driving force behind a newer perspec- tive of hunger, one associated instead with humour and togetherness. Quoting anthropologist David E. Sutton, the food events in Totò's work convey a "burning desire," both for certain foods and for the commu- nity and creativity that once surrounded hunger: a return to the Naples illustrated more positively by Moro and Niola. As seen most poignantly in *Miseria e nobiltà*, that desire is satiated through sensory, deeply phys- ical experiences, which evoke local knowledge, revalue a domain of experience (hunger) that has fallen into disuse, and conjure feelings of great emotional affect: "wholeness, or fullness in experience."[34]

Since food and its absence are so central to Scarpetta's play and to the identity of the greater nation, in order to anticipate the physical sensations among the audience, as well as to illustrate the viscera of Totò's desire, Mattoli emphasizes the physicality of food in his film. From a tear-jerking raw onion, to a steaming vat of spaghetti, to the ice cream splattered on Totò's nose, these foods play upon the body's five senses, prompting physical sensations and desire among the cast and audience. This sensory overload is a symptom of the connection that Mattoli forges between hunger, spectacle, history, and city, shared between the stars and the audience, despite the barrier of the movie screen. Considering the viewers' absence from the set, and that they are encouraged to *imagine* all of the smells, textures, and tastes of the foods, the act of imagination forges a connection between hungry Felice/Totò and the audience. It is almost as if we can interact with the products of hunger-induced hallucination: to feel the warmth of the pasta or smell the garlic in the sauce; alas, those foods and feelings are also out of the viewer's reach, not available for consumption, instead stuck inside the mind's eye.

From the very outset of Scarpetta's play, and, by extension, the film, hunger is apparent. Naples is depicted as squalid, poor, and hungry, leaving much to be desired; Pupella (Valeria Moriconi), Pasquale's daughter, is seated by a window – looking outward, as a sign of longing – and cries to her mother, "I am hungry! I am hungry!"[35] In the opening scenes of the film, Pasquale chastises Pupella for "allowing herself the luxury of waking up with an appetite" – never mind that she is biting into a raw onion, attempting to satiate her hunger by likening the pungent, acrid vegetable to a piece of fruit. This scene is minor but crucial to a discussion on the reconfiguration of hungers. Exactly as the form of an onion symbolizes, with many rings wrapped around a hard core, Pupella's strange food choice reveals the desperation of the families' hunger and the many layers of their desire. The hunger that was first and fundamentally alimentary – where Pupella would eat whatever was available, no matter how implausible – is soon translated into other forms of desire: for economic improvements, for love and conviviality, for a woman's flesh. The rest of my analysis of *Miseria e nobiltà* focuses on these last two tenets: the corporeality of flesh, and the importance of imagination: envisioning and hungering for what is not real. The desire for a woman's flesh is a topic discussed more profoundly in later chapters. Here, the focus is entirely on Totò and how his theatrical excesses, as well as his power of imagination, correspond to society's remembrance of a hunger that no longer exists and which was supplanted in this decade by desires for other satisfactions.

The above desires are intertwined in an early scene of the film, when Felice, Pasquale, and Felice's son, Peppino, visit Nadia, the Piedmontese seamstress (Franca Faldini, Totò's real-life partner) who lives downstairs from them. Through the *mise en scène*, as well as through Mattoli's experimentations with colour, Nadia's apartment is framed as a pleasure palace for the three men, a venue in which their alimentary hunger and – at least for promiscuous Felice – sexual frustrations could be satisfied. The rosy hues of Faldini's body and, later, of poultry are not to be read as just a conflation of "flesh" – *la carne* – but, instead, as the multiplicity of desire; the men's desires for food, warmth, fullness, and sexual pleasure are compounded together.[36] Additionally, Mattoli utilizes colour contrasts – Nadia's lacy black bodice against her pink skin, her red lipstick, and the men's drab brown clothing juxtaposed with her luminous, colourful apartment – not only to illustrate this plurality of desires, but also to accentuate a series of disparities. These contrasts convey what, and who, the men want but cannot afford.

More poignantly, this scene reveals the differing attitudes towards food between North and South: a significant theme across Totò's oeuvre.

For example, Peppino seeks to satiate his hunger by smelling heaps of burgundy jam that Nadia leaves untouched on a plate. What is striking about this scene is not just the gross quantity of food present, but also Nadia's blasé attitude towards food: circumstances opposite those against which the Neapolitans struggle. Whereas Peppino is reprimanded for attempting to fill his stomach with mere fumes of jam, Nadia responds, "I am not so hungry, but I have to eat anyway."[37] Nadia, who we must remember is a transplant from Piedmont, an affluent region of the North, has little regard for food. Her use of *dover mangiare* – to have to eat – instead of *poter mangiare* – to be able to eat – marks the divide between her personal wealth and her poor surroundings. Whereas the men cannot eat because they cannot access food, she actively chooses not to eat; she has no desire for food because, for her, it is always present, so she eats only out of habit – indeed, as Felice remarks bitingly to Pasquale, "When the time comes, the lady *has* to eat."[38] In addition, as she eats in front of them, spreading butter and jam on bread, she states how she, a Northerner, is still unaccustomed to their food. In her conversation with Felice and Pasquale, gastronomic differences between North and South are further elaborated, but the overarching distinction is that of presence versus absence. The audience, meanwhile, watching this scene unfold in 1954, is situated along the spectrum of continuities and ruptures portrayed by Totò; having recently satiated their own hunger, viewers both sympathize with the starving Sciosciammoccas and welcome newfound luxuries afforded by Nadia: butter, jam, and the sizeable quantities of these foods. Through the following dialogue, the audience is inclined to snicker at Felice's repeated jabs at Nadia's ignorance, but they can also recognize the positionality of the more affluent Northerner:

NADIA: I'm not yet accustomed to your cuisine.

FELICE: To our cuisine?

PASQUALE: And how does one get accustomed?

FELICE: We're not accustomed, either!

NADIA: No, I meant Neapolitan cuisine. Here in Naples, everything is cooked with oil, while by us, up in the North, everything is made with butter.

FELICE: Oh yeah? You make *everything* with butter?

NADIA: Everything!

FELICE: Instead, we make everything with oil. We consume jugs of oil. We put it on salads! Even stains, we stain them with oil!

PASQUALE: And in the North ...?

FELICE: They are butter stains!

NADIA: Oh no, maybe not that, but we certainly eat a lot of it, no? We even put butter in our coffee! (*pours coffee from a porcelain kettle into a cup, with Felice looking on*)
PASQUALE: We don't put anything into our coffee.
FELICE: Neither milk, nor coffee.
NADIA: (*smiling, laughing*) Oh, Sir! They don't put in anything!
PASQUALE: Let's talk about something else.
FELICE: You don't like coffee and milk? (*His eyes widen, eyebrows are raised, and his lips begin to pout*) Would you prefer a cup of cocoa? (*Smiling wide*) With some brioches, some *maritozzi*?[39]

Their entire conversation is laden with Felice's sarcasm, reflecting a set of schisms: hungry versus full, rich versus poor, and North versus South, explored further in Totò's later films, such as *Totò, Peppino, e ... la malafemmina* (1956).

From the concluding line of the conversation, Totò begins to exhibit a physicality that mirrors the men's desires, both for food and for women. His bulging eyes and wide smile communicate the immense pleasure that arises not only from imagining foods and the satisfaction they provide, but also from Nadia's sex appeal. Returning to the jam, Felice commands Peppino to "*non guardarla*" (not to look at it), which presents the viewer with a sexualized double entendre. One may read the feminine "*la*" as jam – sticky, sweet, and connoted as a feminine food – and as forbidden fruit, and, thus, in a similar position to Nadia, whom the men can ogle but not touch. The men exit from this scene with their stomachs mostly empty – after having stolen collectively one piece of bread and jam from her – but they leave with satiating visions of her supple body; unlike foodstuffs, these memories shall be recuperated for later, repeated enjoyment. Indeed, the men must rely on imagination to satisfy themselves in non-alimentary ways, as a response mechanism to feel full and pleasured by the pretend, the nonexistent: the impossible to obtain. As Pupella must imagine that the raw onion is appetizing, like a similar-looking but infinitely sweeter apple, imagination is a driving force in Mattoli's film. As evidenced through the primary *furbizia* of the film, the Sciosciammoccas must get creative – they, like Totò the actor, must embrace the *maschera* and pretend play – to quell their hunger pangs, even for food that is entirely imagined.

As stated in the synopsis, in order to win over Gaetano, Gemma's father, Ottavio the marquis enlists Pasquale, Felice, and their relatives to pretend to be Ottavio's extended family. They must thus perform within the performance, attending a luncheon at Gaetano's house, donning costumes and going by new names to convince Gaetano that

Figure 1.2. Two scenes from *Miseria e nobiltà*, while Felice (Totò) and Pasquale are in Nadia's apartment.

Gemma and Ottavio are a suitable match. The objectives are that, by the end of the meal, Ottavio will officially be engaged, and the families will finally eat; indeed, Ottavio states matter-of-factly to Pasquale and Felice, "If you act well, you will be compensated well,"[40] and Felice affirms towards the end of the film, "If we work, we'll earn ourselves some soup!"[41] Complete with a roasted chicken, whole fish, a platter of cheeses, bruschetta, and ice cream sundaes, the marquis's luncheon is the ultimate prize, the moment when the Sciosciammoccas' hunger finally dissipates – although their road to consumption is far from straightforward. Reminiscent of the excesses of the *maschera*, elaborated upon in the coming paragraphs, Felice's ravenous hunger and crass behaviour outdo the aristocratic appearance of *il Principe di Casador* – which, always preoccupied with food, Felice mistakes for *cassarola*, or casserole. The Principe's costume fails to contain Felice's destitution, deteriorating to allow the real Felice to shine through: He[42] eats off part of his glove while gnawing on chicken, and his moustache falls off in a brawl between his wives. In addition, reminiscent of Nadia's jam, Felice enjoys little morsels of food – bits of chicken so savagely consumed that he eats his glove off – but these moments are *coitus interruptus*, in that Felice's chances of eating are soon jettisoned by, for example, watching Gemma in the ballet, and the unexpected arrival of Luisella. Once more, external circumstances dictate when food is available, barring Felice from satiating his massive appetite. But as his impatience, wait-time, and hunger level increase, the film reaches its climax, when Totò is at his most Totò; viewers are immersed in his excess – an overwhelming grandiosity, a boom in food, but one that is entirely imaginative.

Before the luncheon, and thus before their rigorous play of "make believe," imagination again subsumes the characters. Their long-standing hunger forces them into a hallucination that not only epitomizes Totò's relationship with food but is also one of the most memorable scenes of consumption in all of Italian cinema. Scarpetta's treatment of this scene is little more than stage directions, which Mattoli elevates by not only his use of colour but also the vast creative liberties that he extends to Totò, allowing the actor's physicality to flow most freely and even violently. The directions, ending Act 1, are as follows:

> *Exchange of insults and invectives at the discretion of the actor. This scene must be performed with a lot of enthusiasm. Then everyone follows. From the door in the back to stage-right, a servant advances, along with a porter who brings forth a big stove. Without speaking, they approach the table and place the stove at Felice's feet. The porter goes away but comes back with two flasks of wine. Out of the stove, the servant takes out a huge vat of macaroni, then two chickens, some fish, two large pieces of bread, napkins and settings, while the porter puts the two flasks of wine on the table. He and the servant take back the now-empty stove, arrive under the doorway in the back, turn, bow their heads, and leave. Pasquale, Concetta, Pupella, Luisella, and Felice approach the table. Then they suddenly get up and, all on their feet before the table, they fling themselves at the steaming macaroni with great longing, devouring and grabbing hold of it with their hands. The curtain falls.*[43]

From these stage directions, of particular interest are two aspects: the wordlessness ("*senza parlare*") of this scene, as well as the "*grande avidità*/great longing" with which the characters devour the spaghetti. Totò transforms the scripted instructions of "flinging themselves," "devouring," and "grabbing" the spaghetti into unforgettable actions, a wildly outlandish aesthetic that cements contemporary spectators' own recollections of the hunger of the *dopoguerra*.

To further summarize the scene that unfolds in Mattoli's film, Ottavio takes leave of the families, and Luisella, Felice's new wife, is offended that Ottavio excluded her from the scheme; if she stays home, she cannot act or, thus, eat. Frustration stems from their unrequited, dire, and even animalistic hunger; Felice exclaims, "Here we eat only poison!"[44] and then begins to bark, as a dog does when he is bothered and/or needs something, as if talking about hunger is no longer a viable coping mechanism. Indeed, for the rest of the scene, words are practically nonexistent, allowing for heightened focus on the characters' hunger and, consequently, the power of their all-consuming hallucination.

Felice's barks are answered when a chef enters the room and assesses the number of guests, returning moments later with assistants, carrying picnic baskets brimming with loaves of bread, bright red apples (which again contrast the stone-grey of the walls and distressed wooden beams), and wine. The chef sets the table for his seated guests: a beige tablecloth, sparkling wine glasses, and porcelain settings. The assistants unpack the baskets, revealing a roasted chicken, platters of fish, and, most famously – as the music crescendos and Mattoli zooms in for a close-up – a crock of steaming spaghetti. The chef departs, leaving the families alone with the table of plenty. Anxious and confused, the characters glance nervously at each other, all the while sliding their chairs closer to the table. They abruptly seize the spaghetti – Totò at this point growls and jumps up to kneel on the table, allowing him to dominate the crock and also to hide from outsiders as he continues to enjoy his handfuls of noodles; he even eats Pasquale's handful, hiding behind his back. The scene fades to black as Totò stands atop the table, stuffing handfuls of pasta into his pockets; similar to Nadia's flesh, this is yet another figment of imagination stored for later enjoyment.

Confusion, anxiety, and even shame are the emotions that surround this table. First, the characters do not know what to make of the feast that magically "appears" before them. When the chef arrives, Felice and Pasquale widen and rub their eyes, stating simply, "A mirage,"[45] and "I dreamed of the ballerina's father, the cook."[46] The characters then hide their ravenousness from one another; Felice momentarily dances on the table, for example, instead of devouring the dream-food. In an attempt to make sense of the feast before him, Totò maximizes the use of his senses; if he were to touch, see, smell, and taste elements of the feast, those sensations would confirm their existence. He reaches for the basket sitting at his feet, removing the cloth covering to reveal the plate of fish; he "sees" and "touches" the food. He also repeatedly exaggerates his olfactory sense, tilting his chin upward and flaring his nostrils to get a whiff of the foods that pass right under his nose. And, of course, Totò engulfs the spaghetti, shovelling noodles into his mouth and stuffing more into his pockets. Valeria Moriconi, who played Pupella, was amazed by the massive creative liberties that Mattoli had granted Totò, as well as the excessive, even harmful, measures Totò took to make himself one with the pasta: to eat the pasta, but also to make the pasta an extension of his body, bulging from his pockets. The following reports her reaction:

> The director had explained to us that our chairs should scooch over a little at a time, and then we would throw ourselves onto the pasta. It's clear that the scene was then ad libbed; no one said "end scene" because Totò was

being so inventive and Mattoli let him go on. I look up and see that Totò had gotten up, climbed onto the table and proceeded to put the spaghetti in his pockets. Who knows how long the scene would have gone on for? But the director had to put an end to it because, as he was filling his pockets with spaghetti, Totò had also taken one of the heat-coils, which was used to create the smoke, and the coil was burning through his pocket.[47]

Through this scene, Totò stuns not only his fellow cast members but also the audience. Smells and tastes are impossible to share with movie-goers, who are shown only images; likewise, it is difficult to recall these sensations without an image. It is easy to imagine a colour without a stimulus; for example, if prompted to envision a Granny Smith apple, most people experience little difficulty in mentally producing that shade of green. Smells, meanwhile, require a visual stimulus. Before imagining the smell of garlic, one needs to recall an image of garlic cloves. Once in the presence of that object or image, any associated smells can be recognized for extended periods of time. Mattoli's combination of images and smells – as evoked by Totò's reactions – doubles down on the (non)existence of the feast.[48] Totò's sniffing, in combination with visual stimuli, draws the viewer in, leading *her*, too, to insist on the reality of the feast. The viewer cannot smell the pasta, but the steaming pot of spaghetti is in clear view within the frame; the filmic image evokes and affirms the scents, and the tastes, that the food exudes. Despite the verity of this image – the fact that the viewer recognizes the pasta, the steam, and the characters' reactions to the food – the viewer is jarred by the realization that this feast is imagined. The hunger, that on-screen and the recent collective experience, sparks a hallucination that both the characters and the viewer negotiate by way of their senses. In so doing, food moments of the past are not only captivated, but remembered.[49]

Moriconi's testimony underscores the prowess of Totò's *maschera*. The way in which Totò overtook the scene and captivated his audience matches the excessive amounts of spaghetti. As the central persona of Scarpetta's hallucinatory consumption, Totò functions in a world where there appear to be no limits: The food will not run out, and there are no rules and regulations subduing the consumers, because the spaghetti is all in their minds; as in a dream, they are free to act as they see fit and eat as much as possible, because the spaghetti and its limit concepts are nonexistent. Such excess has long defined the concept of the *maschera*.[50] Pulcinella, another archetype of the *commedia dell'arte*, also interacts famously with spaghetti; Moro and Niola remind their readers of "the reddening lava of spaghetti that springs from the hands of a Pulcinella that welcomes visitors

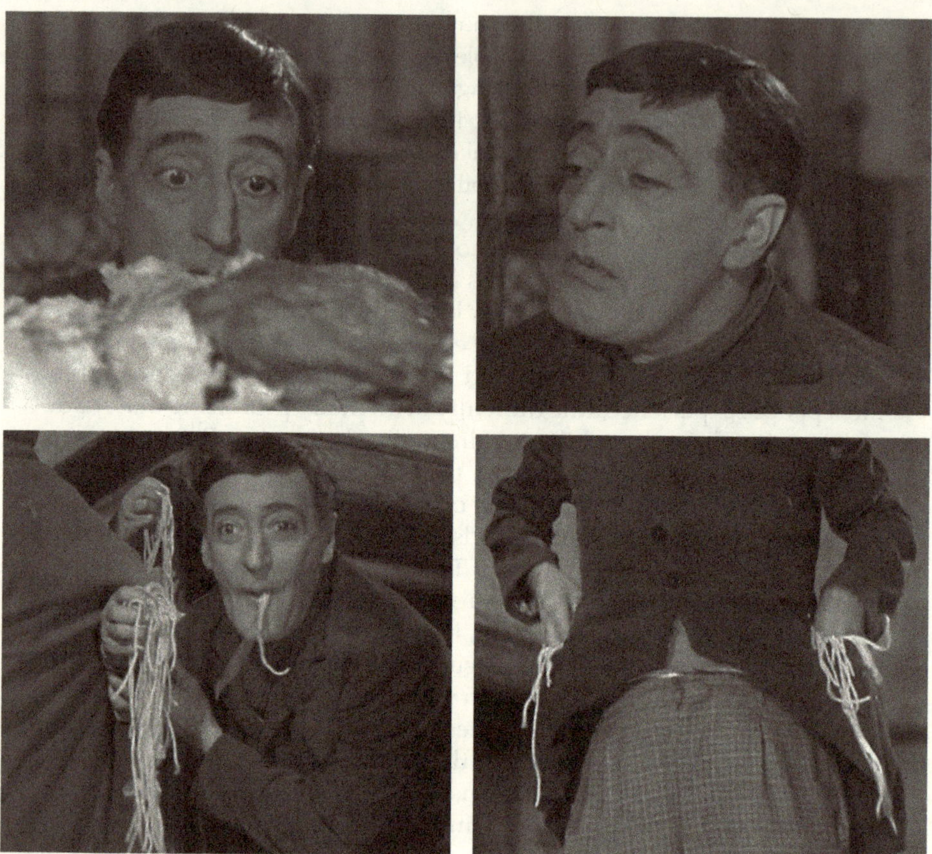

Figure 1.3. Four shots depicting Totò's hallucinatory feast. Each image targets a different sense: sight, smell, taste, and touch.

who enter the majestic, underground stables of Palazzo Sansevero."[51] This allusion solidifies the connections between Totò, food and hunger, and comedic traditions – particularly as one progresses further into the 1950s. Indeed, this free-for-all could be read as a microcosm of the Economic Miracle: After decades of austerity and severe controls on consumption, the 1950s, by contrast, presented a world of new products and extensive consumer freedoms. One could liken the mountain of pasta to the terrain of Cockaigne, an imagined land of promises and plenty, reminiscent of an affluent America across the Atlantic, completely opposite to Italy's autarkic austerity. As one gathers from *Miseria e nobiltà*, satiation was once possible only through imagination; appetites were curbed by way of mind-games. But once such abundance arrived at Italy's shores, the atmosphere was one of confusion, unrecognizability, and uncertainty; now what do we do with such things? The spaghetti scene epitomizes the lack of restraint but also a sense of continuity in consumer attitudes, even in the face of novelty: a duel between bodily needs and psychological habits. This scene is especially telling because this nexus of a very real, lived *miseria* and the imagined prosperity of *nobiltà* represents a crossroads that Italy approached in the 1950s: a web of possibilities and concerns surrounding the *boom*.

The next film, *Totò, Peppino e ... la malafemmina*, is primarily concerned with the widening stratification between North and South. *Totò, Peppino e ... la malafemmina* is once again full of *furbizie* demonstrative of people trying to "get by." The film also exhibits a deep-seated attachment to the foods of the South, the home of Totò and his co-star Peppino De Filippo. Wherever the Southerner may be, always close at hand are the foods of his native village: a ridiculous vision at which any Italian would laugh, but a recognizable image intended to provide comfort and normalcy in otherwise turbulent times.

Totò, Peppino e ... i comfort del Sud

Directed by Camillo Mastrocinque, *Totò, Peppino e ... la malafemmina* (1956) is the first of the four-part *Totò, Peppino e ...* series,[52] in which both comics, Totò and Peppino De Filippo, develop and get entangled in their harebrained schemes of "getting by." Across the films, Totò and Peppino commit *furbizie*, scamming loved ones and sabotaging rivals; in *Totò, Peppino e ... i fuorilegge* (1956), for example, the two men stage the kidnapping of Antonio (Totò) by the outlaw Il Torchio, so as to procure ransom money from Teresa, Antonio's rich, greedy, and tyrannical wife. Yet, beyond the formulaic narrative – the messy teleology of achieving a goal, followed by the film's happy ending – at the core of these films are psychosocial crises, where the struggle to "get by" is to withstand the myriad of changes of the 1950s. The backdrop of these films is no longer the painted set of a play or a Naples of the distant past, both of which were the case in *Miseria e nobiltà*; these films illustrate an Italy "on the move," in a state of geographical and socioeconomic flux. The premise of these films, released during the peak of the *boom*, is internal migration: the exodus from South to North, and from rural provincialism to the hustle and bustle of the industrialized city. In this period, families took leave of their crippling farms to pursue work in the factories of the North, Fiat chiefly among them, or, perhaps, to go in search of more emotional prosperity, such as love or stability. This film portrays the exploration of uncharted territory: the passage from the recognizable to the unrecognizable, from "what was" to more alien surroundings – no matter that Italy was at once the protagonists' point of departure and the destination. In particular, the imaginative tendencies surrounding food in *Miseria e nobiltà* begin to vanish as society rises in affluence and food is henceforth available; thus, continuity is most clearly manifest through a physical attachment to food. In *Totò, Peppino e … la malafemmina*, Totò will once again stow away food for later, but not only will the spaghetti he once stuffed in his pockets become real, but these foods of the South will now accompany him on a faraway journey, as he navigates what he envisions to be a place as cold and foreign as the North Pole: Milan. Food, then, is the attempt to root oneself in two worlds at once: while consuming *caciotta* and pasta fills Totò with essences of his home, Naples, he meanwhile struggles to make sense of the striking contrasts of the North.

At the centre of this film is no longer the monolithic icon of Totò, but two *pulcinellesche* figures, both with strong ties to provincial Naples. De Filippo, son of Eduardo Scarpetta and, hence, raised in Naples's theatre scene, also underwent extensive training to develop a *maschera*: a stage persona that, perhaps even more than Totò's, mirrors Pulcinella. De Filippo once said:

> For me, the connection to a great actor like Salvatore De Muto was like "blood and bread" for my artistic tendencies. De Muto was a *pulcinellesque* "mask" of great resonance for our theater world … In the years that I was close with him, when I was young, I learned a lot about the spontaneous and improvised art of De Muto, studying and imitating it in planning each of my characters in a farcical way.[53]

In his formation, then, Peppino turned towards the *pulcinellesque* tradition, distancing himself from the persona of Felice Sciosciammocca and, therefore, from the theatrical innovations of Scarpetta. However, over the course of Totò and Peppino's collaborations, one immediately recognizes how Totò's excesses overpower Peppino. Totò's presence electrifies the space, whereas Peppino appears meek in comparison; Totò goes to great lengths to distort his body to captivate his audience, the image of his jutted chin and bulging eyes, so recognizable, practically cemented on the viewer's brain, whereas Peppino's physicality is alarmingly static. It was almost as if the figure of Peppino could not stand alone but instead represented an alter ego of Totò.[54] As filmic evidence, one may recall Mattoli's

Signori si nasce (1960), a film featuring two estranged aristocratic brothers, Pio (Peppino) and Zazà (Totò), who "come from the same tree" but whose personalities and lifestyles could not be more different. As Pio says bitingly to Zazà on the night of their reunion, "Our father rightly left even you a part of the inheritance, and you used it up frolicking, on vices, on the ugly life, on luxury! Not I. I instead, thank God, capitalized on my inheritance, and now I am a well-to-do tailor!"[55] Indeed, across the twelve films in which Totò and Peppino co-starred, what emanates is Peppino's more introverted conservatism and Totò's outlandish antics; Totò proposes some wild scheme and Peppino follows Totò's instructions, no matter how debilitating.[56]

Peppino appears to lack autonomy, and Totò's *maschera* easily engulfs that of Peppino, yet it is as if "Totò e Peppino" form one holistic presence in these films; the conservative *yin* of Peppino contends with the outrageous *yang* of Totò to perform one narrative, therefore upholding the contrasts displayed in not only *Miseria e nobiltà* but in greater Italy in this period. Indeed, the antagonizing forces between the two stars of the *Totò, Peppino e …* series are the binaries of North versus South, provincial versus city, and home versus elsewhere. The duo mirrors the socioeconomic bifurcation of greater Italy, unsure of whether to gravitate towards consumer novelties or tried-and-true traditions. Totò, embracing the spendthrift possibilities of Italy's new consumer era, is put into check by Peppino, who is more cautious and, perhaps, more nostalgic than his co-star. These differences are amplified within the consumers' paradise of Milan. Throughout their travels, Peppino is as strong a reminder of Italy's provincial, austere past as the foods from home packed in their suitcases, which are discussed in greater detail in the coming pages.

At first glance, *Totò, Peppino e … la malafemmina* is a love story with an objective similar to that in *Miseria e nobiltà*. A young Neapolitan student, Gianni (played by popular singer Teddy Reno), falls in love with an aspiring actress, Marisa (Silvana Pampanini), who is considered by Lucia, Gianni's mother, to be a hussy and bad influence on her son. When Marisa announces that she is leaving for Milan to pursue her career, Gianni follows her northward, sending his family into a panic. Lucia and her brothers – Antonio (Totò) and Peppino Caponi – venture to Milan with the goal of locating Marisa and verifying whether she is marriage material. Lucia confronts Marisa directly, while Antonio and Peppino, fumbling around these strange, new surroundings, decide to write Marisa a letter, bribing her with 700,000 lire – which the brothers frame as consolation money – to leave Gianni. Marisa refuses the money, choosing to marry Gianni. Indeed, the closing shots reveal a resolution: Marisa and Gianni remain together, have children, and although their windows of quality time are small, they manage to bond over the occasional pizza. Most pertinent to this discussion are such feelings of community and togetherness over food – and, moreover, how that wholesomeness is jeopardized by migration. There are not one, but two, settings of the film: Naples, framed as a hub of tradition, and Milan, a city of the *boom*, of economic promise. Anxiety surrounds the Caponis' trip to the North, as made evident through certain cultural manifestations of fashion choices, language, and food.

Part of the title of the film, ... *la malafemmina*, alludes to a song of the same name written by Totò in 1951. The lyrics of the song depict a woman who was born to deceive her suitors, to poison one's soul. However, Marisa – the supposed *malafemmina* (evil woman) of Mastro-cinque's film – turns out to be quite honest, and just flirts and utilizes her body with the sole purpose of furthering her acting career. Why, then, does the title code Marisa as a "bad woman"? The concluding lines of the song do not speak of a faulty moral compass but, rather, of how the woman is representative of changing times: "I still love you, / but you don't know why ... / Because the only love / Was you for me! / And you, *out of caprice*, / Destroyed everything ... / But God does not forgive you / For what you did to me ..."[57] The caprice, the unpredictable and perhaps even dangerous changes that the *malafemmina* embodies, is the source of Totò's negativity. Marisa, affiliated with the affluence and dazzle of Milan, thus frightens the Caponis, whose radius of worldly knowledge is – at least until this point – centred on their farm in Campania. She functions in a space outside the Caponis' comfort zone, and the young nephew's pursuit of such "dazzle" within the uncharted territory of the North jeopardizes all that Antonio and Peppino thought they knew about their native Italy, on geographic, generational, socioeconomic, and cultural levels.

Antonio and Peppino are farmers in the South, a profession that was drastically waning in the 1950s. They seem to defy the trend of destitution, however, as they are seen in the beginning scenes of the film conducting various transactions, and Antonio even gifts their maid a necklace. Marisa evaluates their wealth in terms of food; when Gabriella, her friend, asks if Gianni is wealthy, Marisa exclaims, "Super-rich! He had a whole wheel of sheep's cheese!"[58] The farmers' easy access to food marks their economic well-being, but this wealth fails to buffer the changes impacting society at large: the increased technologization of society, as well as the widening stratification between North and South.

In terms of technologization, Antonio purchases a tractor for their farm, hoping to squash the Mezzacapa family, their rivals. In this scene, one recognizes the consumerist differences between the two men. Peppino calls the tractor "an armed car,"[59] implying both its prowess and menacing appearance, and he all the while asks Antonio how much and with whose funds he paid for the tractor. Antonio/Totò, meanwhile, literally swats such questions away with his hands, reframing the vehicle as "a mechanical ... gem,"[60] which signals a simultaneous praise for and confusion about the new innovation. Overall, the tractor is a symbol of unrecognizability. It is soon apparent that neither brother knows how to operate the machine; they are much more accustomed to animals – horses, oxen, etc. – pulling their ploughs. They nevertheless dismiss the instructions written on the tractor, claiming that since the tractor is from Milan, the instructions are thus in Milanese, an apparently foreign language; Antonio encourages Peppino to mount the tractor, commanding him to *civilizzarsi* despite Peppino's hesitations. The investment in the tractor is meant to bolster the Caponi farm – to "civilize" them, consonant with the depictions of Naples mentioned earlier – but the tractor turns out to be completely harmful; in two minutes, they damage their wooden fence and, after a series of haphazard burnouts on their land, continually repositioning their bodies to keep the tractor upright, they crash through the Mezzacapas' concrete wall, seriously injuring them both. The tractor, a second emblem of Milan, is yet another foreign presence that the Caponis fail to understand, and which thus endangers the men and their farm: the locus of their wealth which suffers because of the urbanization and increasing prosperity of the North. The tractor's damages are inflicted upon the bodies of Antonio and Peppino; with his head bandaged and arm in a sling, Totò's body is no longer a site of hunger, as it was depicted in *Miseria e nobiltà*, but it now receives the blows of societal changes.

The tractor is a Milanese import on Southern soil, but what happens when the Caponis are transported to Milan? The tractor demonstrates a violent physicality against the provincial farmers, but how does that physicality change when Antonio and Peppino themselves become the imports? In their travels to Milan, food becomes the connective tissue between their native Campania and the alien characteristics of the North. On the tractor, Antonio and Peppino shift their bodies to preserve a centre of gravity; the tractor would have tipped if the men had not repositioned their bodies against the bumps and turns in the soil. Once in Milan, food provides that sense of stability; the Caponis fill their bellies with the foods they brought from home in order to feed their Southern roots, to keep their sense of home alive, while exploring the North.

Although Milan and Naples are part of the same Italian nation, the Caponis nonetheless imagine Milan to be as foreign and distant as Mars; Milan is viewed as far outside Italy. When Lucia declares that they will follow Gianni to Milan, Antonio is shocked by the idea of such an expedition, exclaiming, "It'll take four days by sea to get to Milan!"[61] This statement is completely erroneous; Antonio believes that Milan is in neighbouring Calabria, but then corrects his answer – wrongly – to Sardinia. More ridiculous questions and predictions are revealed as Antonio asks Mezzacapa, who did his military service in Milan, how the Milanese walk and how they greet one another. Likewise, on the subject of climate, the word *bufera* (blizzard), repeated multiple times, is new to the Caponis' vocabulary, as the men are unaccustomed to snow; the men also do not know how to handle *la nebbia* (the fog), failing to understand its vaporous intangibility, treating it instead as a phantom blanketing the city. Milan poses an otherworldly challenge for the Neapolitan farmers. These conceptions of the North, although absurdly comical to the contemporary viewer, reflect the Southerners' minuscule radius of geographic knowledge in the 1950s, as well as the consequent anxieties about such areas that extend beyond the hub of Naples but present the Southerner with a wealth of (employment) opportunities. Totò, whose knowledge of the world is thought to have spanned from the South to Cuneo, is no exception to such a trend.[62] In playing Antonio, then, Totò treats his character's trip to the North as a global expedition, amplifying the supposed alienness of the North through his outfits, his speech, and his food choices. These extensions of his body exhibit the confusing labyrinth of changes Italy was undergoing in this period: a mix of "what was" (in this case, in the impoverished, backwards South) and "what will inevitably be" (the urbane prosperity of Milan and the North, both of Italy and continental Europe).

From the moment the Caponis disembark from the train in Milan, the only words to describe the juxtaposition between the business-class Milanese and the bewildered Southern farmers are "contrast," "bizarre," and indeed "alien." However, the Milanese – wearing suits and dresses, carrying briefcases, and rushing through their day's commute – are not presented as foreign creatures; the Caponis instead offer a striking contrast to the bourgeois, urban surroundings. Having prepared for their trip with only the information that Mezzacapa provided them, Antonio and Peppino dress as if they were travelling to Siberia; the Cossack dance music playing in the background further likens Milan to the Russian wilderness. Fur hats top their heads and stoles cover their shoulders, canteens and binoculars hang around their necks, and under their arms, viewers find a framed portrait and packages brought

Figure 1.4. Totò and Peppino arrive at Milan's central train station, dressed in furs for the *freddo caldo* of the North. From *Totò, Peppino e … la malafemmina* (1956, dir. Camillo Mastrocinque).

from home. The Milanese ridicule their excessive costumes and props; indeed, Antonio and Peppino's ignorant and blatant stereotyping of the North backfires, making *them* appear extraterrestrial. What outdoes the laughter, however, is Antonio/Totò's stubbornness; he claims to see the fog and feel *un freddo caldo*, "a hot coldness," ignoring his siblings' complaints about the heat, which is only aggravated by their fur accessories. Antonio's defence of the Milanese stereotypes is one way of assimilating to his new surroundings, arming himself with mechanisms to cope with the supposed differences of the North, adopting a sort of "when in Rome" mentality. Or, this is a means of resisting change, of upholding continuity despite the surrounding novelties, as he continues to treat the North as a distant other, reinforcing the polarizing stratification between North and South, and attaching himself to his native South despite his new geographical positionality.

This attachment to the South is made most apparent through the Caponis' food choices. At the hotel, the siblings begin to unpack their suitcases, all of which contain foodstuffs that they believe can be found only in Naples. Mastrocinque's focus in this scene is entirely on the food; the characters' faces are initially out of view as the camera captures their hands, pulling out foods sandwiched between their undergarments. The foods are regarded as objects as personal and intimate as what is worn behind closed doors, not to mention as fundamental a staple as underwear. Bread and underwear are both seen as equally immediate extensions of the body – one to cover the most vulnerable parts of the body, under one's street clothes, and the other to fill the belly and keep the body in motion. The foods include three bottles of wine, a loaf of bread, a *caciotta*, and four kilograms of pasta; in the background, already on a clothesline that the siblings put up, hang cloves of garlic, eight sausage links, and an entire leg of prosciutto. The *mise en scène* is, in a word, excessive, considering that these foods are meant to nourish the three Caponis during a three-day journey. This excess is not the same as the imagined table of plenty in *Miseria e nobiltà*; whereas Felice Sciosciammocca second-guesses his senses around the spaghetti, Antonio has no doubt that he can touch and eat these four kilos of pasta – he even questions whether four kilos will be enough food. Not only does this excess match the growing quantity of food in postwar Italy in general, but this moment is also similar to that of the Siberian outfits showcased in the previous scene; the abundance of foods of the South, and the familial conviviality that these foods promote, are meant to combat the frigidity of the urbane North.[63] This clothesline of foods is a portrait of the South recreated in the mostly bare, grey space of their hotel room; the viewer is immediately reminded of the alleys of Naples, where clotheslines of colourful garments hang over the streets, bridging two apartment buildings. Indeed, the clothesline and the foods it holds are the means of retaining and recuperating the Caponis' Neapolitan culture while in Milan. Although certainly available for purchase in Milanese groceries, these foods – which the Caponis select to represent Naples, pack for their journey, and treat with the utmost care in their "cold" living quarters – create a foothold of stability and recognizability for the Neapolitans, as they navigate across Milan and attempt to free Gianni from Marisa's grasp. Although Milan appears to be uncharted territory and a site of unpredictability (remembering the caprice of the *malafemmina*), the Caponis can at least control their food consumption. An active recollection of Southern, rustic traditions, these foods comprise "what was" amid such newness.

And yet, these foods hold a solely symbolic value, as the viewer never sees the Caponis eat them; the rest of the film focuses on their encounters with Milan and its people, and how Milanese customs compare to those of the South. Indeed, while the four kilos of pasta are

Figure 1.5. A look inside the Caponis' hotel room in *Totò, Peppino e … la malafemmina*.

left unconsumed in the hotel room, when Lucia encounters Marisa and evaluates whether she is suitable for her son, she asks Marisa, "Do you know how to make pasta?" The provision of food, and particularly of pasta, is thus framed as a crucial criterion for marriage and motherhood. With this aspect elaborated upon in the next chapter, for now, the focus will instead be on the buffoonery and decorum – or lack thereof – of Antonio and Peppino as they dine with Marisa's theatre troupe at the Gran Milan, a decidedly bourgeois eatery.

The restaurant space could not be more different from the Caponis' hotel room, and it is a true site of tensions between North and South, Milanese industrialist and quintessentially Neapolitan street urchin. This scene illustrates, in a word, differences: the major disparities between the affluent, urbane North and the provincial South. First, reminiscent of the conversation Felice has with Nadia, the Piedmontese seamstress, in *Miseria e nobiltà*, Northerners eat and cook differently. Ingredients popular in the North, such as butter and cream, starkly contrast the ubiquity of olive oil and tomatoes, two staples of the Mediterranean diet. Second, at the Gran Milan, there is a luxurious refinement that is not as prominent in Southern eateries, which instead boast simple meals such as pizza, made with inexpensive, filler ingredients. These differences come as a shock to Antonio and Peppino, Neapolitan farmers who likely have never eaten out before, so they fail to fit into restaurant culture. At the Gran Milan, Antonio and Peppino retain a sense of provincialism, as they do not know how to manoeuvre the niceties with the front-of-house staff, and as their "poor" dietary choices clash with those promoted by the restaurant.

Indeed, the restaurant setting upholds an unspoken code of etiquette that all participants, staff and customers alike, are expected to follow. There is a certain chronological rhythm and decorum involved in one's dining experience, and the Caponis miss these cues ingrained in Gran Milan's culture. First, Peppino is infuriated by the coat-check system, accusing the attendant of stealing his hat, because he does not understand that the ticket will be used to retrieve his hat at the end of the night. Even more comical are Antonio and Peppino's troubles communicating with the maître d', a French term for the front-of-house manager that the brothers mistake for "metro." When the maître d' says "Buona sera" to the two men, Peppino questions whether Antonio knows the maître d' because Antonio reciprocates the greeting; Antonio dismisses the confusion, stating matter-of-factly, "In Milan there are well-mannered people."[64] In addition, they take the maître d's questions literally; for example, Antonio and Peppino are bamboozled by "Quanti sono i signori?" – a question meant simply to assess how many will be dining that night – because, as they respond, they do not know how many *signori* live in Milan. When the maître d' clarifies, Antonio proceeds to introduce himself and his brother: "Two. There are two of us. We are the Caponi brothers. Ca-po-ni. I am the oldest, and he … the second-oldest."[65] The information that he provides, however, is both excessive and irrelevant to their dining experience that night, as Antonio and Peppino are actually joining Marisa's fellow cast members. Much like their arrival in Milan, when the Caponis stand out as exceedingly bizarre creatures who do not belong, at the Gran Milan, too, their presence is the subject of ridicule. The viewer hears laughter directed at the brothers as they trip up the stairs leading to the *salotto superiore*, the upper dining room; their hand-holding, as well as Antonio's kicking Peppino after his stumble, only draw more attention to the anomalies. A final sign of comic excess is when the maître d' closes the curtains that separate the *salotto* from the other diners – a spatial move that casts the brothers aside as different – and the brothers mistake the sound of the curtains for their garments being torn, frantically checking each other's backsides for rips. The atmosphere can thus be described as "alien," as the noises and gestures comprising the restaurant space confuse, anger, and even frighten the Caponis, but their crass behaviour offers an equally bewildering contrast to the refinement of the restaurant.

Likewise, as the Gran Milan is coded as a bourgeois space, the restaurant's cuisine is a far cry from the Caponis' clothesline of foods, or even the vat of saucy spaghetti in *Miseria e nobiltà*. The word "cuisine" is used to underline the fine art and polished techniques of cooking, versus the necessity to eat to survive. Thus, food itself is another factor that distinguishes the refinement of the Gran Milan from the Caponis' more quotidian *caciotta* and *pasta bianca*, and these foods come at a high price. Initially, when realizing that they only have 20,000 lire to host a "little dinner" for seven people, Antonio suggests bargaining for a cheaper experience. This ridiculous idea devolves into further malaprop misunderstandings and, eventually, panic. The Caponis first protest against the obligatory *sette coperti* (seven cover charges), because, mistaking *coperte* (the general word for "covers") for "blankets," they do not understand why they would need seven blankets in a city that is not as cold as they anticipated; they do not realize that the restaurant requires a cover charge per customer. Then, perennially concerned with costs, and since the maître d' explains that all meals begin with a soup course, the Caponis reject the decidedly exotic turtle soup in favour of *pasta e fagioli*, which involves cheap filler ingredients meant to stretch one's resources; the *pasta e fagioli* would feed seven mouths considerably more cheaply than turtle soup. This counter-suggestion is immediately dismissed by the maître d', and the brothers panic about how to finance the dinner; Antonio even prays to his patron saint, asking for a miracle. Fortuitously, the actresses arrive, carrying with them the consolation money that Antonio and Peppino gave to Marisa. Antonio's prayers, as well as the girls' exclamatory requests for champagne and turtle soup, have thus been answered. Debauchery ensues as the Caponis squander the 700,000 lire – the bribery money – on the restaurant's myriad of expensive offerings; Antonio cries out, "Let's eat! Vegetable soup! Turtle soup! Seafood canapés! African fish! Champagne! Champagne!"[66] As the scene fades, Antonio – feeding off the youthful, spendthrift energy of the five actresses – is seen tossing the banknotes into the air, much like a child playing with fallen leaves. Again, as seen in *Miseria e nobiltà*, Totò elevates scenes to utmost excess; with the box full of money thus vanishes the idea of a modest meal such as *pasta e fagioli*, subsumed by the exotic luxuries of the Gran Milan, and the viewer is caught once more in a frenzy of consumption.

This frenzy, the abrupt transition from a bean soup to turtles and African seafood, is no longer the animalistic pursuit of food that we saw in *Miseria e nobiltà*. Instead, this is a commentary on the gross increase in food in this period and on radically changing tastes. In his work *Distinction: A Social Critique of the Judgement of Taste* (1979), sociologist Pierre Bourdieu constructs and interprets axes that correlate one's class affiliations and level of education to her leisurely interests and consumption tendencies. With respect to food consumption, his findings reveal that upper-class members of society prefer meals that are "original, exotic, and delicate," whereas those of the working class choose dishes that are "simple and well-presented."[67] The before-and-after in the *salotto* exhibits a shift along Bourdieu's axes; the surprise of 700,000 lire – a massive spike in the Southerners' budget – allows the Caponis to eat like the other diners, not merely to eat but enjoy Milanese cuisine. The Caponis forget about the *fagioli*, as well as the array of foods hanging in their hotel room, and they embrace the idea of turtle soup.

This jump towards "exotic" foods is an exciting move, but the allure diminishes when we realize that Totò's hunger and provincialism – and even Totò himself – are just an *act*. Although de Curtis was born and raised in Naples, and although his collaborations on *Miseria e nobiltà* and, later, Vittorio De Sica's *L'oro di Napoli* (1954) celebrate "a world and a culture that seemed proud, joyous, and self-sufficient,"[68] Totò and Sophia Loren, the basis of my next chapter, do not share the poverty and provincialism of their fellow citizens; class differences separate the average Neapolitan from the stars. Totò is not even a real person. Totò, as de Curtis's on-screen persona, is but a character; he is just a mask worn by someone else, detached from the Italian public. He is a fictional creation, imagined and executed by a man of nobility and wealthy tastes. One laughs at Totò's excessive role as *il Principe di Casador/Casserola*, but beneath the façade of the imposter prince lies a royal truth; de Curtis was adopted in 1933 by the marquis Francesco Maria Gagliardi Focas di Tertiveri, and de Curtis thus inherited not only the noble titles of Tertiveri but also a name that forever guaranteed him food, despite the war, black market, and devastations of the South.[69] De Curtis's daughter, Liliana, discusses the simple tastes of Totò, but even a description of bread and oil speaks of bourgeois tastes; whereas Felice Sciosciammocca would have gone to great lengths for a slice of bread in his hand, de Curtis required a more elegant culinary experience. Liliana writes, "Every food, according to Totò, was curated in its simplicity. If one decided to eat bread and oil, both ingredients should be top-quality and eaten at a well-set table, because the eyes and the stomach have equal rights."[70] How do we believe Totò's excess and *furbizie*, tied to an animalistic level of hunger, when a privileged de Curtis was excused from Italy's hunger pangs? The viewer thus questions the authenticity of the connection that Italians share with Totò, as well as his ability to perpetuate feelings of hunger, especially since he is not even real, and is instead an extension of someone not like his Neapolitan counterparts. Just like the spaghetti in *Miseria e nobiltà*, the artificiality of Totò compels the viewer to imagine continuity as well.

Conclusion

Antonio de Curtis, known universally as Totò, was a source of continuity and connectivity, restoring a sense of harmonious brotherhood to those left hungry and distraught in the wake of the Second World War. As the neorealist movement – decrying the social injustices of the 1940s – came to a close, the *commedia all'italiana* of the 1950s, by contrast, viewed the hunger pangs of the *dopoguerra* in a new light: filling empty stomachs with laughter. Through his body language, from bulging eyes to exaggerated gestures, Totò reflects the difficulties of procuring food and, later, of upholding food traditions amid geographic and socioeconomic stratifications. In stuffing his pockets with imaginary spaghetti, Totò reminds his viewers at once of their recent hunger and, also, of the importance of *pasta bianca* to Italy's longstanding food heritage, thereby bridging together past and present, suggesting a harmony missing since before Fascism. As the closing sequence of *I soliti ignoti* conveys, pasta remains the true gem: a versatile, rustic culinary mainstay of Italy, despite the rapidly revitalizing North and the influx of "exotic" and American products.

This ridiculous scheme makes the audience laugh because Totò functions within a world of imagination. The spaghetti is imaginary, the love stories are clouded by charlatanism, and even Totò is but the *maschera* of de Curtis. As an abundance of new products and ideas floods Italy's marketplace, we are left to imagine hunger: a sensation, at least in the physical sense, hereby lost to the past.

Chapter Two

From *Pizzaiola* to Phenom: Sophia Loren, the Nexus of Networks

The year is now 1971, and we return to another filmic world of Mario Monicelli: this time, that of *La mortadella*, or *Lady Liberty*, as it is known to English-speaking audiences. The film opens on a plane; this particular flight is en route from Italy to New York City, the establishing shots framing its descent. A montage of signs – "No Smoking/No Fumar" and "Lavatories Occupied/Toilettes Occupées" – reminds the viewer of the usual rules and regulations of air travel. These rules are perverted, however, when combined with a close-up of cigarette butts in the bathroom, along with cries of an orgasm off-screen. The opening shots underscore motifs of copulation and transgression: of sexual awakenings and inter-twinings that deviate from what had been codified as societal norms until the late 1960s and early 1970s.

The camera then rests on the protagonist, Maddalena, a passenger who is ultimately woken from a deep sleep, her arms cradling an enormous mortadella. The mortadella, wrapped in cellophane and adorned with the red, white, and green of the Italian flag, is a gift she received from a coworker for her upcoming marriage; her trip to the United States marks her reunion with her fiancé, Michele, and the start of their chapter together in America. Mortadella in tow, Maddalena exits the plane and heads to Customs, where an agent asks her if she has anything to declare – to which she naively responds, "Oh, yes, I am very happy to be in your country." The Customs agent then gestures to the mortadella and declares that she cannot bring meat into the United States. Maddalena insists that mortadella is exceptional, citing its supreme quality and categorizing it differently from meat: "I don't know how you call it, it's not in the dictionary, but … it's a special kind of sausage … it's like salami, but mortadella is better, you see, it's more delicate." The agent's supervisor then intervenes, concluding that the mortadella – for fear of its bringing contaminants into the country – must be burned, despite

Maddalena's protests that "It's just a mortadella ... Is America really scared of mortadella?" Losing her argument to the laws of US Customs, and silenced by Michele, who has broken away from Italy's code of conduct and commands her to follow the ways of "the most civilized country on Earth," Maddalena chooses detainment. Yelling at Michele to go home, she remains in a standoff in the Customs office, all the while holding tight to the mortadella.

The precariousness surrounding Maddalena and the mortadella reflects the sociopolitical upheaval of the late 1960s. Maddalena dismisses Michele, claiming that he has drastically changed since coming to New York, and thereby rejects the patriarchal expectations touted by Italy's Christian Democrats. Meanwhile, she protects the mortadella with motherly instinct, clinging to a powerful gastronomic symbol – but one she has trouble defining. The mortadella is indeed not to be seen as meat; neither salami nor sausage, it is instead a symbol of exceptionality. This "in-between" nature of the mortadella mirrors the settings of the establishing shots, all of which are of transit: the plane in the air, suspended between two distinct cities, followed by US Customs, where Maddalena is no longer in Italy yet barred from entering the United States. She cannot legally enter the country with the mortadella, so what is to be done? Maddalena chooses to remain sequestered for several days, gradually consuming the mortadella. The process that follows is twofold: The iconic Italian meat is broken down by Maddalena's digestive organs, sustaining her as she exits the airport and must now negotiate the norms and praxes of New York City. Supported not by a man but by the nutrients, flavour, and national reputation of the mortadella, Maddalena has to learn how to succeed in America: find a job, procure housing, and navigate the cultural expectations of her new country. How can she thrive in New York while staying true to her Italian roots?

These negotiations will be explored in greater detail through Sophia Loren, the actress who played Maddalena, and whose interactions with food on and off screen convey historic changes in domesticity.

Defining Loren and the "Nexus of Networks"

Across Loren's career, spanning more than sixty-five years, and as mass media constructed a portrait of her identity for readers and viewers worldwide, food has served as a North Star: not only a formative part of her films' *mises en scène*, its presence (and glaring absence) a litmus test for the socioeconomic and political circumstances described at large, but also a pillar of Loren's personal happiness. Food is part of the lifeblood of both her fictitious work and her real life. Loren *is* the mortadella: a filmic object for consumption and a complex metaphor for not only cultural hybridity but also the complicated rules, expectations, and transgressions defining her existence and popularity. Food was her compass as she navigated the conformism and rigidity of Hollywood and Anglo-American cinema, with eating and cooking as glorious and sacred daily rites;[1] likewise, the very first page of her 2014 memoir does not lament the trials and tribulations of the movie business, or the war, or harsh critics of her work, but instead shares worries stemming from her family's Christmas celebration: "Tomorrow is Christmas Eve and we'll finally all be together. The truth is, though, that I'm not ready. How will I manage to feed so many people? How can I possibly fry all those *struffoli*?"[2] This chapter, thus, unpacks such complicated dynamics, connecting food – tropes and recipes alike – to Loren's stardom: her status as a working woman worth millions of lire[3] and even more in symbolic capital, yet fiercely determined to be a mother, longing for the day when she could be holed up with her child, where no one could touch her, journalists and photographers fighting for crumbs of updates.[4]

Loren became a critically acclaimed film actress and sex symbol of the revolutionizing 1960s – but not until the "Toothpick" ate more to fill out her frame,[5] to exhibit a "height of 1.72 [metres], bust 95 [centimetres], waist 58 [centimetres], hips 95 [centimetres], weight of 60 kilograms, all assuring her a million dollars, or 600 million lire, therefore 10 million lire a kilo."[6] Growing up poor and hungry, Loren thanked cinema for "not being hungry anymore … To you all that might not mean much, but I was starving for so long that I believed one couldn't live any other way."[7] Acting was her way out of destitution; her elders described her otherwise as "deeply studious," attending school "with great discipline and advantage" and earning a teaching certificate by age sixteen.[8] What *does* one do with a woman who, from 1950 to 1960, worked on five to ten films each year, thereby generating enormous wealth and fame for herself, yet who longed to be a mother and wished to feel "womanly, weak, protected by a man," believing that "women can be independent, but within certain limits"?[9] What, then, does Italy's postwar filmic foodscape mean for, and by, Loren – whose stardom felt all but limitless, but perhaps was not always or necessarily so?

This chapter investigates Loren's struggles towards stardom amid radical socioeconomic and cultural transformations in postwar Italy: how she fitted into the Christian Democratic heteropatriarchy of the *boom*, and how she both upheld and challenged societal norms previously instated under Fascism. Working within a capitalistic, man-made star system, and facing harsh scrutiny for her early relations with producer Carlo Ponti, Loren had to fight to become an icon, recognizable among not only networks of Italians but also viewers and women worldwide. For such a reputation to incubate, she required space, hereby called the "nexus of networks": At the intersection of various sociocultural and international arenas, defined below, she functioned as a validated actress, a wife whose romance was splashed across tabloids for over a decade, and, after much patience and drive, a mother.

Loren's work and navigation of greater society were largely controlled by men – not only inspirational male figures in her life and the laws dictating Catholic Italian society, but, of special interest to this chapter, also mass media reports on both the international and the microscopic scales: the big sociopolitical transformations of the "swinging 60s," existing alongside one forceful sneeze tearing Loren's dress, scaring her from eating anything at a gala.[10] Loren was both designed by and confined to a male-dominated star system, her reputation responding to sociopolitical and classist expectations. These criteria were largely determined by four macrocosmic cultural networks that comprised Italy's patriarchy in the postwar years.[11] First, Italy's attachment to the Catholic Church provided a stronghold of sociopolitical governance. Second, boasting the largest Communist party outside of the Soviet Union, Italy's Left was strong, upholding the values of the working class. The Left also scorned the third cultural influence – the oncoming waves of American products and ideas. And finally, there were also the urban poor of Rome and Naples: underbellies of two cities that defined Loren's upbringing. Satisfying all four subcultures proved arduous, but food paved a way.

Loren's ascent to stardom, in combination with her struggles and triumphs with maternity, is peppered with her interactions with food. The use of food in her cinema is a poignant way to document the trajectory of women in the 1960s and 1970s, as they struggled against Catholic, heteropatriarchal norms and legislation for equal rights. Her public demonstrations of cooking and eating spoke volumes to the millions of women across the peninsula, who were inundated with directions for domesticity but beginning to acknowledge that their status was changing. Loren was *not* just a "mobile of fruits and melons," as she was described in 1962 by *TIME* magazine.[12] Instead, through close readings of Vittorio De Sica's *L'oro di Napoli* (1954), *La ciociara* (1960), and *Ieri, oggi, domani* (1963), as well as her own cookbooks, this chapter underscores the combination of Loren's sex appeal with the sensual pleasures of food. In each of the case studies, the notion of desire is multiplied: the viewer simultaneously desires Loren's body and the foods with which she interacts. This doubled desire fuelled her stardom; she attracted a fan base across the four subcultures, reversing their respective criticisms, and all the while championing women who, similarly, sought to find their own space within the patriarchy.

L'oro di Napoli: The Promiscuous *Pizzaiola*

Loren's connections to Naples are noticeably different from Totò's root-edness to the South, a major premise of Chapter 1. Totò's iconicity is mostly limited to Italy, his performances consonant with the changes impacting the country, and particularly the South, in the 1950s. Loren, by contrast, fondly remembers her upbringing in Pozzuoli, but she utilized her Southern autochthony as a means of symbolic capitalism, enabling her career to extend beyond the peninsula. Loren's Southern-ness stands opposite the filth of Naples described in the previous chap-ter; instead, the desires and the sensory overload surrounding earlier portraits of Naples, as well as of Totò's hunger, are now channelled through the body of Loren. The viewers no longer desire just food; they desire Loren herself, who embodies the exotic, picturesque aspects of the Italian South. Through Totò, Naples had been a point marking the end of the civilized world, beyond which lay uncharted territory, unrecognizable to the Northerner – and, likewise, the Southerner felt alien in the North. Through Loren, though, that unrecognizability is romanticized and exoticized, rendering Naples a place of desire. Over-looking the filth and the dusty streets, the outsider imagines a beautiful spectacle: volcanoes, blue seas and green fields, multicoloured dawns, all of which offer a picturesque contrast to the squalor.[13] One need only remember Giovanni Verga's short story "Fantasticheria" (1880), in which he describes a woman who imagines the allure of the Sicilian town of Aci Trezza, clapping her hands in wonder at the deep blue sea and its giant rocks, looking out her carriage window onto Aci Trezza and exclaiming, "I'd like to spend a month down there!" Within forty-eight hours, however, the woman grows bored and restless, ultimately leaving her to question "how people can spend the whole of their lives in a place like this."[14] The viewer experiences this same desire towards Loren, but she escapes that ultimate feeling of boredom, perpetuating her allure for decades. She does so through an act of Northernization, opening herself and her career up to the rest of the world. Loren, born as Sofia Scicolone, changed her name twice, willing to change a major signifier of her identity for her career, thereby solidifying an interna-tional recognizability and memorability. During her career in photo-romances, in which she was frequently cast as a gypsy temptress or a slave girl because of her darker complexion, she was known as Sofia Lazzaro, implying that her beauty was so violent it could awaken even the dead.[15] The change to "Sophia Loren," meanwhile, reflects the need to Northernize her identity and to increase her viewership beyond Italy – to overcome that eventual ennui described by Verga. In a conversation with producer Goffredo Lombardo, which, in her autobiography, Loren named her "artistic christening," Lombardo wanted to give her "a short name that was easy to pronounce, a name with a certain allure." Inspiration came from a poster of Swedish actress Märta Torén. Loren added, "While we were at it, he also decided to replace the *f* with a *ph* and voilà, it was the right name for an international star." The change to the consonant cluster of "ph," one foreign to the Italian register, granted Loren a recognizability beyond Italy's shores, particularly among Anglo-Saxon audiences, but it also increased her exoticization, a cultural displacement, among her native Italians. To this end, Loren concluded, "People in Pozzuoli somehow became convinced I'd changed my name to Sopìa, with a *p*, although they didn't understand why."[16] As this chapter proceeds to show, this is just one way in which Loren negotiated the contours of her iconicity; indeed, as an article in *Corriere d'Informazione* once concluded, "Now her name is in the papers: There's no longer any fear of her changing it. With the h, or without the h, it is hereby engraved in the history of cinema."[17]

Loren's career began to blossom in 1954, following the production of *L'oro di Napoli*, the first of her eight collaborations with De Sica.[18] In this film of six vignettes, adapted from Giuseppe Marotta's novel of the same name, De Sica had intended to paint a prewar portrait of Naples: a beautiful and primitive world, not yet touched by the overbearing influence of America and the rapid industrialization of the new West. Indeed, over the course of *L'oro di Napoli*, audiences encounter some of the quintessential stereotypes of the Italian South: a family subservient to a local Mafia boss; a hopeless gambler; a prostitute whose life turns to shambles; and an earthy, sexy *pizzaiola*. As seen across Totò's oeuvre, the setting of the vignettes, Naples, is an important component – a protagonist perhaps as central to the films as any human role. The Caponis' misadventures in *Totò, Peppino e ... la malafemmina* (1956) have Naples as the "home base" for which the farmers – and audiences at large – long, comparing the alien Milan to the more comforting surroundings of the Mediterranean. It makes sense, then, that Totò stars in the first vignette of *L'oro di Napoli*, portraying a man who explodes against and expels *Il guappo* from his home, because *Il guappo* commanded them to eat a lean preparation of fish for Christmas instead of the traditional fried cod. As in the hotel room of *La malafemmina*, laden with mortadella and *pasta bianca*, in *L'oro di Napoli* Totò is once again championing tradition, rooting his tastes in and upholding his allegiance to his native South. With

Loren, meanwhile, the viewer hungers for the foods with which she interacts, on one hand because she extends a sexualizing, tantalizing component to these products; on the other, perhaps, because we wish that *we* were those foods, being touched and consumed in the ways seen on screen. In so doing, however, Loren negotiates *against* certain societal traditions.

Loren's role is, like Totò's, centred on food, as she plays the *pizzaiola* in a later vignette. With "his third eye, which was trained to discover the actor behind the appearances,"[19] De Sica extracted Loren's autochthon, unearthing and projecting her Neapolitan roots to the world at large as his explosive, blowsy pizza girl. Loren related to A.E. Hotchner, "He [De Sica] said I had a quality of spontaneity, an outgoing impulsiveness, typically Neapolitan, that he wanted to capture in this part … It was a part made to order for me: an explosive, earthy Neapolitan woman, a type I knew so well; she was even called Sofia."[20] From this role, with the *pizzaiola* nickname following her throughout the 1950s, Loren acquired the first of her fan base: those living in the poor, urban South who immediately recognized De Sica's Naples, meanwhile wary of the cultural traces left behind by the American GIs. She did so with an Italian product as iconic as she: pizza.

Pizza perfectly embodies Neapolitan culture. In a book dedicated entirely to pizza, food historian Carol Helstosky claims that pizza started as a street food consumed largely by the poor of Naples, eaten on weekdays (so as to pay for a more lavish meal on Sunday) and paid for on credit.[21] It makes sense, then, that De Sica's vignette, appropriately titled "*Pizze a credito*," was shot mostly on the street, centred on the small, makeshift pizza stand managed by Rosario and Sofia, husband and wife. The episode is centred most specifically on Sofia, her body portrayed as more mouthwatering than her pizzas, and more supple than the dough. The viewer is immediately jarred by her presence; through a series of long shots, we meet the tall, buxom woman, dressed in white, whose appearance commands her fellow street urchins. Despite Sofia and Rosario's egregious shouts of "Come have a snack!" and "Eat today and pay within eight days!", it soon becomes clear that their clientele flocks to the stand not for the pizza, but, rather, to get a glimpse of Sofia. As she kneads the dough, her customers stand on the street and consume not only the fresh pizza but also her voluptuous body; viewers, watching from within the male gaze, eroticize both the pizza and the *pizzaiola*. When Rosario yells at her to cover herself, we are reminded that Sofia's curves match the suppleness of the dough she shapes into pizzas, and she embodies the fertility of the yeasty dough with which she works. Loren's star power is strongly rooted in her body, hearty and

Figure 2.1. Sofia the *pizzaiola* (Sophia Loren) working the pizza counter in *L'oro di Napoli* (1954, dir. Vittorio De Sica).

rounded, like the iconic pizza. But her allure is also carnal and scandalous, as this episode underlines.

While De Sica shot most of the vignette outdoors, the shots that take place indoors are far more revealing. The vignette begins not at the family pizza stand, nor at church, as Sofia has her husband believe, but at Sofia's lover's house. Worse yet, Sofia lies to her husband not only about her whereabouts but also about her ring, which she claims she accidentally misplaced in the dough and ultimately baked into a customer's pizza. While intended as a simple alibi, this scenario bears deep consequences. In Sofia's attempt to jettison an adulterous reputation, the couple ventures to the customer's house and demands to inspect his pizza. The pizza, however, was the man's snack-break from mourning his wife. Rosario and Sofia disrespect the man's privacy, as the pizza ultimately becomes a sign of betrayal: in not joining the funerary proceedings, it is a betrayal of communal solidarity as well as of Sofia's fidelity.[22] The sexualized metaphor of the dough is furthered and dirtied, amplifying the use of Sofia's hands on both her dough and her lover, and the emblem of her marriage gets lost, even forgotten, in the amorphous, sticky substance. But, were we to look back on Loren's budding career in the 1950s, in this moment, we would recall her own messy, illegal romance with Carlo Ponti, producer of *L'oro di Napoli*, which subjected her to years of chastisement by the Vatican, by the government of Italy, which refused to recognize their marriage, and by fans alike.

Ponti and Loren first met in 1950, when Loren was a contestant in a beauty pageant and Ponti was one of the jurors. Upon meeting her, Ponti recognized that, with enough money and encouragement, he could transform Loren into a star rivalling Gina Lollobrigida and Silvana Mangano. He not only pumped a staggering 60 to 70 million lire into her campaign but also provided her with protection, counsel, and moral support.[23] What began as a platonic and even fatherly relationship, however, soon escalated to a secret, illicit romance, as Ponti was still legally married to his first wife, Giuliana Fiastri. In terms of its secrecy, Loren related to Hotchner:

> Carlo was aware of my fears and reticence, aware that I wasn't just another accessible starlet (how I despise that word!) and he never tried to go very far with me. From what I gathered, Carlo had always had little affairs with actresses, and his wife didn't seem to mind as long as he didn't see the same girl very often and there was no threat of a serious relationship. That's why we saw each other secretly, so that his wife wouldn't become aware of me.[24]

There was media frenzy, pandemonium throughout periodicals for the next ten years, while their lawyers sought grounds upon which the marriage of Loren and Ponti could stand. They looked to Mexico, in particular Ciudad Juárez, known as "the little divorce capital," where a proxy marriage was honoured and registered by Judge Fernando de la Fuente in September 1957.[25] While it was not so difficult to arrange, because Loren was in Hollywood and Ponti in Rome, they got word of its approval only moments before the press. Loren expressed her shock in her memoir: "I almost fell off my chair. Even Carlo, although it was he who had unleashed his legal office in search of a solution outside of Italy, was taken by surprise. His lawyers, evidently, had gone ahead with it without his knowing."[26] Her mother, Romilda Villani, meanwhile, reported differently to *Il Giorno*, implying that the couple had known that they were to be married but unsure exactly when:

> IL GIORNO: But you, when did you find out that Sofia had been married?
> ROMILDA VILLANI: Yesterday, shortly before it hit the papers. Sofia called me from Hollywood and told me, begging me not to say anything to anyone. "Let them find out from the papers," she said, so I kept quiet.[27]

Regardless of the timeline, because Ponti's marriage to Fiastri had not been annulled religiously, neither the Vatican nor the Republic of Italy would officially recognize the union. The proxy was valid everywhere but their home country: a thorn in Loren's side well into the 1960s.[28] Not unlike the *pizzaiola* of three years prior, she was portrayed as an unfaithful saboteur: a stark contrast from the universally adored star we know today. Indeed, in the months that immediately followed their proxy marriage, conservatives attacked the budding star; among women in particular, Loren "became the concubine and the home-breaker, the siren who had stolen a man from the breast of his family without regard for morality or the sentiments of others."[29] (Ponti, "the stolen man," had faced more lenient criticism.) More macrocosmically, the Church – already confronting a period of radical secularization – condemned Loren. Cultural historian Stephen Gundle noted, "Sophia was not a practicing Catholic but, as she later said, 'emotionally Catholicism was my heritage and ex-communication was a chilling threat.'"[30]

Loren and Ponti, however, responded swiftly: They whisked off to Switzerland, seeking Swiss citizenship to uphold their marriage. The move was strategic. Not only would they be recognized as legally married throughout Europe, but leaving Italy also opened Loren up to more global opportunities. *Houseboat* (1958), *The Key* (1958), and *It Happened in Naples* (1960) began a legacy abroad, untapped founts of fame overflowing for the skyrocketing star.

As Loren bounced between continents, from Los Angeles to London to Madrid and Jerusalem, relaxing at her Bürgenstock villa in between, her ties to Italy were shaky and even invalidating despite her ballooning stardom. Reminiscent of Totò and Peppino out of their element in Milan, food cured whatever angst and homesickness lay within. In the summer of 1960, amid magistrate Guido Guasco's public cries of bigamy against the couple, among Loren's self-defences was food. Her memories of London, while shooting *The Millionairess* (1960), are rich with "unforgettable mozzarella-stuffed macaroni, or spaghetti with peppers and anchovies, prepared in her cottage before going to bed."[31] Likewise, she fondly recalls the sauce, pasta, and eggplants of her *paese*: "I have dreamed of them for so long, fried and golden, on a layer of mozzarella and tomato, a clove of garlic, a little sliver of pepper, fresh out of the oven, hot and fragrant."[32] While she was not depicted as a traditionally chaste, virtuous housewife, nor was she a mother, her marriage worthless paper in Italy, she nevertheless sought diversion at stoves across various hotel rooms, inventing recipes alongside her secretary, Ines: "Discovering the conformism of Hollywood, in England the pleasure of strolling through the woods, and in Paris the joy of going to

Figure 2.2. A newspaper clipping depicting Loren and her husband, Carlo Ponti. Translated into English, a caption underneath reads, "Sofia Loren and husband Carlo Ponti at Victoria Station in London, shortly before departing for Switzerland." *Quotidiano Nazionale il Giorno*, 24 November 1957. Courtesy of Luca Ceroni, Editoriale Nazionale S.r.l.

the theatre, all these experiences remain alive in Sophia's heart through some culinary invention."[33] Not only did cooking keep her grounded as she rose to superstardom and navigated life outside Italy, but these recipes also formed the basis of her 1971 cookbook, a project developed while she was pregnant with her son, Carlo Jr., as will be discussed at length later in this chapter.

For Loren, Hollywood was dizzying: In her first interview on American soil, she stated that it made her nervous; she feared going insane from such an impossible, crazy city.[34] She was inundated with requests, parties, invitations; the clamour around her was feverish. Actress Janet

Figure 2.3. Translated into English, the caption reads,
"It's Sofia's big moment: the *pizzaiola* from five years
ago, once used for just supporting roles, is today the
centre of attention in Hollywood: parties worth tens
of thousands of dollars organized for her, attended by
the likes of Gregory Peck, Frank Sinatra, John Wayne.
But her celebrity does not come without 'troubles':
The other day brought an attack by Social Democrat
Deputy Preti, struck by the fact that the *diva* declared
an income of 16 million [lire]; and yesterday a breach of
contract was cited by Burt Lancaster. Where the girl from
Pozzuoli never wavers, however, is in her aggressive
and majestic Venus-like state." *Il Corriere Lombardo*, 29
June 1957. Courtesy of the Archivio Fotografico *La Notte* –
l'Università degli Studi di Milano, Centro Apice.

Leigh, who had befriended Loren after a 1955 trip to Rome, declared that "Sophia conquered Hollywood, at her feet from the first moment."[35] Director Cecil B. De Mille added that, within three months of her arrival, Hollywood would become "Lorentown."[36] But was Loren's acting any good? Was her fame exclusively derived from her sex appeal – Western media exoticizing and eroticizing her *italianità*? Loren commented to *Il Giorno* in December 1957, "I now want them to judge how I act. I've almost finished the film [*The Key*] with [William] Holden, directed by Carol Reed. If I appear 'sexy,' I haven't done so deliberately: It just means that I am that way. But now I want to use my brain, and I hope one day to act so well that I'll win an Oscar."[37] Farewell, *pizzaiola*. Enter *La ciociara*.

La ciociara: A Mother's Greed to Feed

Then there were the Marxists, wary of light-hearted, Hollywoodized pulp, and, hence, Loren's early "confectionary" performances.[38] Following the success of *L'oro di Napoli*, however, Loren got the opportunity to work with De Sica once again, this time on a film that documented the struggles of motherhood and of survival in occupied, famished Italy. Now separated from the war by fifteen years, De Sica – a forefather of the neorealist movement[39] – was able to revisit the devastations of the war and explore *la carestia*, material deprivation, through the lens of Italy's new consumer economy.[40] *La ciociara*, adapted from Alberto Moravia's 1957 novel of the same name, is a narrative of hunger, but one drastically different from the hallucinatory buffoonery that Totò illustrated for his audiences, as discussed in Chapter 1. Totò's hunger is comical and imagined, whereas the hunger of Cesira and her daughter, Rosetta, is carnal and violent; they forcibly become objects for consumption, as they struggle to survive in la Ciociaria, Cesira's native province.

Production of the film was, similarly, a struggle. This collaboration between De Sica and Loren was, in a word, serendipitous. Originally, the film was to be directed by George Cukor, and Anna Magnani, the *doyenne* of Italian actresses and queen of neorealism, herself an Oscar winner for *The Rose Tattoo* (1955), was to play Cesira; Loren was supposed to play Rosetta. However, Magnani had regrettably rejected that dynamic. Hotchner's biography of Loren reduces these qualms to Loren being "too tall,"[41] but Magnani's lamentations reveal a greater paradigm shift: "'Ever since Ponti discovered that the roles I've always played could also be done by Sophia, there wasn't any room for me in cinema,' Anna Magnani affirmed in an interview with a reputable weekly press."[42] She continued:

In not doing *La ciociara* … I lost three hundred thousand dollars. But how could I have? I was supposed to play Sophia's mother. To persuade me to take the role, they said that whenever I appeared alongside Loren, they would put a stool under my feet. It wasn't so much about our heights, but I found it absurd to put us together as mother and daughter. And I wasn't the only one to think that … Not having done *La ciociara* has caused me pain for years. When De Sica insisted, I told him to stop it, as it was making me feel bad. Despite that, I suggested giving the role of the mother to Sophia. And I must say that Loren was by no means bad in that film.[43]

Magnani had abandoned the project, and, without her, Cukor lost interest and withdrew. Ponti had bought the rights to the film and made De Sica his director, and Loren had been promoted to the role of Cesira, the mother. In Moravia's novel, Rosetta is eighteen years old, but when twenty-six-year-old Loren was cast as Cesira, De Sica and screenwriter Cesare Zavattini decided to make Rosetta even younger: only *twelve* years old.

These changes made the Left nervous: How could Loren, by this point a Hollywoodized bombshell, possibly portray a valiant mother weathered by war? At certain points, De Sica's film is a drastic departure from Moravia's anti-American, anti-consumerist work. In his novel, Moravia draws a binary between American GIs and Italian civilians, treating their relationship like a market exchange: Americans offer gifts and good cheer to the hungry, distressed Italians, thus cementing the image of Americans as supreme victors and, in line with this role, generous benefactors in the places they occupied. Yet, according to Moravia's text, these transactions – the gifting of niceties such as candies and cigarettes – did little more than boost America's public relations. Cesira observes bitterly:

In those few hours, what had already formed was an atmosphere that I had observed in Rome for the whole Allied occupation: The Italians asked for things to please the Americans, and the Americans gave it over to please the Italians; neither group realized they were not pleasing each other whatsoever. And I think that no one wants these things and they happen on their own, as if by unspoken agreement. The Americans were the winners and the Italians the losers, and that was that.[44]

De Sica's film, by contrast, avoids the Americans' hubris, and it upholds the Italians' feelings of celebration and gratitude towards the Americans, which was in line with the propagandist visions of the Marshall Plan ten years earlier.[45] In one scene of the film, the Italians cheer the Americans, celebrating their liberation; the Americans dole out their rations, but the Italians receive these with joy. Through such transactions, both material and emotional, Italy is illustrated as accepting America's growing hegemony. De Sica's criticism of America and its soft power, then, is to be found in his keen employment of Loren.

The decision to cast Loren as Cesira, though happenstance, is one that brilliantly transports Moravia's war recollections to the peak of the Economic Miracle, complete with its questionable traces of Americana. Loren, who by 1960 was a recognizable figure on both American and Italian screens, thus took on an ambassadorial role amid such cultural transactions; as an Italian not only recognized but also strongly desired by the American public, viewers of either country were inclined to follow her into a darker, more politicized agenda. Moravia remembers this difficult time through Michele, an intellectual and anti-Fascist who bides his time with Cesira and Rosetta, accompanying them on their quest for provisions while decrying both the war and commodification: the selfishness and greed that blind Cesira and block her from protecting her daughter in wartime. With Loren at the helm of such a story, De Sica was able to continue a directorial mission dating to his neorealist days: underlining moments of social injustice, and ultimately holding Italians accountable for sustaining the Fascist *ventennio*. Whereas in, for example, De Sica's *Ladri di biciclette* (1947), the glaring absence of the bicycle signifies the painful absence of solidarity, community, and any chance at material prosperity, in *La ciociara*, the focus is no longer on banal objects. Rather, the new central object is Loren's body. The star's pin-up is torn down as Cesira's body is violated, thereby exposing the moral privation and wilful ignorance blatant throughout Italy's Reconstruction: a key objective among leftists.

Readers acknowledge that Marxists were against two tenets, both of which informed the backdrop of Moravia's narrative: war and capitalism. To this end, readers are meant to praise Michele, a proponent of Resistance, and sympathize with Cesira, who falls victim to the alluring spell of consumerism and, consequently, the Allied occupation, as she and Rosetta become spoils of war. Michele could even be read as a spiritual leader of sorts, who encourages Cesira's conversion from selfish shopkeeper to humanitarian, a trauma victim reckoning with her wayward materialism. Indeed, Cesira is seized by material goods, whether she possesses them or strives endlessly to restock her personal supply; among the objects she values is her daughter, feeling a similar joy in motherhood as in being a keeper of goods, profiting from the scarcities of war.[46] From the very first page of the novel, lists, inventories, and accumulations of stuff come to define this *nouveau riche*. Having landed a husband who, before his death, ran a successful grocery store in Rome, Cesira is able to move to the capital and live continually immersed in goods:

The market was there, a few steps from home, and I would circulate around the stalls, for over an hour, not so much to buy anything, because most of the stuff we had at the store, but to look around. I would go around the stalls and look at everything, fruits, vegetables, meat, fish, eggs: I would get to know all of it, and I liked to calculate the prices and profits, evaluate the quality, uncover the vendors' scams and tricks. I liked just talking, weighing the stuff, leaving it there and then coming back to discuss it again, and in the end, not buying anything.[47]

Cesira is, in other words, obsessed with the *spectacle* of commodity goods: the abundance of commodities and people's interactions with these goods. The spectacle diminishes, however, with the invasion of the Allies, as pantries are emptied and shelves lie bare. Hunger drives her and Rosetta to Sant'Eufemia, Cesira's hometown in the Ciociaria. Hereafter, Moravia emphasizes the trivialities of Cesira's search for food, especially amid bombardments, partisan resistance, and severe threats to human life. The store once provided a nourishing cocoon, enveloping and protecting the two women from the looming war and accompanying famine, but *La ciociara* follows the mother and daughter *out* of such containment, documenting the decisions that Cesira must make to continue feeding herself and her family.

It seems that only when extracted from the store and positioned with respect to another mother does Cesira acknowledge the pangs of war. One moment in both the novel and the film that is especially grotesque is Cesira's encounter with Lena, a young mother whose infant son was recently killed by the Nazis. Lena, in turn, is psychotically traumatized, obsessed with her leftover breast milk, the remaining link to her son. In the novel, Cesira, noticing that Lena is meandering aimlessly, asks Lena if she has seen any Nazis, and is perturbed by Lena's reaction:

> I grabbed her by the arm, repeating the question; and she, lowering her voice, said, "If I tell you, you won't go and tell where I keep my provisions?" I remained agape at these words, because at the same time they kept with the circumstances and were completely absurd. And she, shaking her head: "They come and take … they come and take … the Germans, you know … but do you know what I told them the last time they came? I don't have anything, I said to them, I don't have flour, I don't have beans, I don't have lard, I don't have anything … I just have milk for my baby … if you'd like it, take it … here."[48]

De Sica's filmed portrayal of this moment is, while only roughly ninety seconds long, decidedly more shocking. He provided his audience with a visual that Moravia's written words could not fully convey. De Sica captured Lena's lunacy, as she, through tears, re-enacts the Nazis

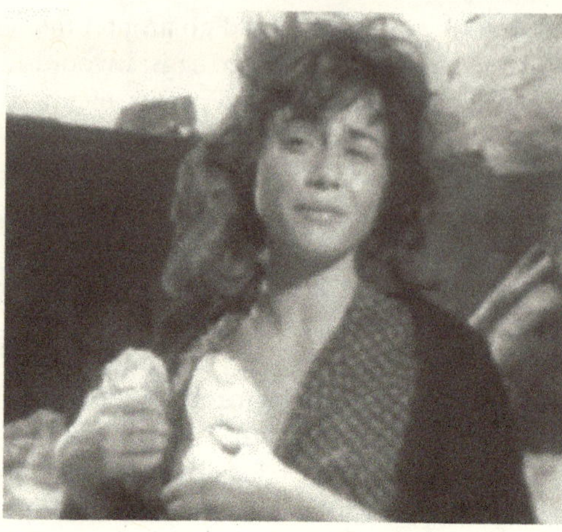

Figure 2.4. Lena, a young mother whom Cesira encounters while looking for food, with her breast out for consumption, revealing just how distorted Cesira's priorities are. From *La ciociara* (1960, dir. Vittorio De Sica).

shooting her baby, and then – without skipping a beat – pulls out her breast for Cesira, causing Cesira to flee; Lena meanders off, exclaiming madly, "Who wants milk?"

Let us consider the usage of milk in these scenes. A fetus grows in the mother's womb, receiving her nutrients by way of the umbilical cord, but, upon birth, it is milk that connects mother and child. Breast milk is produced by the mother, but it *is* the mother in liquid form: her immunity, her energy, a store of nutrients from all that she eats or drinks. In consuming breast milk, the child takes on her mother's shield, and she is readied for the tumult of the world beyond the womb. Milk, then, is the symbol *par excellence* of life and of a mother's loving protection – a message, however, that Moravia and De Sica invert. When Lena's son is killed by the Nazis, but she not only survives but continues to lactate, she functions at a caloric surplus but is overcome with loss: at once full of milk and grief. Cesira solicits Lena for food, and Lena offers her breast, thereby revealing both mothers' *modi operandi*, and just how differently these women view the world at this juncture. Cesira sees milk as a product to be consumed, whereas for Lena it represents a loss of innocence. Lena does not seek the commodities that Cesira so desperately craves, but rather, with breast out and body on raw display, she *is* the commodity. Because Cesira is too enamoured with the spectacle of material items, the striking spectacle of Lena fails to shake Cesira's ignorance; hence she runs away. Lena not only signifies the stark contrast in mentality between the two mothers – victim of the war in 1944 versus victim of the *boom* in 1960 – but it also foreshadows Cesira's own fate as a mother. No matter where Cesira goes, and no matter how much potential she believes her wad of cash wields – hidden under her skirt, under the false impression that "no one would think to look there" – she cannot escape the horrors of the war on Fascism, including and especially witnessing the brutal rape of Rosetta. This act of violence reveals the fallacies of a consumer economy; no amount of money, or chewing gum or candy or cigarettes gifted by the Americans, is a guarantee of one's security, nor can these goods erase the continued commodification of, and threats against, the female body. With respect to Marxist subculture, the capitalist ideals promoted through America's hegemony only distracted from greater socioeconomic and sociocultural inequities. Loren's body does, to a certain extent, serve the same purposes of appeasement and of distraction: her body could be read as analogous to the Americans' candy, something sweet we desire. However, through the ways in which she exhibited the gravity of the mutual exclusivity between one's capital and one's safety, Loren curried the favour of Italian Marxists. She won the Oscar, Hollywood's top prize, for this role, indicating her acclaim among American audiences, but her portrayal of such desperation and defeat, running counter to her usual "star" qualities, impressed the Marxists as well. Unlike in her lighthearted comedies and saccharine romance films, in *La ciociara* Loren communicated a solemn message on accountability, the absence of solidarity and of total equality, and the nation's struggle against Fascism and its haunting legacy, which – as will be underscored in my analysis of *Ieri, oggi, domani* – De Sica wove into their later collaborations.

Despite her Academy Award–winning performance, for which she earned the admiration of fans worldwide, as well as Marxists at home, some remained unconvinced by Loren's acting and, thus, continued to question her place among the stars. Some newspapers assessed her win as a power play, a move to stabilize the hegemony of Hollywood against new waves of European cinema. In 1957, *La Settimana Incom* foresaw that, so long as Loren stayed in Italy, her influence would greatly contest that of Hollywood, contributing instead to a European *divismo* that would undermine the American star system.[49] The response, then, was to cultivate Loren's prowess – her popularity, style, and calibre of acting – on American soil; the soft power of Hollywood would appear global. Guido Aristarco of *La Stampa* published an article berating such a ploy and, by extension, diminishing Loren's win – indeed "putting some bitters in her champagne."[50] He proceeds, "The Academy pretends to select an Italian actress. Our newspapers highlight the fact that this is the first time the award has been given for a non-English-speaking performance. But Hollywood, hiding its true objectives, is only interested in creating the myth of Loren, who for some time has been part of American productions."[51] Even with an Oscar, Loren is still not met with universal praise.

There was a paradigm shift, however, as Loren not only continued to play "motherly" types but also struggled to become a mother off screen. While newspaper correspondence provided extensive, even invasive, coverage of her pregnancies and miscarriages, my reading of this period is more through her interactions with food: foods signifying the fertility that Loren herself hoped to eventually embody, both in a Fascist world where fecundity was intensely treasured but monitored, and later, at the turn of the 1970s, when the once-dichotomous, unequal arena between men and women underwent significant levelling.

Ieri, oggi, domani: "Gestations Like Fruit"

This next section analyses Loren's performance in *Ieri, oggi, domani*. Critics argue that the film, among other late works by De Sica, is "miles away from his neorealist art"; De Sica himself lamented his ultimate ruin by money and "big Hollywood."[52] Despite these criticisms, it remains a cornerstone of the *commedia all'italiana* movement, as well as of Loren's career. *Ieri, oggi, domani*, composed of three vignettes based in Naples, Milan, and Rome, respectively, illustrates a fundamental transition in Italian history: disentangling from the Fascist *ventennio*, and, against a backdrop of secularization and economic revitalization, progressing towards the age of the emancipated woman. Loren, as the star of all three chapters, is at the helm of this fictionalized film, embodying the collective spirit of women beyond the screen: mothers, wives, and economically independent free-thinkers alike.

The film begins in Naples, the *"ieri"* of the film, where we are immediately absorbed not only into the black market but into a world dominated by sex, food, and procreation: fertility abounds. The premise of the film is as follows: There is a warrant out for Adelina's (Loren) arrest for selling black-market cigarettes. The announcement of her pregnancy, however, puts her punishment on hold. Come December, when she gives birth to the child, she almost immediately thereafter gets pregnant again. This cycle persists, and Adelina and her husband, Carmine (Marcello Mastroianni), ultimately welcome seven children into the world. When they fail to have an eighth child, Adelina is sent to jail, but she is soon released and happily reunited with her family.

This vignette speaks to the interference of civic offices in women's most private, intimate moments: the conception and gestation of a baby. In this episode, a woman's pregnancies are not only for public exhibition but they are also historicized. While Loren and Mastroianni dominate the screen, one could make the argument that History is in fact the greatest protagonist in this first vignette. The idea of bearing seven children – to avoid a prison sentence, no less – is, certainly, laughable. This sort of behaviour, however, would have won the family prizes and great acclaim under Benito Mussolini's rule. How, then, did the once-fervent encouragement of fertility by the government and, thus, the media, change – or not – in the 1960s? And how does Adelina take advantage of such a system? To underline the conditions that women fought to overcome in later decades, and to highlight the prowess of women in the postwar period, one must recall the economics and gender politics of Fascism.

We can begin our discussion with the setting and *mise en scène*. This vignette takes place in Naples, a city which, with the invasion of the Allies in 1943 and the requisitioning of foodstuffs by the Nazis, became the central hub of Italy's black-market economy, developed in strong collaboration with American GIs.[53] The black market was an economy of crime built in response to Fascist autarky, but one that was hardly curbed. Contraband goods filled the homes of Italy, but predominantly the Neapolitans'.

One sees this bounty in Adelina and Carmine's neighbourhood and apartment. De Sica fills these spaces with not only heaping amounts of colourful produce – watermelon rinds in a bowl, green grapes at dinner, a tumbling mountain of oranges – but also symbols of Americana: Lipton tea, canned chicken, and, of course, the ubiquitous red and white of Coca-Cola. These choices have prompted critics to suggest that De Sica was viewing the postwar with thick, rose-coloured glasses; film scholar Stephen Snyder writes, "It is as though a large screen painting of overflowing fruit bowls has been placed in front of *Umberto D.*, rendering the world of that film effectively invisible."[54] Snyder is referring to De Sica's neorealist film, in which a retiree debates suicide when he and his dog, Flike, are threatened with eviction from their Roman apartment. *Umberto D.* underscores the vast social injustices against marginalized groups – in this case, the elderly – in the years following the Second World War. In other parts of this book, the kitchen has been portrayed as a warm, welcoming, and indeed maternal space. However, in *Umberto D.*, Maria, the building's young servant and Umberto's companion, reveals to Umberto that she is pregnant and does not know who the father is. This news is disclosed in the kitchen, and, all the while, Maria ignites newspaper and burns pesky ants while she speaks. The joy and warmth typically associated with new life is negated by fire and destruction: helpless creatures are burning to death. Motherhood takes a grave turn, intensely sombre when juxtaposed with the fresh fruit of *Ieri, oggi, domani*. Nevertheless,

Figure 2.5. A scene from Adelina and Carmine's kitchen in *Ieri, oggi, domani* (1964, dir. Vittorio De Sica).

the fruits and big-brand goods in Adelina's kitchen do not merely replace *Umberto D.*, adding colour and warm light to the frame. Instead, they signify something much more poignant: the promise and fertility of the *boom*, and the tumultuous birth of modern, mechanized, even Americanized Italy in the aftermath of Fascism.

Fruit hints at fertility and virility, the heart of gender politics under Fascism. The germination of seeds is analogous to Adelina's booming family. Featured a number of times in the vignette, Pasquale, the nut vendor outside Adelina's home, likens her gestational periods to the seasons of commercializing produce.

> *He still tries to read [Adelina's certificate of pregnancy];*
> *he's finally able to do so.*

PASQUALE: … *Sra, sga … sgravata … Ah, sgravata!* October 20th, I was selling prickly pears …

> *He stops reading and counts on his fingers.*

PASQUALE: Six months of lactation: November, December, January, February, March, April … April, May, when the first cherries blossom, her immunity expires.

CARMINE (*sure of himself*): Well, we're in January. There's still time …

PASQUALE (*joking*): If you want help, no offence …

CARMINE: *Pasquà*, if you want a kid, I'll come by and set you up.[55]

De Sica affirms Pasquale's analogy in the following shot, focusing his camera on the bright cherries of May. Pasquale is selling cherries to the passersby, and it is announced that the police are camped outside Adelina's home, waiting to arrest her – that is, until she dupes the officers once more, presenting them with yet another certificate of pregnancy.

> *We follow Elvira, who reaches her husband's stand.*
> ELVIRA (*excited*): The cops have arrived into lower 'Mellino. Carmine is alone, Adelina's not there. But the cops have said that they're waiting for her, that they're not leaving.
> PASQUALE: The devil with them! But look at the cherries …[56]

Pasquale needs insemination as much as Adelina; if the nuts – read botanically and crassly – are available and in good shape, both of their businesses thrive. However, Pasquale's business is presumed legal, whereas Adelina's is not, thus requiring pregnancy for her to persevere as the default earner. Indeed, through her multiple pregnancies, Adelina remains the default earner, not the default parent, as was long expected of women, and she "gets by" the police and prison systems – the very institutions closely monitoring a woman's most intimate, personal moments – through pregnancy itself. Thus, in this moment of defiance, Adelina brings into question a "woman's place." Women were thought to belong to the domestic, private realm, and, in particular, the kitchen, providing not only children but also food: traditional elements of hominess. Increasingly so in the 1960s, women were engaged in uncompensated reproductive work *and* paid employment outside the home, seeking value outside the domestic sphere. Adelina manipulates the reproductive (her pregnancies) to remain active in the *public*, commercial realm: to conquer a new place of belonging.

Adelina's defiance of the law, and of the patriarchy of the police, might remind readers of the "unruly woman." Coined by Kathleen Rowe in her book *The Unruly Woman: Gender and the Genres of Laughter* (1995), the term refers to "a woman who disrupts the norms of femininity and social hierarchy of male over female through outrageousness and excess."[57] This excess functions similarly to Totò's *maschera*, in which his kinesthesis and bodily engagements outshine his fellow cast members, as well as the role itself. But the excess of unruly women is not exclusive to acting; it is a way of life, and a way of navigating amid – and despite – power structures. Thriving on the power of her femininity, the unruly woman embarks on a life of independence, rebelling against traditional, oppressive gender structures. Instead of being tamed and subsumed into the greater patriarchy, the unruly woman resorts to body performance to achieve her goals,

Figure 2.6. A metaphor for Carmine's inability to bear fruit.

thereby fending off the *inetto*: the impotent, inept male. Adelina's constantly pregnant belly, quite literally paraded around Naples, is, thus, a sign of the unruly woman in action. Adelina does not become a mother to assume the traditional tasks of wet nursing and child rearing; instead, she utilizes maternity to defy the police (itself a signpost of the heteropatriarchy), evade her prison sentence, and continue to provide financially for her family. The "outrageousness and excess" of the unruly woman persona are Adelina's six pregnancies in incredibly quick succession: the bearing of fruit to fight the Law. Further inverting the traditional notion of "father works, mother rears the children," it is Adelina who goes to work each day and Carmine who takes care of their several children; the unruly woman breaks into the public domain, long occupied by men alone, as the *inetto* retreats into the private sphere, once predominantly a woman's space.

The idea of the *inetto* also underlines sexual potency, or, rather, a lack thereof. Referencing the fieldwork of David Gilmore, Jacqueline Reich calls the phallus the most determinant sign of manhood; to "be a good man" is to procreate.[58] When Adelina fails to conceive an eighth child, not only does her cigarette enterprise come to a screeching halt with her imprisonment, but we also question Carmine's manhood. An exhausted Carmine drops a box of oranges on the street; he is unable to carry the fruit, sustaining his family's growth. Since Carmine fails to continue to "be a good man," Adelina is arrested by the police (the "Man"). One could read this as a metaphor for women's subordination to Man, which women in this period began to resist.

This said, despite her increasing star prowess, combined with women's protests against patriarchal laws, Loren received universal praise only when she became a mother herself. After repeated miscarriages, Loren landed the new, long-coveted role of "mother" in 1968. This dual struggle towards universally recognized stardom and motherhood will be unpacked in the next section, as read through Loren's first cookbook.

In cucina con amore: Recipes from Mamma Sophia

The room is entirely redressed with woodwork and glass cases that contain the innumerable awards that Loren has received during her career. The Bambi d'oro, the Donatello statues, medals, the Oscar that form for Loren a triumphant frame. Fitting for a champion of the screen. Now, though, what's most important to Sophia is that the living room in which we find ourselves is just a few steps from her son. She needs to go and see him constantly, to hear him breathing if he's sleeping, to caress him, if he's awake, the dark, faint hair (like a little bird, she says) on his round little head … as if to assure herself that he didn't disappear, that he's not a mirage.

"But he's there," I assure her. "It's a clear fact. He exists: I even touched him …"

She smiles. "I realize that a little bit each time, but I still can't convince myself completely," she confesses. "Let's say that I'm 80 per cent convinced."[59]

In 1969, journalist Anita Pensotti painted this picture for her readers: an image that demonstrates most vividly Loren's longtime struggles with pregnancy and maternity. A critically acclaimed master of the cinema, winner of numerous awards, recognizable star across the oceans, sultry pin-up … but, until December 1968, "mother" seemed but another fictional role.

Throughout the mid-1960s, American and European periodicals captured Loren's fervent desire to have children. *La Gazzetta del Mezzogiorno* quoted her, "I would give anything to have a child, and if I had to choose between continuing to work as an actress and being a mother, I would choose the latter without hesitation."[60] Likewise, in a feature for *Oggi*, Pensotti herself recorded Loren as saying that "women feel beautiful only when they are expecting."[61] The media then tracked almost microscopically Loren's gynecological visits and procedures, "station[ing] reporters and photographers outside the hospital in round-the-clock shifts," and obliging readers to sympathize with her pregnancy losses.[62] In this vein, we are reminded of the State's surveillance of Adelina, where Loren and her character's (in)fertility were nearly one and the same. In fact, Loren was pregnant while shooting *Ieri, oggi, domani*, miscarrying mid-film:

> For the Adelina episode, attached to Sofia was a foam belly, its size in accordance with the different trimesters, and every time it had to be put on, her eyes shone with satisfied pride. It was at precisely that moment that Loren realized she herself was expecting. No one knew, not even De Sica. And since the film was well underway, not to be interrupted, Sofia continued to go before the camera, waking up at dawn, putting herself under all kinds of strains and risks (even a car crash in the third episode), following her professional conscience. In so doing, unfortunately, she lost the baby.[63]

Most telling, however, are not the media portrayals – both real and diegetic – of this deeply intimate, private time in Loren's life, but instead the texts she herself authored. In her memoir, for one, she lamented the miscarriages that she suffered: "I felt gutted. It was as if the world had been turned off forever. I tried, but I could see nothing ahead of me, nothing that could console me … My life as a star was nothing compared to the happiness of the new mothers I'd glimpsed at the clinic, getting ready to breast-feed their newborn babies."[64] This section, however, focuses on a particular contribution to the filmic foodscape: Loren's cookbook authorship.

Once she got pregnant for a third time, under the authoritative watch of a Doctor Hubert de Watteville, Loren moved to Geneva to be near her obstetrician, retreating from the public eye to focus in earnest on motherhood.[65] As a way of distracting herself from her pregnancy, Loren returned to cooking with Ines, her secretary. She recreated recipes both from her childhood and from her recent travels around the world, all the while taking copious and meticulous notes on her experience. This compilation was published three years later: *In cucina con amore* (1971), Loren's first cookbook.

At first glance, *In cucina con amore* is a typical cookbook of the 1970s: The table of contents outlines recipes for festive appetizers, soups, meat- and seafood-based dishes, desserts, and side dishes containing eggs and vegetables. Her first section is "*I piatti per party*," such as tuna meatballs, bruschetta, and eggplant crostini: hors d'oeuvres to kick off a festive occasion, dishes curated and promoted by Loren for their quick preparation times and portability, making them easy to serve and to eat.[66] Later sections, meanwhile, showcase Loren's renditions of the mainstays of Italian gastronomy: food traditions to be easily replicated on a daily basis. Besides entire sections devoted to polenta and *minestra*, Loren suggests ways to enjoy pizzas in the comfort of one's home. She also recounts a history of pasta in Italy and lists "the eight commandments for preparing *la pastasciutta*," insisting that doneness of the pasta is determined only through taste, and emphasizing the importance of adding a teaspoon of olive oil to the water before straining.[67]

Loren's recipes are, thus, situated along a gastronomic crossroads: iconic Italian fare adjusted to the flavour profiles and changing social, political, and economic circumstances of the 1960s and 1970s. Her writing underscores a household's increased budget for food, the emergence of the working mother, and the influx of cooking products and innovations from America – a story in which the many dimensions of Loren are at the centre. In the cookbook, Loren is a Neapolitan; a daughter of a poor, single mother; an actress and sex symbol; and a wife and working mother. Presenting her recipe for spicy avocado, which reads as deconstructed guacamole, she recalls her first time in Beverly Hills, living at director Charles Vidor's villa, complete with an orchard full of the robust fruit.[68] Later, she associates lobster cocktail with Cary Grant and memories of her first American, English-language movie. While in Madrid in 1956, Grant introduced her to a combination of shellfish, ketchup, Worcestershire sauce, cognac, cream, citrus, and spices; Loren fondly remembers not only the immense comfort that the lobster provided her, the new flavours mirroring the newness of the Hollywood bubble that she was entering, but also Grant's smile at being blessed to have been the one to introduce her to such a pleasurable experience.[69] Her cookbook is an anthology of such stories: narrations of food, as the author illustrates how these foods intertwine with life beyond the kitchen.

Loren's cookbook narrative is at once personal and political, as she combines food with her imminent motherhood and, more macrocosmically, womanhood. Through an approachable tone, she provides a sense of warmth, homeliness, and nostalgia, feelings that the star sought to embody as a mother, but which also conjure notions of conviviality and wholesomeness, in that all are unconditionally welcome to partake in the pleasures of cooking and eating. At the end of her preface, she writes, "There is nothing left but for me to give you best wishes and recommend you pay the most attention, because I want you to have great success with my recipes. It's also a matter of personal pride. I beg you, don't make me look bad. By opening this book, you are welcome in my kitchen. Eat with me."[70] As can be gathered from the preface, where she hopes in earnest for her readers' success in the kitchen and implores them to not embarrass her (as a mother asks of her children before any outing), this cookbook is the means by which Loren prepared for what she, and the Catholic patriarchy under which she compiled the recipes, coded as her biggest role yet. More than any of her films, the cookbook held tremendous weight, as it signified the success of her pregnancy with Carlo Jr.; it was cooking that carried Loren along to her long-awaited due date, and, even today, the cookbook stands as her personal reminder of those days of expectancy.[71] But considering the position from which she was writing, as well as whom she was addressing, this cookbook achieved much more, both for Loren and for women overall.

Prior to the *boom*, cookbook authorship was decidedly a man's work. Pellegrino Artusi's *La scienza in cucina e l'arte di mangiar bene* (1891), considered the exemplar Italian cookbook, is a compilation of "family recipes" that are written by a man, based on his experiences in restaurant and university settings: spaces where women were long excluded and unwelcome. For decades, women, though charged with executing such recipes, had limited agency and practically no authorship in their cooking. Thus, for female authors of the postwar period, the cookbook became a means of being recognized: of inscribing oneself and one's womanhood into domestic culture, of gaining individuality and ownership inside and out of the kitchen – of carving a woman's space in what was once a wholly man's world. Cookbooks penned by women became their point of entry into public life: a way to explore their femininity in such changing times. Loren, not just acting within texts but now a *creator*, not only committed her struggles with pregnancy to the public domain but was also able to comment on the shifting of traditional gender roles through a medium traditionally read and appreciated by women, wives and mothers like herself, who had to navigate and decipher the myriad messages of mass media. Using *In cucina con amore* as her platform, Loren acknowledged and even celebrated these transformations and the construction of spaces for women by women.

As I had wondered about her Oscar, does her cooking have merit? Did Rizzoli, her publisher, capitalize on one of the first celebrity cookbooks – published not for its culinary worth, but its star status? Let us consider, for example, how she treats soup, *la minestra* in Italian: a family meal that domestic literature once celebrated as a way of "making do" with scarce ingredients and tight budgets. In her cookbook, the pages in question show two brief paragraphs, headlined with flowery writing. On the left, there are the recipes for cauliflower soup (top) and pasta-and-potato soup (bottom); on the right, there is a full-body shot of Loren, her focus off-camera, seated at a table piled with various fruits, vegetables, and strands of spaghetti. Staged this way, the priority is not the soup, but how effectively *Loren* can sell vegetables. Her recipe for pasta-and-potato soup is translated below.

Difficulty: Easy
Preparation: More than an hour
INGREDIENTS for 6 people:

- 1 kg potatoes
- 400 g pasta
- 1 carrot
- 1 tomato
- basil
- olive oil
- salt

The "poor man's soup," but how tasty it is. Peel and cut the potatoes into small pieces. In a pan, sauté the carrot and tomato, minced, with some basil leaves and a little oil; then, add the potatoes and salt, and when you see that it's just about cooked, add the pasta (best to use spaghetti broken into short pieces, or *cannolicchi*), and at the same time add hot water to your base. When the pasta is cooked, and the soup appears dense but not runny anymore, serve.[72]

The recipe is nothing special; her photo is more compelling than the "poor man's soup." What, then, makes Loren an authority?

Of special interest is her *tone*: the maternal love embedded into every page, the stories of the "*superpromessi sposi* of modern Italy" from whence the book came.[73] Her language meant to achieve maximum conviviality. Her recipe is quick and brief, and she omits exact quantities of salt, basil, and olive oil. One might argue that the recipe was designed this way to evade the precise, bookish cooking presented in American texts (the work of Julia Child, for example), but as Loren transitioned to motherhood, her cookbook represents this new call of duty: simultaneously assembling dinner for six *and* caring for a newborn and, by extension, the mother herself. Loren encourages women to *consume* the meals they have created with, one hopes, enjoyment: an unorthodox message that contrasts the reproductive labours and high, yet unpaid, expectations of mothers, as well as the dainty food advertisements of domestic manuals. She commands her readers directly to "eat with me," welcoming women to eat and to the social pleasures of mealtimes: a space traditionally reserved exclusively for men.[74] She had carved a space within the nexus of cultural networks, and now she was inviting all to join her.

Indeed, only through Loren's miscarriages and relentless pursuit of motherhood did she win the favour of the Church and of Italy's Catholics: the fourth and final cultural network to render Loren a true icon. As

Figure 2.7. Loren featured in her 1971 cookbook, *In cucina con amore* (95). Photo shoot by Tazio Secchiaroli. ©David Secchiaroli

the large-circulation Catholic weekly *Famiglia Cristiana* acknowledged in 1967, "The misfortunes of Loren render her more human and bring her nearer to us. They make her poorer than she appears, more simple and therefore more worthy of compassion."[75] Loren's cookbook, an exposé of her very public struggles with pregnancy, was a sign of her "reduction" from a godlike diva to a human star. She was at last fully recognizable because she was a mother: the signpost of womanhood. Once she was "Sophia the happy mom, far from Sophia the home-wrecker,"[76] Loren had become Italy's icon.

With her stardom conflated with her success as a mother, providing food for her children[77] and her readers at large, Loren appears to remain inscribed in the patriarchy. Her remarks in *Women & Beauty* (1984), her manual on health and beauty regimens, only further such problematics: "When I became pregnant, my concern for my career evaporated. Nothing mattered to me but my baby. If necessary, I would have given up my work to have a child. If this means I am not modern, then I am not modern."[78] This conservatism matches interviews that she had given in the early 1960s; when asked what she thought of women fighting for equality between the sexes, she responded bluntly, "Maybe they feel a bit manly." Funnily enough, she was then asked if she would ever write a book, and she said no, because she was afraid to do so.[79] How things changed!

Yet, in her cookbook, Loren comments on the continuous struggle for emancipation for tens of millions of women: the fight to cook and to be a mother by choice only, and to control their own bodies and lives. In the introduction, Loren acknowledges that Italy's social arena has changed greatly, that "equality between the sexes, even in the kitchen, has almost been reached."[80] Later in the cookbook, however, she takes a stab at her remaining conservative naysayers, most of whom are male. In a digression titled "*I mariti ai fornelli*/Husbands at the stove," Loren suggests that, if men are so appalled at the idea of cooking for their wives and families, perhaps they could learn a thing or two from her recipes: "It is actually they, with their inadequate ideas on the evolution of society, that need this 'culinary therapy.'"[81] After decades of harsh scrutiny, Loren took to her cookbook to suggest that these men could learn something from *her* messages, both filmic and gastronomic. Ultimately, utilizing the subjunctive mood, she expresses her hope that women choose cooking out of love, not by force: "Anyway, since it is natural that most of my readers are women, to them I say: May cooking *please* you, and may it not be a bothersome routine."[82] May their food choices continue to give them power. In these concluding words, Loren expresses solidarity with her fellow countrywomen, as they weathered the changes both within and beyond the kitchen.

Conclusion

These first two chapters have shown how Totò and Sophia Loren capti-vated audiences of the 1950s and 1960s, putting their bodies, including their pursuit and consumption of food, in conversation with history. Their narratives, however, could not be more different. Whereas Totò's performances are consonant with the overcoming of hunger, progress-ing towards material excess, Loren's life and work are read as instances of surveillance, codifications, and marketing strategies: all practices left over from Fascism. Loren's films and her authorship depict at once a depar-ture from the Fascist policing of women's bodies and a quest for agency: agency that food providers had in choosing goods for consumption and, at large, restructuring the public and private spheres of society – freely gravitating towards spaces where they felt they belonged, enjoying the fruits of their labours, reproductive, culinary, or otherwise.

Although Totò is an icon of postwar Italy, his fame is not international or political like Loren's. His fame is contained to the peninsula; her star-dom speaks to ideals of womanhood and housewifery in this period. The foods of this chapter speak to the stakes of womanhood, as well as the problematics and dreams surrounding motherhood, during a piv-otal moment in Italy's social arena. Loren has assumed countless roles, bringing to life some of the most beautiful characters ever to grace the screen, recognizable through several generations, and across a web of cultural networks: Italy's South, Americanized youth, and Catholic con-servatives. Food, and the culmination of her cookbook, were the means through which Loren attained such relatability, allowing her to carve a space into the heteropatriarchy in which her stardom could blossom, unchecked, but also in which she could be a working mother of two.

Yet, Loren's struggles with pregnancy were so public precisely because she was a star: a woman of the highest social and economic standing. This chapter analysed her cookbook with respect to her pregnancy, but, on the other hand, one may read her cookbook as an exhibition of her wealth, as a compilation of recipes for "exotic delicacies, discovered and adopted over the course of my many travels ..."[83] In other words, Loren's cookbook is just one example of her upper-class life, offering the average reader glimpses into her luxurious travels: the story of her miraculous escape from poverty and entrance into the extravagant, jet-setting ways of the rich and famous.

As an additional example, Ponti gifted Loren a piece of jewellery for every film debut since *L'oro di Napoli*, a collection that by 1960 was worth half a billion lire – in today's currency, a value just shy of $280,000 US. While she was shooting *The Millionairess* in London, however, the jewels were stolen from her Elstree accommodations. In the short run, her co-star Peter Sellers gave her a gold bracelet, "the first part of a new collection."[84] The media, in turn, jabbed at her privilege, the inability to relate to her viewers from such a high socioeconomic standing. The punchline of one cartoon in *Corriere d'Informazione*, sarcastically titled "Vita Dura," read, "Poor Sophia, to make back those jewels she'll have to work at least a month!"[85]

Like de Curtis, who through his nobility was exempt from his nation's hunger, Loren is an extremely rare case. Though her films and books present a narrative aligning her with Italian women at large, we must isolate her because of her extraordinary wealth. What, then, about the working class – or even those devoid of class altogether? In a radical departure from the lifestyles of the rich and famous, the next chapters consider the plight and the invisibility of some very different residents of Italy's filmic foodscape.

Chapter Three

"Feels Like Home": Elevation and Containment in the Patriarchal City

The undercurrent of this next chapter continues to be women's gravitation towards food production and provision. However, the following women are not of the middle class, nor are they of the social elite, like Sophia Loren, discussed in the previous chapter. This time, food turns a profit, the means of livelihood for a particular group: prostitutes exiting the profession to navigate life on and off the street by way of food vending. This chapter, with *Adua e le compagne* (1960, directed by Antonio Pietrangeli) and *Mamma Roma* (1962, directed by Pier Paolo Pasolini) as its bases, examines the paradox of street-walkers – public-facing women of the city – who seek to enter the private, domestic sphere, but who continue to be policed by the codes of the patriarchy: laws and systems of governance, buildings and urban plans, and even modes of language, keeping the would-be entrepreneurs in check. Their chances at success are only fleeting: As these women function under such heteropatriarchal neo-capitalist systems, born of and furthered by the legacy of Fascism, they continually rely on the patronage of men and their city. They thus ultimately fail not only at independence but also at being working mothers.

This chapter addresses the changing contours of one particular *casa* – *le case tolleranza*, or *le case chiuse*, otherwise known as the brothel – and the continuous policing of domestic and work spaces. What happened, in other words, when the walls of the brothels could legally no longer keep prostitutes in, thereby ejecting them to the street, which was also policed? What happened when prostitutes' work in the brothels was forbidden, but their registration with the police – which had once rendered them visible and legal members of the workforce – continued to surveil them, keeping them from pursuing what the patriarchy had coded as honest, less dangerous work? How do livelihoods persist in such a paradoxical space: prostitutes exiting with no way out?

This chapter focuses on this muddied arena, considering the slippage in transactions for food and sex. In an age where more women were working outside the home, the value of a woman and her contributions, both to her home and to society at large, was renegotiated. When these prostitutes were themselves the item for sale, exchanges mediated by a pimp or madam, there was little public outcry, but the prostitute was without agency. Now that the kind of flesh for consumption had changed, shifting from human to that of meats and fruits, sold not by an intermediary superior but by the prostitute herself, questions were not only raised to hostile levels but perpetuated into later decades. In the early 1980s, anthropologist Carole Counihan conducted an oral history in Florence, and Giovanna, one of her subjects, recuperated the very issues of women's mental load and their undervalued worth. Giovanna explained:

> Sure, fine, he brings home his salary, but is that enough? If you had to pay someone to prepare your breakfast, wash your clothes, prepare your lunch and dinner, and then go to bed with you, well, look, it is impossible to put a monetary value on it. Right? Think about how much prostitutes earn. You have to realize that a woman has to satisfy the needs of so many people and it would be impossible to pay someone to do it all; it would take so much money. Women's work is taken for granted from generation to generation. But there are problems if the women are increasingly working outside the home to gain some independence.[1]

The problems referenced by Giovanna resound throughout this chapter as former prostitutes strive for socioeconomic elevation but the patriarchal orders of operation remain the same. The pleasure of the foods that Adua and Mamma Roma sell, which were historically prepared by women for free and in accordance with men's expectations, replace the pleasure they once directed at the phallus – playing on objects that penetrate the mouth, soliciting whole-body sensations.[2] But once they seek to generate their own income for food production, a domestic task in which women had full responsibility but no compensation, they continue to work in spaces established and perpetuated by the codes of men, over which they have no control. By way of threatening male bodies, laws, architecture, and even cinema itself, the women's attempts at autonomy are ultimately rejected. Neither Adua nor her friends, nor Mamma Roma, nor their children, successfully endure the world of modern, male neo-capitalists.

Pietrangeli and Places of Prostitution

From his film criticism, in which he scorned the saccharine movies of Hollywood and Italy's white-telephone films of the 1930s, to his direction of some of the most acclaimed films of the 1960s, Antonio Pietrangeli capitalized on the uncomfortable. Hollywood presented the world with the "American dream," complete with notions of beauty, wealth, and success, which appealed especially to Italian audiences left devastated in the wake of the Second World War. Pietrangeli's cinema, meanwhile, safeguarded his viewers *against* such spectacles of Americana, instead presenting sociopolitical commentaries by way of dark comedy. The first chapter of this book is grounded in the comedic therapy of loss and hunger; though operating under the same premise, Pietrangeli is focused on trauma, particularly that of women. His assessment of *Adua e le compagne* is as follows:

> "Thus," Pietrangeli concludes, "the film means that if these disgraced women had been helped at the most difficult time (their reinsertion into normal life) maybe they could be saved because no one, no matter how broken, is completely so. But 'the good people' consider them forever branded and push them into an existence somehow more degrading than the one they previously led. And seeing as how I believe in *this truth*, I believe in my film."[3]

Pietrangeli is widely considered the feminist director of the decade, centring his work on women's journey towards autonomy – hence his biographies have titles such as "the director who loved women" and "the director of women." A "director of women" signifies a power dynamic: control over actresses and the characters they portray, directorship implying a determinative hand in women's fates. Pietrangeli exhibits the *laceration* of women, not their emancipation: the objectification, sexualization, and commodification of women's bodies under the male gaze, including that of Pietrangeli himself. His women do undergo a "radical, profound interior revolution,"[4] but there is special focus on Italy's institutions – legal and otherwise – holding women back and ushering them into defeat. These codes, inscribed into the society in which women struggle towards more promising, less dangerous lives, determine the fate of Pietrangeli's protagonists.

Prostitutes had been a fixture of society since Roman antiquity. Upon the Unification of Italy in 1861, under the government of Camillo Cavour, prostitutes were officially recognized. Their legal status and visibility, however, needed to satisfy certain conditions: regulations that carved a "safe" space for their sex work, but forever codified them as prostitutes. Cavour's "Regolamento del servizio di sorveglianza della prostituzione/Regulation of Surveillance of Prostitution" stipulated that prostitutes needed to register with the police, undergo biweekly health examinations, and, as necessary, seek treatment for venereal diseases in specialized hospitals, *i sifilicomi*.[5] Other requirements included a minimum age for prostitutes of sixteen (no age was specified for their clientele), and that prostitutes be well dressed, maintain sobriety, and stay off the streets, conducting sex work in fixed residences or brothels.[6] These rules not only gave the prostitute legal definition but monitored her entire existence; the prostitute was at once recognized and reinforced by the police. While the expectations of the prostitute were strictly enforced, the spaces in which she functioned were more precarious – so much so that if a woman was found alone on city streets in the evening, she could be apprehended and forced to register as a prostitute.[7] My analyses focus on the brothel and the city, the confusing, misconstrued settings for the paradox of exiting prostitution.

The historical premise of *Adua e le compagne* is the Merlin Law of 1958, which forced the shutdown of *le case chiuse*, Italy's brothels: the space in which Adua and her three friends service their clients. Co-authored by leftist Senator Angelina Merlin and Christian Democrat Boggiano Pico, the Merlin Law called for the closing of such state-run brothels, in part to keep pace with the rest of the Continent, closing a gap of almost forty years: Denmark, Finland, Spain, Bulgaria, and Holland had all closed their brothels between 1890 and 1914; the United Kingdom closed theirs in 1886, and Czechoslovakia and Poland, in 1922.[8] It was also Merlin's intention to signal a beginning to the women's movement: Free from the *case chiuse*, women could potentially exit prostitution and earn their own income, no longer subject to a madam. Indeed, in its original phases, Merlin intended to keep prostitution legal but criminalize those who exploited the prostitute. However, co-authored by Pico, of more conservative leanings, the law ultimately criminalized the *prostitute*, subjecting her to continued surveillance and regulation by the patriarchy. The law perpetuated prostitution as what feminist Andrea Dworkin described as "a social bottom beneath which there is no bottom. It is the bottom. Prostitution women are all on the bottom. And all men are above it."[9]

In his film, Pietrangeli further problematizes the top/bottom hierarchy, underscoring the nebulous demarcation of "honest" and "dangerous" workspaces. Adua and her friends are at an impasse: Forced out of the very kind of residence that Cavour had validated for prostitutes, do they continue their sex work, but outside the regulated spaces, now illegal themselves? Or do they pursue "honest" work, opening a restaurant that Adua envisions, but face the financial, bureaucratic, and psychological obstacles forever accompanying their prostitution licences? An elevation from Dworkin's "bottom" seems impossible, not only because their licences create a paper trail that codifies the women as social delinquents but also because there is a stigma continually surrounding a prostitute, no matter how long ago she exited from the profession. Sociologist Roger Matthews elaborates:

> Many will have low educational levels and few skills and qualifications. For others there may be unresolved psychological problems caused by a history of abuse. Further, after a period of involvement in prostitution many of these women will have difficulties in forming and sustaining normal relationships and have difficulty in trusting others, particularly men. For some it is the money and the difficulty of earning similar amounts in other ways. For others it is the growing familiarity with the lifestyle and the flexibility of the working arrangements that may be hard to give up. Hoigard and Finstad (1992) suggest that the problems of leaving prostitution are bound up with feelings of shame, problems of identity, feelings of insecurity and overcoming marginalization and stigmatization.[10]

Thus, when these prostitutes were, essentially, laid off, questions abounded about their future. One woman wrote to Merlin on the eve of the law's passing: "I admire and am almost content about your project; but thinking of the perhaps short time that I have left to exploit my years in this abject work, and then I won't be able to feed my children, makes me feel almost bitter. Will the government give us jobs? Or will we be scorned and isolated then as we are today?"[11] Adua and her friends are challenged with these very questions, as they plan, but ultimately fail, to transition from *casa chiusa* to *cucina casareccia*, attempting to dispel their past of prostitution and replace their brothel, the only home they knew, with the "homely" profession of food service.

From the *case chiuse* to "*Da Adua*"

The establishing and closing sequences of *Adua e le compagne* are nearly the same: Pietrangeli bookended his film with long shots of a mostly empty, quiet street in Rome – so the viewer is forced to gaze at a woman, walking alone. This may be read as Pietrangeli's continuation of male-oriented scopophilia, surveilling and even endangering the woman outside the home. However, his opening shots underline that women are the *protagonists*: the active subjects of his narrative, and not passive objects of pleasure. The atmosphere that Pietrangeli constructs is one of confidence and optimism, a stark contrast to the fears and questions that one imagines women would struggle with throughout their exit from prostitution; the women appear fearless. The night before the Merlin Law is to go into effect, the women celebrate this exciting moment, as a palm reader predicts "Good fortune and money on the horizon" for one prostitute, and as they smile upon a funerary parade of men, mourning the end of the *case chiuse*. Unlike Dworkin's assessment of the prostitute as the "social bottom," these women believe themselves to be free and able to pursue legitimate, "honest" work. The transition from prostitution to food provision, then, actually seems attainable for Adua (Simone Signoret) and her friends: Marilina (Emmanuelle Riva), Lolita (Sandra Milo), and Milly (Gina Rovere).

As soon as the brothel closes its doors, a fifth prostitute, Fosca, reveals to the protagonists that, for five years, she has been sending money to Dino, presumably her boyfriend, to establish a dairy business in Milan. Within a matter of days, she will migrate to the North and begin her new career as a food entrepreneur. Such an endeavour could be read as an elevation in several dimensions. It marks a successful exit from prostitution, as well as a geographic and socioeconomic shift to the booming Economic Triangle of the North, from the streets of the capital to an industrial farm. And milk, a drink binding female producers – quite literally – to those whom they nurture, becomes a commodity, generating not only a distance between producer and consumer, amplifying the intimate connections between a mother and her child, but also a profit. Fosca's growth is, however, anomalous: Most exits from prostitution were not so seamless; without the rehabilitative interventions in place, and with the continued stigmata and circulation of codes reinforcing the women's ties to prostitution, sex workers continued a life in policed containment.

On their last night at the brothel, Adua and her friends discuss their first steps in opening, ostensibly, a simple country restaurant. In the same vein as Fosca's transition from prostitution to dairy, Adua's "simple country restaurant" requires a signification different from her street-walking in Rome. The city is a space of movement, at once of anonymity and independence; the rural, meanwhile, implies fertility, germination, and a rustic innocence.[12] The mobility of Pietrangeli's female protagonists from country to city, and vice versa, symbolizes the changing nature of their roles in society and their navigation of the transforming social arena.[13] When Dora of Pietrangeli's *La parmigiana* (1963), for example, abandons her fiancé, Michele, and his patronizing lectures on how to be a good wife, she runs to catch a bus to Rome, seeking autonomy and independence within the urban space. Adua and her friends, meanwhile, move in the opposite direction. They, too, are navigating a changing social arena, but the Rome they know is coded as surveillant, a space occupied and controlled by men, so their transition to more rural surroundings is loaded with their own hopes of autonomy, independence, and innocence. To run a restaurant demands a sense of utmost control: the ability to be, as Adua emphasizes, their own boss at last. The setting for their restaurant must, therefore, be a space removed from the capital, to which their lives of prostitution and subordination to a madam were linked. The viewer soon learns, though, that the restaurant will evolve into a front for a continued prostitution business upstairs: a brothel without the nomenclature, thereby evading Merlin. The restaurant represents a site of "honest" work, but the space compels the women to continue earning money as they had before. Customer service and the commodification and sale of flesh thus exist on two planes: food production and sex work. Adua and her friends are at the helm of both enterprises, but their well-being remains subject to men's tastes, wallets, and authority.

Even if the restaurant is meant exclusively as a site of food service, the women are forced to continue prostitution. The restaurant has to serve the dual purpose of selling food and bodies because of a loophole in the Merlin Law. In Articles 8 and 9 of the law, rehabilitative and re-educational services were promised to exiting prostitutes, who were to remain anonymous:

Article 8

The Minister for the Interior will provide, by promoting the foundation of special institutes of patronage, as well as assisting and subsidizing existing ones, which effectively correspond to the purposes of this law, for the protection, assistance and re-education of outgoing women, as a result of this law, from houses of prostitution.

In the institutes of patronage, as envisaged above, in addition to the women who have left the houses of prostitution abolished in this law, they will also be able to find shelter and assistance for those others who, even if already initiated into prostitution, intend to return to honesty of life.

Article 9

With determination of the Minister for the Interior, the funds necessary for the exercise of the activities of the institutes referred to in the previous article will be assigned, to be taken from the fund allocated in the State budget in accordance with the present law.

At the end of each year and no later than the following 15 January, the patronage institutes founded in accordance with this law, like the other institutes envisaged in the previous article and which enjoy state subsidy, must transmit an exact report of their activity *omitting the names of the people they have received.*[14]

Former prostitutes, evicted from their brothels and forced to transition out of state-run prostitution, were to be offered interventions to help rehabilitate them into mainstream society: drug and alcohol rehabilitation, vocational training, and strategies to rekindle estranged relationships with relatives and children. These initiatives were designed with the intent of increasing women's skills and self-confidence. To ensure that they exited prostitution altogether, these women's social, emotional, and economic issues needed to be addressed.[15]

A restaurant entirely devoted to food service, then, could have come to fruition if the tenets laid out in the Merlin Law were actually fulfilled. If the women received proper training in, for example, basic arithmetic, reading literacy, and menu design, as well as the more hands-on skills of food preparation, handling, and service, they would have the tools to open and maintain a restaurant – and, in accordance with Article 9, without the public revelation of their former professions. But their licences continue to identify and register the women as prostitutes; despite the promised "omission of names," not only do the licences permanently inscribe the four women as prostitutes, forever linking them to their now-illicit sex work, but they also perpetuate a constant surveillance over the women, whether in bed at their Roman brothel or serving meals at their simple country restaurant. Indeed, Adua and her friends are caught by surprise when the letter arrives denying their petition to open a restaurant; "they know who we are at the police station." Unable to shake the past, the women cannot assume control – over the restaurant, over their lives – that they had anticipated. After repeated rejections, an educated, bourgeois man, Dottor Ercoli (Claudio Gora), comes to provide a sense of legitimation for their enterprise. When he demands a million lire each month from the women, an impossible sum for a simple restaurant of the 1950s, the viewer recognizes that *Da Adua* is not, in fact, run by Adua, but by Dottor Ercoli, their post-Merlin pimp. The licences, then, continue to have more agency than the women, because they determine the plot of the film and, thus, the women's fate; they restrict the women to the "bottom." Nevertheless, despite the near-certainty of defeat, the optimism of the establishing shots travels with Adua and her friends as they try to transform a ramshackle country house into a prosperous restaurant.

It is obvious that Adua is the leader of the prostitutes. Whereas her friends are financially and emotionally indebted to men, or suffering from mental health issues and substance dependencies, Adua embodies the relentless determination, independence, and street savvy typically required of a businessperson. Upon the closing of the brothel, the restaurant is her idea, as she lays out and spearheads the steps to establishing their new business venture: overseeing the clean-up of the property and the moving of their personal and business furnishings; pooling their savings as they attempt to secure a licence from the bank; and appealing to Dottor Ercoli when their application is rejected, thereby rendering *Da Adua* an underground brothel. She brands the restaurant with her name; Adua, in name and flesh, defines and embodies the restaurant. However, without proper training, Adua does not know anything about maintaining a restaurant: culinary, inventory, and food-service skills are all lacking. Once the restaurant is officially open for business, Milly notes that their first customers only "had a beer, dirtied the cloth, and even asked for a date." A later customer asks for a side dish to accompany his steak, but, with no vegetables or mozzarella in stock, he has to settle for an apple. Their sauce is salty, their meat is burned. Lolita does not know how to hold and deliver plates to guests. The beginnings of the restaurant are, to say the least, shaky. The question thus persists: Without the appropriate vocational training, how does a long-time sex worker navigate the food industry? In addition, Adua has demonstrated leadership qualities, but what about her younger *compagne*? The other women, too, face significant setbacks over the course of running the restaurant. Marilina, for one, struggles against substance abuse and mental health issues, which she attempts to reconcile by bringing her son, Carletto, back into her life. Milly, meanwhile, tries to win a man's heart by way of his stomach, thereby subscribing to longstanding patriarchal expectations of women in the home. Through these two women, the viewer sees the restaurant evolve into a home-space, where familial relations of old and new are nurtured, but because of the continued codification of the women as prostitutes, these ties are severed.

Marilina: The Dependant

On the eve of the closing of the *case chiuse*, while Adua is busy with the logistics of the restaurant, the viewer meets Marilina upstairs, lying on her bed. Positioned in the bedroom and going through the motions of sexual satisfaction – lying on her back, smiling dreamily, smoking a cigarette – Marilina is in stasis: Pleased to be in bed, captured in a state of reverie, she is unready for the great changes ahead. While her future is uncertain, her past is also troublesome, as her years of prostitution have taken their toll on her mental health. She is at an impasse. The restaurant comes to be the site of Marilina's arduous rehabilitation, where she recognizes and rectifies the pains of her past: chiefly, her estranged relationship with her son, Carletto, whom she claims to have seen only ten times.

Marilina's attachment to the restaurant is not automatic. At first glance, she immediately calls their restaurant a "dump," and she regularly antagonizes Adua, pointing out her old age and desperation, going as far as saying that Adua would sell herself for two hundred lire. The two women share a dark commonality, however: painful memories of motherhood, which come to the surface during a heated argument. Adua forgot to apply for electricity service, forcing the women to spend their first night at the restaurant in the dark. As they bicker over the lights, the bleak dialogue that follows matches the room's darkness:

ADUA: Your mind is sick. And you'll never get better. Never! You even had a baby.
MARILINA: And what about your baby? The one that was stillborn!

[What follows is a close-up of Adua, whose face freezes, then she looks down. Pietrangeli's choice of high-angled shots to document such tension demonstrates the power Marilina wields in revealing such sensitive information. But it is Marilina who then storms off, exiting the restaurant.]

In response, Adua exhibits a hardened resilience, returning her focus to the restaurant, barking more orders at Lolita and Milly, and snapping at Lolita's childish question of what is for supper: "Oh, *Gesù*, we'll eat the candles!" Meanwhile, Marilina exits from the restaurant. She returns to the city, away from Adua/*Da Adua*, a space where her failed motherhood had been summoned, amplifying the absence of her son. She exits the dark restaurant and, to fill the void left by her son, gets inebriated at a nightclub in the city centre, stealing a vase and hugging a statue – seeking affection from an inanimate object. When it is time to go home, Marilina does not venture towards the restaurant, considered a sobering, uninviting, unwelcoming space, so she unconsciously returns to the old brothel: "*casa mia, casa mia.*" While she is in her bedroom, the alcohol catches up with her and she conjures hallucinations of a mother hen. Lying in her old bed, Marilina stares at the cracks in the ceiling, saying lovingly, "There's my hen. And how are my chicks? One, two, three, four, five [*as the camera pans across the ceiling, following her gaze*] … Five? Just five? One's missing!" [*She jolts out of bed, manically searching the floor for the missing chick, chanting, "Più, più! Più, più!"*] The missing chick is, of course, Carletto. Despite her attempt to evade her shortcomings in motherhood by returning to the only home she knew, Marilina upon waking from her bender realizes that the country restaurant is a site of domesticity appropriate for the boy. She soon thereafter brings Carletto to the restaurant. The consequences of this decision, however, prove turbulent.

At first, Carletto's arrival at the restaurant only deepens the hostilities between Marilina and the other prostitutes. Again Adua questions Marilina's sanity, but Marilina defends herself by way of her equal investment in the restaurant:

> ADUA: What possessed you? Couldn't you leave him with his nanny?
> MARILINA: This is my house, paid with my money. So I'll bring anyone I
> want. I've only seen him ten times. At least for a few days … You're not
> getting up to anything. It's like a convent here!

Capitalizing on her financial stake in the restaurant, as well as recognizing the purity of the idea of the restaurant in its rustic location, Marilina feels justified in having Carletto live with them. The restaurant is thus coded as "home" for the mother and son. Though its etymology refers to its restorative purposes, restaurants do not typically house families; rather, they function with the purpose of serving dishes in accordance with diners' choices, needs, and preferences. While Marilina comes to view the restaurant as their new home, she fails to see the restaurant for what it ostensibly is – a site of food production and consumption – or as the brothel it eventually becomes. Marilina is the only one of the four women who is never seen preparing, cooking, or serving food, either for the restaurant patrons or for Carletto; rather, her ignorance of both the processes and significations of food, in a setting focused entirely on food service, strikes the viewer.

One particularly jarring moment surrounds Carletto's belated baptism and Communion: the acceptance of Christ's transubstantiation into bread and wine, His flesh and blood given up for all to consume. This scene reveals that Marilina's compass does not align with the Church's, nor with the expectations that society has placed on mothers. She is first chastised by the town pastor for choosing to baptize her son so late in his life; Marilina reduces the ceremony of the sacrament into a game, tricking Carletto into thinking the Body of Christ is just sugar. Instead of taking this opportunity to educate Carletto on Catholic virtues and traditions, thereby fostering a spiritual connection with her son, Marilina reduces God to a sugar wafer; in defining Him as a treat to be eaten on

Sundays, she equates God with someone to be consumed with pleasure. Additionally, Adua, Carletto's new godmother, organizes the backyard party to honour Carletto's initiation into Catholicism. Such conviviality never crosses Marilina's mind – hence her shock at the beautiful cake that Adua purchases for the occasion. Through these lenses of food, Pietrangeli illustrates two outcomes. He demonstrates, first, Marilina's lack of foresight, especially on questions of child development; second, her inability to navigate the expectations established by the patriarchy. The pastor, a figure of the Church, expects that Marilina will both obey and rationalize Catholicism's seven sacraments for her son; the mother is expected to plan and execute a feast for her family to celebrate the love and mercy of Christ. Marilina does not recognize, let alone satisfy, these expectations; one may infer that Marilina's transition to more "honest" work is, thus, incomplete, because she does not interact with food in the ways expected and promoted by the patriarchy at large.

Milly: Once the Cook, Forever the Prostitute

Whereas Marilina embodies an antithesis to food and the restaurant, Milly appears rooted in the kitchen. Her physical appearance, round in stature, associates her with fecundity and, by extension, domesticity. She becomes the chef at *Da Adua*. Despite the restaurant's lack of supplies at the beginning of the film, Milly "makes do," managing to prepare dishes that appeal to the clientele. This is analogous to what housewives did across Italy, who, inspired by domestic literature, were instructed to be versatile and prepare simple yet exciting dishes for their husbands and children, despite a limited budget. Milly's domesticity is also integral to her dynamic with Emilio (Antonio Rais), a land surveyor working nearby who becomes a regular customer and, eventually, her fiancé. Although the viewer only sees Emilio twice on screen, his command over Milly, along with her (in)ability to escape prostitution, is nevertheless powerfully determinative.

Emilio first arrives at the restaurant when it is empty and Milly is home, working alone. When she hears him, she first complains about the restaurant duties she now must complete by herself: attending to the customer, preparing his meal, bussing his table, and cleaning up after he leaves. Because she is alone, however, she can entertain Emilio in ways she could not during a busy service. She serves him bread and a plate of gruyère and gorgonzola cheeses, promising him a chicken liver frittata the next time he comes – at which point he may also pay for the cheese. This first encounter, where his lunch is prepared for free by a woman, initiates their courtship along very traditional, if not exceedingly formal, lines: Even as they get to know each other better, with Milly revealing her real name (Caterina) to Emilio, and even when their relationship evolves into a marriage proposal, they still address each other by the formal *Lei*. While their relationship is a gateway for Milly's social elevation, this formality signals not an amorous kinship but a parental relationship, built on the premise of containment. Emilio, who has a car and his own home in Primavalle, twelve kilometres away, is free to enter and exit the domestic space as he pleases. He visits (a verb that connotes a temporary stay) Milly every Sunday, where she prepares the same frittata for him. He admits that he does not really like chicken liver, though he ate it as a child because that was a dish that his mother had always prepared. But now "it is Milly who cooked it," and he declares shortly thereafter that the restaurant "feels like home" to him. This ritual reinforces a familial dynamic; mother figures are remembered for providing and are continually expected to provide food for their husbands and sons, without compensation – indeed, it remains unclear whether Emilio ever pays for these weekly lunches. What should be transactional is reframed as familial, where a woman's labours are undervalued and unpaid.

Inviting Milly to join him at an unfinished building that he is surveying – a space implying precarity and uncertainty[16] – Emilio discusses with her his hopes and dreams for the future, asking her if she would be his wife. Her response is not a simple "yes," as he was unaware of her past as a prostitute. In fact, expressing humiliation and rage, she laments that, despite her "wifely" ability to cook, she would still be inscribed in the patriarchy as a prostitute. Whether she functions in a brothel, a restaurant, or a traditional home-space, Milly is registered and thus continuously defined as a prostitute – a reputation that Emilio might deem tainted. Her sombre confession, however, does not sway him, as he returns the following week to take her to the movies. He accepts her past, to be kept as their little secret. This sensitive information, however, is at a man's disposal; her status is guarded by a male beholder. Milly's revelation signals a parallel between contracts of prostitution and marriage: Out of pocket or by dowry, men buy access to the bodies, skills, and narratives of women, who become available when the men desire but can also be rejected at will.[17] Milly's cooking teases a social promotion – from a legally recognized prostitute to a wife – but her continued codification as a prostitute solidifies her demise.

Towards the end of the film, Dottor Ercoli visits the restaurant and its upstairs quarters. He barges into Marilina's room, and the camera pans to reveal a child's bed, a tricycle, and toys strewn across the floor. Ercoli grows enraged: He invested in a brothel, not a restaurant, and certainly

Figure 3.1. The scene in which Emilio (Antonio Rais) proposes to Milly (Gina Rovere) in *Adua e le compagne* (1960, dir. Antonio Pietrangeli).

not a "rehabilitation centre," as he exclaims. He demands that the space lose all signs of its domesticity and maternity and be reconverted into a brothel under a restaurant's name. He insists, in other words, on the women's containment: They may do as they please, so long as he gets his million lire each month, a sum attainable by sex work alone.

> ERCOLI: Good wishes and sons … get married, become nuns, but you must stay here and give me what we agreed upon, a million a month.
> MARILINA: I denounce you!
> ERCOLI: I arranged for your licence, and I can take it away. A trattoria can't be run by four women like you … do you understand that you are registered, yes or no?[18]

Made aware that they are but goods in a transaction, the women destroy the restaurant, overturning tables and breaking plates. In destroying the restaurant, they efface what they had considered a space of hope and prosperity, full of glasses and plates that, just like them, amounted to fragile property.[19] Ercoli has the women arrested. Once their story makes the front page of the newspaper, not only does Emilio immediately break up with Milly but the press memorializes their pasts as prostitutes; once a prostitute, always a prostitute.

With the restaurant destroyed and their ties to Ercoli severed, the women are forced back onto the street: an illegal, sometimes lucrative, but entirely vulnerable space. The closing shots depict a lone woman on the street: This time it is Adua, working in the rain. Drenched, wizened, and drunk, Adua cannot pick up clients. As she idles, she fondly remembers her restaurant. The restaurant distanced her from the streets for long enough that, psychologically, she is blocked: she is neither restaurateur nor, through her failed solicitations on the street, a working prostitute. She does not appear to belong in any world she once knew, and the alcohol only further blurs her conscious. As she murmurs repeatedly, "I can't do this anymore," her image diminishes as the long shot zooms out further: dialogue and cinematography reduce her existence under the male gaze.

Indeed, the male gaze brings Pietrangeli's feminism back into question. Yes, he addresses the problem of prostitution and attacks the loopholes of the Merlin Law, but as a male director of women, Pietrangeli is in the position of recording the laceration and demise of his female characters. His female characters *act*, but Pietrangeli demonstrates more agency in filming the women's "break with nature," documenting the changes within his characters against certain ideological constraints. In other words, Pietrangeli captures the women's codification and containments from *the outside*.[20] He zooms out at the end of the film, diminishing Adua and freezing her forever under the surveillant male gaze; he decides that Adua is finished.

As for the film's reception, *Adua e le compagne* was praised for its acting but overall eclipsed by hallmark films of 1960: Federico Fellini's *La dolce vita*, Luchino Visconti's *Rocco e i suoi fratelli*, and Michelangelo Antonioni's *L'avventura*. *Adua e le compagne* has been cited as a "lone voice in *commedia all'italiana*, and arguably in cinema more widely."[21] *Adua* will now join another filmic voice: Pier Paolo Pasolini's *Mamma Roma*, released two years later. Pasolini's film, too, follows a woman's tormented exit from prostitution and her reunion with her son. Once more, of particular focus to my study are both women's ill-fated attempts to work in food service and live in the patriarchal city, a setting that continues to subvert and subdue its hopeful residents.

Mamma Roma and the Deathly Spectacle of the *borgate*

Mamma Roma extrapolates the paradox of the city streets, reinvoking the question of spaces that are "safe" for not only women who exit prostitution but also their families. In particular, Pasolini's film is his commentary on the postwar urban space of the *borgate*. The *borgate* formed a tentacle of the city reserved for its social underbelly: street urchins, disillusioned workers, wayward youths, and prostitutes. This section examines how the city is demarcated to determine and signify one's social status, or the ability to live altogether. Through the barren landscape of the housing complexes, the exploitative acts of selling sex and food within the same space, and the growing tensions between visceral physicality and the bourgeois spectacle, *Mamma Roma* is Pasolini's exhibition of the death of the archaic.

My synopsis will begin with the film's title, *Mamma Roma*. Pasolini named his prostitute Mamma Roma (Anna Magnani), revealing no Christian name or other moniker for his protagonist. The nomenclature signifies the two key markers defining Mamma Roma's identity: She is a mother who is tied to the capital city. The migration pattern that Pasolini illustrates is opposite Pietrangeli's: The brothel and country restaurant of *Adua e le compagne* have been replaced by the streets and new housing constructions of Rome. The rural safe haven of *Adua e le compagne* is abandoned, as Mamma Roma celebrates her freedom from Carmine (Franco Citti), her pimp, and procures an apartment in the *borgate*, which will have room for her estranged teenaged son, Ettore (Ettore Garofolo). What unfolds are the tensions between a mother and her son, but also the challenges that both characters face in living and working in unfamiliar arenas. There are moments of derision in the conflict between Ettore's country-bumpkin, *burino* upbringing and the urban bourgeoisie by which Mamma Roma is deluded. Indeed, her delusions are rampant: Pasolini's *borgate* are unrecognizable, and as she attempts to climb Rome's social ladder, she and Ettore are bamboozled by *double entendres*, trickery, and costly betrayal, revealing that, ultimately, the city is a king not to be usurped.

"*I campi di concentramento*": Confounding, Fascistic Backgrounds[22]

Of great importance to *Mamma Roma* is the artificial construction, the fictionalizing, of Rome's housing projects. Pasolini's Rome is, in other words, textual: a pastiche of cultural quotations, underscoring the falsity and inauthenticity of the city.[23] In his two novels, *Ragazzi di vita* (1955) and *Una vita violenta* (1959), followed by his films *Accattone* (1961) and *Mamma Roma*, Pasolini chose the background of the *borgate*, or housing projects situated along the periphery of the revitalizing capital. "*Background*, not landscape," Pasolini insisted, journalling his reflections of *Mamma Roma*. "… None of my shots begin with a wide field of vision or an empty landscape. There will always be, even minuscule, a human figure. But he'll be tiny for an instant, because right away I call out to my faithful [cinematographer Tonino] Delli Colli to put on the

75 and zoom in: a close-up of his face."[24] Indeed, while his narratives unfolded along Rome's *terrain vague* – the overgrown edges of the city, where natural landscapes were bulldozed to make way for, ideally, new housing developments – his focus was human. Pasolini zoomed in on the people of the *borgate*, depicting their activities there, often precarious and illegal.[25]

The particular setting of *Mamma Roma* is based on INA-Casa, a housing initiative developed in the early 1950s to expand housing for workers and provide jobs for the unemployed.[26] Despite being marketed as a solution to remedy unemployment at the start of the Economic Miracle, the *borgate* were not a new phenomenon to booming Italy. In fact, Pasolini's oeuvre comments on the complexes' problematic descendance from Fascism, with state-subsidized housing passing the ideology through a spectacle of hope: state surveillance under the guise of an elevated quality of life. These new houses embodied a key remnant of Fascism: virtual consumption, or consumers looking to buy into a state-controlled initiative that was meanwhile advertised to bolster the image of the consumer and her country. They were spectacles designed to dazzle their inhabitants, founded on the false pretence that purchasing such a house validates not just one's existence but one's respectability among Rome's bourgeoisie.[27]

Over the course of his early work, Pasolini compared the *borgate* to the concentration camps of the Holocaust, connecting them by their Fascistic relation of state power to the urban poor, and going as far as sprinkling "Buchenwald" and "Lager" across his writings set in the *borgate*.[28] *Mamma Roma* is no exception to such Fascistization. Mamma Roma is duped, as are the viewers. When Carmine gets married, Mamma Roma is released from prostitution. Having saved sufficient funds, she loosens from Carmine's control and gains autonomy over her career and her housing situation, and she reunites with Ettore. Her ideas of self-control and prosperity are founded on her stake in the *borgate*. However, as her housing remains inscribed with codes of the Fascist patriarchy, Mamma Roma ultimately fails to navigate her new environment. Pasolini amplifies feelings of alienation and unrecognizability through his cinematography, at once confusing his protagonists and the viewer by his shots of the city. His portrayals of the housing projects – a first apartment in Casal Bertone, followed by Mamma Roma's more permanent apartment in Tuscolano II – are conflated through his use of a rhyming shooting style, thereby corrupting the viewers' usual perceptions of shot-reverse shots. His shots blur the two distinct apartment complexes into one giant, engulfing building.[29] This underscores the falsehood of the *borgate*: Though a project "built for the people," through Pasolini's camera,

Tuscolano II exists for no one but itself.[30] The viewers, and Mamma Roma herself, fail to recognize this new Rome. To cite Guy Debord's theory on the Society of the Spectacle, INA-Casa is the "concrete manufacture of alienation."[31] Pretty as Mamma Roma thinks her house is, it never evolves into the site of productive societal participation that she imagines it to be. The prostitute's house never becomes a bourgeois, loving home, and the dynamics of Mamma Roma's family collapse.

Bin and *bauen*: Exploiting One's Existence

The confounding architecture also exhibits the disintegrating human connections within the *borgate*. The architecture is but a backdrop for the interactions, dialogue, and, indeed, defeat of Pasolini's characters who embody the archaic: those who stand outside bourgeois culture and language, so are therefore restricted to the periphery of the city and society at large, associated instead with primitivity and nature.[32] These representatives of the archaic are put into grave danger by the housing projects. Not only do these complexes infringe upon their natural habitats, but the frantic speculation on the land creates divides between "residence" and "life," "building" and "being." Going further, Martin Heidegger differentiated between *bin* (I am) and *bauen* (to build). In his 1951 "Building Dwelling Thinking" lecture, he stated, "The way in which you *are* and I am, the manner in which we humans are on the earth is *Buan*, dwelling … Today's houses may even be well planned, easy to keep, attractively cheap, open to air, light, and sun, but – do the houses in themselves hold any guarantee that *dwelling* occurs in them?"[33] The precarity of dwelling – of guaranteed life within the *borgate* – is the linchpin of *Mamma Roma*. The archaic world from which Mamma Roma departs is prominent in Pasolini's establishing shots, laying the shaky foundations upon which the rest of the film unfolds.

Pasolini's film opens at the wedding banquet of Carmine and his bride, Clementina. This world presents a stark contrast to a "postcard" Rome: Dirt is everywhere, there are flies buzzing around the camera frame, and the very first thing viewers see is not a monument, not a picturesque landscape, but three fat pigs, sporting ties and hats, that a hysterical Mamma Roma swats into the dining area with a broom. Pasolini's conflation of swine and humans presents a wide-ranging commentary on social hierarchy. The animal kingdom of the archaic world, for one, is put into question. Mamma Roma's first line of the film is "Here are our brothers!"[34] which likens the pigs to the human attendees; Carmine adds, "*Fratelli d'Italia*/Brothers of Italy," borrowing from the national anthem.[35] In so doing, Pasolini establishes a polemic

Figure 3.2. "Our brothers / I nostri fratelli." From *Mamma Roma* (1962, dir. Pier Paolo Pasolini).

on the Italian people – perhaps an allusion to George Orwell's *Animal Farm* (1945), a portrait of capitalist pigs. Mamma Roma's line is directed at Clementina, *la sora sposa*, which further complicates the dynamics in the room. Clementina, presumably a prostitute herself, functions on the same plane as Mamma Roma and the pigs, perceived as dirty, as flesh to be consumed – sometimes violently. However, Mamma Roma's verticality, as well as her use of a broom, establishes dominance over the pigs: a sign of her impending social elevation once she moves away from Carmine and the *burini*. Yet, with the pigs described in Pasolini's screenplay as "a handful of lunatics, of those condemned to death, like a little dance," Pasolini evokes a festive sendoff for not only the pigs, who will be sold as pork, but for Mamma Roma, who, too, will confront delusion and death in the city.[36]

Pigs/pork and prostitutes/flesh are just two conflations of food. Over the course of the film, but particularly in the establishing and closing shots, food commits false pretences. The sale and hospitality surrounding food are the gateways through which Mamma Roma visualizes her livelihood among the bourgeoisie, and food suggests a nurturing connection between mother and son, but these expectations remain largely unfulfilled, revealing instead the exploitative nature behind producing, selling, and consuming. Likewise, the mood of the wedding is both blithe and brooding, with the food as a focal point of both celebration and contention between the *burini* farmers and the bourgeois consumers of Rome. Alcohol is flowing and people are joking and laughing, but despite the mood of fervent conviviality, Pasolini illustrates, through Carmine's father-in-law's wedding toast, the drastic disparateness between the rural sub-proletariat and the urban bourgeois; neo-capitalism and the pre-industrial archaic; "us" and "them." There is talk of tuberculosis and of provisional freedom, and self-deprecating awareness of the farmers' exploitation.[37] Curiously absent from Pasolini's screenplay, but captured in the English subtitles, is the deeply political, rhetorical question: "They call us hicks, but if we didn't work the land, what would the rich folks eat?" These are all jabs implying the continuous degradation of the *burini*.

Aggravating tensions, Mamma Roma interrupts his speech, further cementing her positionality above the *burini*. She calls for him to sit down, because she does not want to hear him preach any longer, exclaiming that Mass should be sung. This "Mass," which evolves into a biting war of words between Carmine, Clementina, and Mamma Roma, sings of Mamma Roma's freedom:

> MAMMA ROMA (*in a fury, happy, concluding*): Flower of shit, / I have been liberated from the rope, / Now it's someone else's turn to serve! (*And then, yelling agitatedly*) Oh sister, no jealousy! I'm free! I'm free![38]

Mamma Roma wishes not to hear the father-in-law's toast on the enslavement of the *burini*, because she – for the time being – is no longer Carmine's slave. The glee over this new chapter in her life most closely mirrors the conviviality of the wedding: Free from exploitation, the wine is now flowing, and Mamma Roma may finally drink. What she realizes only belatedly, however, is that the festivity is only a spectacle, joy ostensible at best.

Food symbolizes the exploitation of the *burini*, but for Mamma Roma, Carmine, and Ettore, it seems to be the gateway to a more promising life. Yet, through further conflations of food-signs within the spectacular city, all three of their livelihoods are upended. Pasolini's film follows the consequential damages that these three characters incur, particularly the disintegration of their relationships by such commodities and falsehoods. Let us first consider Mamma Roma, who believes that she has successfully exited from prostitution and earned a place among the Roman bourgeoisie, but ultimately is duped; all the while, her imitations of bourgeois life further distort her relationship with Ettore. Their interactions are an uncomfortable combination of derision and materialism; very little is authentic.

Mamma Roma is inauthentic right down to the actress who played her. Anna Magnani, who by this time had already won an Oscar for her performance in *The Rose Tattoo* (1955), emphasized her status as a trained performer, very much distinguished from Pasolini's cohort of non-actors. Never mind that she had gained traction throughout Italy's neorealist period, a core component of which is the employment of non-actors; Magnani underscored, "Even with their instinctual intelligence, they become your robots. I am not a robot."[39] In this conversation with Pasolini, she lamented her inability to laugh on cue, revealing questions of authenticity in her acting. She continued, "On the one hand I feel that I should be able to perform the way you want by relying purely on my acting skills. On the other hand I see that sometimes we don't always understand the character in the same way: I feel out of balance. And so I'm neither a good actress (God willing, and thankfully!) nor an obedient robot … The boys you direct, whom you mould and maneuver, are far more authentic than I am. And this is a paradox that I can't let the public see."[40] Questions arise as to why Pasolini cast Magnani if she was not only so different from his "boys" but also so far removed from the abject poverty of the *burini* and even the *borgate*. His choice is strategic: He needed someone who fully represented the bourgeoisie and its popular culture – a woman born and raised in Rome, but who was also emblematic of Cinecittà, Italy's world of movies. Mamma Roma needed to be played by someone "from that other world," who was already a fixture of the rising, threatening petit-bourgeois ideology.[41]

Additionally, the film's plot is rife with false pretences. Having saved 200,000 lire for a home of her own, as well as for a vegetable cart, Mamma Roma is able to take leave of her sex work, thereby evading threats to her body and life, and she goes into business for herself. Curiously, the vegetable cart is only on screen four times, and she is seen selling fava beans and artichokes only once. Nevertheless, the cart sets her a world apart. As the owner and sole operator of the cart, not only is she no longer bound to a pimp's enterprise but she has also promoted herself to an entrepreneur. Her food business positions her on the street on her own terms; she is free to work by day and conduct legal, unstigmatized transactions with all passersby. Vegetables are now the commodified products, as her body loses its price tag; the transactions surrounding her flesh have been replaced with the fruits of the earth. In addition, she is also now able to maintain a home; retiring to her apartment at night, she is distanced from the illegalities and vulnerability of night-time streetwalking, able to sleep *above* those who were once her peers. These transformations impact Mamma Roma's psyche, however, for the worse: The cart offers a false security, which feeds into her deluded sense of self. In an interview with *Filmcritica*, Pasolini confirms:

> … there is already something in her of the other world, which is our bourgeois world, in other words, a petit-bourgeois ideal. In fact, when she goes to pick up her son and bring him to her place in Rome, she already knows very well what she wants, she already has an ideology, a misguided and confused one: a petit-bourgeois ideology, which she has absorbed from the bourgeois world, through familiar sources.[42]

Indeed, by way of the cart, she is able to convert sixteen years of street-wise knowledge into a business opportunity, one where she performs "good" work on the streets and can usher her son back into her life. But she is unable to connect genuinely with him.

(Mis)constructions

Having arrived in the *borgate* and settled into her apartment in Tuscolano II, Mamma Roma reconnects with Ettore. However, while they are physically together, language serves as a point of division between the mother and son. Language will continue to be a point of contention in the next chapter, but with respect to *Mamma Roma*, one sees the tensions between the dialect of the *burini* and the bourgeoisified standard Italian, developed and centralized farther north in Florence. Also prominent are the misunderstanding and slippage of signifieds. As with the pigs discussed earlier, there is conflation of the status of animals and prostitutes. As with the city, Mamma Roma misreads its codes, continuing to practise, even boast, a false bourgeois consciousness, distancing her further from her son and from reality – culminating in a bewildering epiphany far too late.

Almost immediately after their reunion, Mamma Roma and Ettore struggle to have an authentic connection. A teenager who has just been uprooted to the capital, away from his friends and usual diversions, Ettore complains that there is nothing to do in Rome; Mamma Roma, in turn, gives him an earful, calling him an asshole/*a stronzo*, and exclaiming that she did not bring him into this world only for him to be a hick/*un cafone*.[43] He is unaware of what she had to do and sacrifice to arrive at this very moment; she, meanwhile, in conducting sex work, bypassed typical teenage rhythms and rituals.

The ways in which they speak, too, present another barrier – one which conveys the extent of Mamma Roma's delusions. Pasolini wrote the screenplay in Roman dialect, utilizing the linguistic codes of the city, the outskirts, and those who lived in the margins. He recounted to Jean Duflot that dialect added a layer of reality to his work, mirroring the semiotic authenticity of cinema:

> Already dialect was for me a physical approach to the farmers, to the land, and in the "Roman" novels, the popular dialect offered me the same concrete, even material, approach. Now, I have very quickly discovered that cinematographic expression, thanks to its analogs on the semiotic plane, offered me the same reality, the possibility of reaching life in a comprehensive way.[44]

Pasolini was born in Bologna and raised in Friuli, so his Roman is not native; yet, this directly correlates to Mamma Roma's inauthentic way of conversing, disconnecting her from Ettore. The following dialogue underscores her scorn for his *burino* expressions:

MAMMA ROMA: Are you hungry?

ETTORE: (*with a* burino *accent, and using* burino *vocabulary*) No … I ate this morning. (burino *expression*)

MAMMA ROMA: (*pretending to be mad, wincing*) What did you say? What did you say? (*repeats* burino *word*) What are these awful words? You must speak like your mother, not like those four *bigonzi* over there! If you don't, I'll beat you, you know!

> *Ettore, with his head lowered,*
> *shows a little smile.*[45]

While the dialogue could be read as joking banter between mother and son, it is clear that language is a major point of division between the archaic, represented by Ettore, and the bourgeois, which Mamma Roma purports to be. The most genuine, intimate moment between her and Ettore is, instead, a physical encounter: slow dancing to an old record, reminiscing about Ettore's father. Mamma Roma knows how to communicate on a physical level, but she can afford her son only so much touch, thereby leaving their relationship tense. The tension between written language and physical gestures will be reprised in the next chapter, on Pasolini's later films.

Figure 3.3. Mamma Roma (Anna Magnani) and Ettore (Ettore Garofolo) dancing together in the bedroom of her new apartment.

To immerse most fluidly in the world of the bourgeoisie, one needs to adopt its language: not just spoken words, but the signs that codify the booming capital. Food is one such sign. Recuperating the work of semiologist Roland Barthes, food is a symbol that communicates values, "a body of images" that connotes sexuality, power, and wealth, as well as the divides between work and leisure.[46] Food, then, feeds beautifully into Pasolini's cinematic language, given his intense focus on bodies manoeuvring and working within the neo-capitalist space. Echoing Barthes once more, however, in *Mamma Roma*, the employment of food perpetuates the false consciousness of this new working class. With special respect to advertising, Barthes wrote, "… By now everyone knows that the product as bought – that is, experienced – by the consumer is by no means the real product; between the former and the latter there is a considerable production of false perceptions and values."[47] Pasolini's decision to move his protagonist from the streets to the *borgate*, and from prostitution to food, is doubly poignant, as Mamma Roma struggles against two aspects of the capitalist spectacle: the false belief that selling vegetables will free her from poverty and prostitution, and that her business can be set into motion with the *borgate* as backdrop, which "devour[s] [the immigrants to the capital] without ever digesting their presence."[48]

Despite her attempts to shake the *burino*, Mamma Roma does not recognize the codes of the bourgeois city; she continues to understand, rather, the ways of the street. Despite the vegetable cart and the apartment, two possessions that she believes can offer her agency, elevating her from "the sold" to "the seller," and from "owned" to "owner," her relationship with Carmine resurfaces almost without hesitation. Her return to old ways destabilizes her life once more, initiating a dangerous slippage between her roles as prostitute and provider.

Compared to Mamma Roma and Ettore, Carmine plays a secondary, but nonetheless complicated and deeply jarring, role. The viewer first encounters Carmine on his wedding day, but we do not immediately understand his connections to the rural surroundings in which we first find him. How does a pimp, earning his living off the urban poor, and reliant on prostitutes like Mamma Roma, belong in the world of the archaic? Carmine's presence among the *burini*, and his ability to move so fluidly between urban and rural spaces, signify his inclination to exploit others. The consumption of food by the bourgeoisie is a means of exploiting the *burini*, but Carmine furthers such exploitation: "What" and "whom" Carmine exploits become one and the same; through her acts of prostitution, Mamma Roma is objectified and repeatedly sold for consumption. Before and during his marriage, Carmine focuses on the commodification of flesh. As a pimp, he capitalized on the body of Mamma Roma; later, he sells the meat of farm animals. The flesh of Mamma Roma and the flesh of cows are up for consumption, both of which satiate the bourgeoisie's needs and desires.

Carmine is the human emblem of the omnipotent patriarchy, a presence constantly coercing Mamma Roma to revert to old ways for his gain. The wedding is not the last we see of Carmine; the viewer is surprised to find him at the door of Mamma Roma's apartment, on the day she brings Ettore home for the first time. The viewer is additionally surprised when Carmine exhibits an uncharacteristic bout of emotion as he pleads with Mamma Roma for money to back his new, but still illicit, venture of slaughtering livestock. He stands in the doorway, seeking entrance back into Mamma Roma's life, as he explains the business of selling *bestie*: animals, in the plural feminine.[49] Coupled with his one-sided business proposal is a plea to re-enter Mamma Roma's life on an emotional plane: He presents a strange mix of crocodile tears and regretful memories of his biological mother as he hints at an Oedipal relationship with Mamma Roma:

MAMMA ROMA: My son is here.
CARMINE: Ah! Are you happy! And to think, I was almost his age when I started out with you …
MAMMA ROMA: As if! My son is an angel!
CARMINE: (*suddenly emotional with crocodile tears*) A little boy, I was! I did not have a lick of evil! My mother always said to me that I was the best in the house! And instead I didn't do anything but cause her pain![50]

Indeed, as depicted through Pasolini's close-up shot sequence, their intimacy – grounded in sensual physicality – is the most authentic of the film's fraught relationships. Carmine needs not only funds but also continual approval from his surrogate mother of the streets. Yet, the viewer is reminded that their relationship is one of exploitation when he changes his tone, replacing nostalgic lamentations with his demands for money, falling most naturally back into the role of exploiter. He transitions from a boy asking his mother for an allowance to a menacing patriarch. Because his codes of communication are those which Mamma Roma readily understands, she obliges him.

MAMMA ROMA: OK, OK … I understand. How much do you need … You know I don't have any money …
CARMINE: Two-hundred large.
MAMMA ROMA: And where am I gonna find that? You know that I spent everything I had on this house …
> *Carmine looks at her for a bit in silence,*
> *with swollen lips under his moustache.*
CARMINE: Aaaah, you think I'm playing? So you haven't understood me! What do I have to teach you, how to score the money? What, have you forgotten?
MAMMA ROMA: (*breathless, but still in control*) You're not satisfied yet?
> *Carmine pushes himself away from the railing and starts to*
> *head down the ramp: he speaks turning back.*
CARMINE: (*almost sweet, understanding*) What will it ever be! If you put a little imagination into it, in ten days you'll have the money. Don't you think, 'a Ro'?[51]

In this dialogue, Carmine employs the same capitalist logic that surrounds Mamma Roma's vegetable cart: the idea that, in satiating men by sex, she could realize her bourgeois fantasy. Were she to recommit herself fully to prostitution, she could pay Carmine the 200,000 lire he requires in less than two weeks. As a result, Mamma Roma seamlessly switches from a provider of food to provider of sex; from a vendor of vegetables to, once more, flesh to be consumed. In turn, Carmine's profits are doubly derived from food: the illegal trafficking of meat, and the carnal pleasures of Mamma Roma, which she now enables.

Despite Mamma Roma's continued ties to Carmine, she works to conceal that part of her life from Ettore so as to uphold her bourgeois identity, all the while coercing him to emulate the other boys in their building: "They're good ones! ... Find boys that study, that go to work ... these should be your friends!"[52] Through Ettore, Mamma Roma channels her own dream of penetrating the bourgeoisie; her bourgeois existence just might be actualized through Ettore's formative years in the *borgate*. Her attempts to bourgeoisify her son are similar to her own transformation: Food is thought to be the lucrative key to success, but her misconstructions of the city will result in their downfall.

Ettore, or the Death of the Archaic

Because Mamma Roma communicates most effectively by way of the body, she uses sex as a way of socially elevating Ettore. Their apartment was bought by sex; so, too, will be Ettore's livelihood. Mamma Roma, thus, commissions the help of an old prostitute friend, Biancofiore, for two jobs. First, to land Ettore a job as a waiter, Biancofiore must two-time a promiscuous owner of a reputable restaurant in Trastevere; second, she must seduce Ettore, thereby distancing him from Bruna, a promiscuous young mother herself. Initially, Mamma Roma appears successful. Ettore is hired, and, in the only scenes shot in the city centre, he is seen ferrying plates of pasta to classy diners with an air of theatricality. When she and Biancofiore visit the piazza where Ettore's job is located, pressing themselves against a wall to spy on him, Mamma Roma begins to cry. She is proud of her son but also of herself; through their honest line of work, serving food to the affluent, she has "made it." However, without realizing it, her manipulation and spying perpetuate the same surveillance over Bruna as over a prostitute in the *borgate*. In addition, Mamma Roma does not recognize that Bruna is a proxy for her younger self. To remove Bruna from Ettore's world is to displace the idea of *mamma* to which Ettore had latched sixteen years prior, erasing any tender, motherly memories of Mamma Roma. Placing him in the care of the *burini*, Mamma Roma replaced Ettore with the many transactions under Carmine; she does not realize that to replace Bruna with Biancofiore, an older prostitute, is to disavow the memories and intensity of a mother-infant connection. Part of Ettore's consciousness, too, is hereby artificially constructed.

Pasolini's world of misconstructions and confusing shots takes its toll on Ettore. His way of coping with the city is one of detachment and disconnection altogether. Mamma Roma seeks to embody the elegance and refinement of Rome proper, but Ettore remains detached and disenchanted. Critics have even likened his comportment to that of sleepwalking, unable to participate in normal, waking life.[53] In other words, like the empty, haphazard housing projects, Ettore is *bauen* – a human built out of Mamma Roma's ideals – and not *bin*; he cannot exist in the world of the *borgate*. Such nonparticipation explains why Ettore soon quits his waiter job; unlike his mother, he does not get invested in the spectacle of urban life. Instead, within long takes capturing fields of Roman ruins, Ettore bumbles around, sometimes playing soccer with neighbourhood kids, but mostly meandering, alone. He has a far greater interest in, for example, bird calls – thereby showing a connection with more natural surroundings – than in restaurant hospitality. The city of Rome therefore offers Ettore two polarizing worlds: the ruins of the archaic, the capital of a rich, ancient empire; and the postwar housing boom, sparked by neo-capitalist speculation, but a continuous spectacle of patriarchal Fascism. Caught between these two realities, Ettore responds partly by sleepwalking, semiconsciously straddling the binaries of "asleep" and "awake," and of "capitalism" and "archaic." One who sleepwalks generally returns to bed and wakes the following morning, unharmed. The awakening in *Mamma Roma*, however, is one of death.

Coupled with the act of sleepwalking, shortly after he quits his restaurant job, Ettore develops a fever. A fever is the body's homeostatic response to a foreign, invasive presence. The culprit here, however, is not any bacterium, but, rather, the new environment in which Ettore finds himself; the capitalist spectacle, complete with American contaminations of music, clothes, and roller skates, is like a disease.[54] As Mamma Roma pressures her son to conform to this new society, pushing him to suppress the jargon of the *burini*, landing him the restaurant job, as well as buying him a motorcycle upon which he commutes, Ettore's well-being rapidly declines; he cannot simply be himself, as his body is forced instead to host the strong tension between the affluent consumer and the archaic producer, and the capitalist spectacle and primitive, innocent nature. Ettore's fatal victimhood is, tragically, what brings the spectacle building in Mamma Roma's mind to a jarring halt.

In the final moments of Ettore's life, Pasolini establishes the biting juxtaposition between Ettore, who lies dying in jail after having stolen a radio from a hospital patient, and Mamma Roma, in the kitchen of her apartment, lamenting Ettore's absence while preparing herself a snack of warm milk and bread. Pasolini's screenplay underlines the positionality of Mamma Roma and the food she eats:

> *Cecafumo House. Indoors. Dawn.*
>
> *Mamma Roma is at the window, which she has just opened.*
> *Like an old statue, she watches and says softly:*
> MAMMA ROMA: Poor creature of mine.
> *She gets away from the window, and goes toward the inside of the*
> *house, in the little kitchen. She takes the coffee-pot off the stove,*
> *pours herself milk, puts out bread, and begins to eat.*
> MAMMA ROMA: Poor creature of mine. (*after profound silence … with her eyes*
> *empty*) He came into the world and he was always lost. Alone he's found
> like a Christ-like sparrow, to look around, to wait for who knows what,
> on this earth, alone …
> *She swallows the bite of bread and milk, with her eyes full of tears.*[55]

Through the repetition of "alone" and "poor creature," Mamma Roma realizes her son's tragic situation: Ettore came into the world alone, and he – labelled as a "creature" – continues to stand alone against increasingly capitalist humanity. Mamma Roma proceeds to liken Ettore to a "Christ-like sparrow," emphasizing once more his primitive, animalistic, but also innocent and martyred nature – reflecting his clash with the urban bourgeoisie. Pasolini's description of the space in which Ettore is left to die presents a striking contrast to Mamma Roma's modern kitchen; Ettore, manic, is bound to a structure similar to a crucifix, alone in a dark, empty space:

> *In the cellar there is nothing. A single skylight above, from which enters the light of the moon. There is nothing. The floor, the high walls, the ceiling. And a concrete bed with a hole in the middle.*
>
> *Ettore is tied to the bed. Half-naked, as he was found in the infirmary, when he started to scream.*
>
> *The scene is like a small crucifix, with his arms tied, wrists bound: his feet are also bound, and a belt is tied around his chest as well.*
>
> *Ettore continues to scream, saying incomprehensible words, writhing like a maniac, wiggling around desperately.*[56]

The incomprehensibility of Ettore's language further animalizes him, but the binding of his body to a concrete crucifix signifies a Christ-like death. Christ was crucified by the Romans; so, too, is Ettore. Pasolini deifies Ettore, "replicat[ing] the social problems affecting the *borgatari* and he assigns them a sacral connotation through the construction of

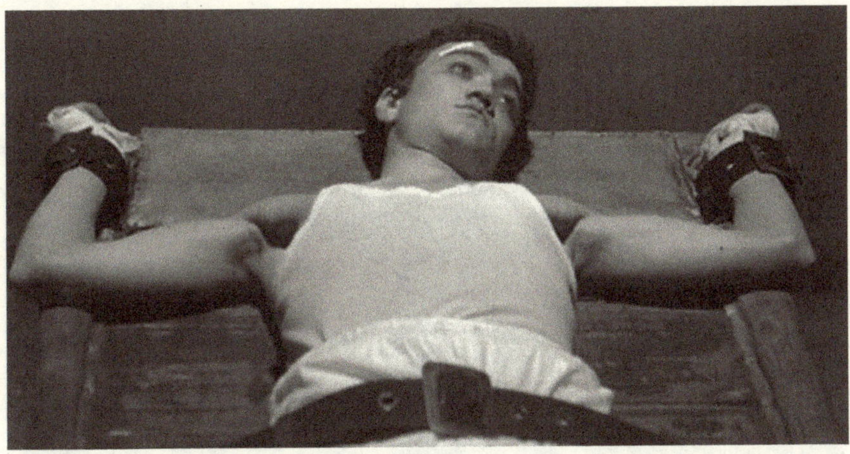

Figure 3.4. Ettore punished, wrists bound to a plank: a depiction of a Christ-like death during Italy's Economic Miracle.

Ettore as a Christ."[57] His nature associates him with the archaic, but he is bound, underground, to a manmade construction: one of concrete, the same material as the foundation of the *borgate*. He dies to atone for the sins of the neo-capitalist. In addition, his plank is horizontal; unlike Mamma Roma's verticality, living above the streets, Ettore's social elevation – his so-called Resurrection – is impossible.[58]

Taking leave of Ettore, we return to Mamma Roma's kitchen, where she is eating as Ettore lies dying. This incongruous dichotomy is the final disconnect between mother and son: She is standing and eating before an open window, taking in fresh air above the streets of Rome; he, meanwhile, is horizontal, static and dying, in a subterranean space. There are several plausible readings of her food choices of bread and milk. These foods might symbolize the abject poverty in which she has always lived, having survived on only the most basic staples, since more luxurious foods, such as meats and exotic fruits, were economically unfeasible. Or bread, representative of the fertile plains, consumed by the mother-prostitute, stands opposite the sunless, barren space in which the son dies. And the milk is a store-bought commodity, not offered freely from the mother's breast. The commodification of milk implicates a chain of intermediaries responsible for its distribution; such profiteering and distance form the very premise of Mamma Roma and Ettore's precarious relationship.

Together, bread and milk symbolize the purity, innocence, and sustainability of life itself: These are the foundations of one's survival. The fact that Mamma Roma is eating these foods – especially within the brightness

Figure 3.5. A shot-reverse shot of Mamma Roma and the horizon of Rome. The difference in perspectives showcases the mother-prostitute and the city that ultimately betrayed her.

and comfort of her own kitchen – at the same moment that her son lies dying is, thus, painfully ironic. Food, and its consumption in a kitchen of the *borgate*, are the lenses through which one detects the hollowed illusions of Mamma Roma's dreams. In swallowing the wet bread, not only is the milk – typically produced for a child's consumption – digested selfishly by the mother, and not only does she consume the crumbs of Ettore's life, as if to take the Communion given up for the neo-capitalist, but also it is foreshadowing: she, too, will be engulfed by the spectacle of the *borgate*.

Only through Ettore's death does Mamma Roma realize the fallacy of the spectacle. She is informed of Ettore's passing while working the vegetable stand. Hearing the tragic news at this location only adds another dimension of betrayal to her food work, as the site of their socioeconomic improvement – of the strides made to establish and foster a home for her and her son in the spectacular capital – is now associated with the death of her son, the archaic. Followed by a mass of colleagues and friends, she abandons the vegetable cart, races home, opens the window and attempts to jump. She is pulled back, rests temporarily on Ettore's bed, and returns to the window. The closing shots of the film are a back-and-forth between Mamma Roma, eyes bewildered, and the distant horizon of a Rome into which, she now realizes, she will never assimilate.

The desolation behind Pasolini's "stupendous, miserable city"[59] comes to the fore, as Mamma Roma, contained inside her once-treasured apartment, looks out at an urban landscape that has ultimately betrayed her. The photograph depicts the shot of the city responsible for Mamma Roma's tragic epiphany. Eyes locked onto a cupola, the architecture's simulacrum of a breast, she realizes the fullness of the spectacle of the patriarchy into which she has been subsumed.

Conclusion

Pasolini's film ends; so, too, does this chapter. All the women therein attempt to exit prostitution to pursue "honest" work, typically done by women without compensation. Stuck within the codes of patriarchal containment – not just the power of their pimps, but also laws and police registrations, linguistic misconstructions, and Fascistic urban plans – they fail to establish stable livelihoods and reconcile strained family dynamics.

As the 1960s progressed, Pasolini's work took leave of the *borgate* and, eventually, Italy altogether. In the next chapter, his focus is not on the pursuit of a fixed home or site for an honest lifestyle but, rather, on wandering and quests: His protagonists meander through parts unknown, in search of food and the bounties of heavenly Paradise amid capitalist exploitation. Evolving into caves and movie sets, the *borgate* are Pasolini's point of departure towards *"un non si sa dove"*: visceral consumption in uncharted time-space.[60]

Chapter Four

Crises and Revolutions in the Work of Pasolini

It's a cacophony, this life, and those lost
in it, lose it cloudlessly, if their hearts
are filled with it: enjoying themselves,
behold the wretched, the evening: powerful.
In them, defenseless before them, the myth
is reborn. … But I, with my aware heart, which is alive only in history,
can I ever again act with a pure love,
if I know that our history is ended?

– Pier Paolo Pasolini, *Le ceneri di Gramsci* (1957), VI[1]

The above citation is from the poem *Le ceneri di Gramsci*, written in 1957 by Pier Paolo Pasolini: poet, novelist, essayist, and filmmaker. This elegiac work is addressed to the late Antonio Gramsci (1891–1937), the pioneering leader of Italy's Communist Party, who died in prison under Benito Mussolini's regime. While incarcerated, Gramsci authored the *Prison Notebooks*, penning ideas on intellectualism, industrialism, history, and politics that deeply influenced twentieth-century Italian thought – including Pasolini's intellectual compass, as undertones of Communism are peppered throughout his work. Facing Gramsci's imprisonment and death, Pasolini laments how life proceeds despite the greatest rupture of all: when our history, *la nostra storia*, is finished.[2]

Indeed, although *Le ceneri di Gramsci* was published in the same period that *L'oro di Napoli* and *Totò, Peppino e … la malafemmina* were released, Pasolini breaks from those "rosy" representations of continuity. Instead of the humour, love, and wholesomeness that exude from the aforementioned films, in Pasolini's work the connections to that harmonious past are severed as he depicts an increasingly precarious, violent future; we are in the realm of *ruptures*. In the previous chapter, by way of Pasolini's *Mamma Roma* (1962), I spoke of unrecognizable backgrounds: His shots of the Fascistic *borgate* confounded his viewers and duped his eponymous protagonist, since her new apartment – and, by extension, her faux-bourgeois comportment – failed to safeguard her son. In this chapter, meanwhile, I examine unrecognizability of a political, temporal kind. Using his later filmography, I question how society functions, and where any sense of continuity can be found, amid sociopolitical upheaval, neo-capitalist exploitations, and, more specifically, the death of a second Communist leader, Palmiro Togliatti (1893–1964), which sent the Party into crisis.

"Crisis," however, must be understood not as an end; history has *not* finished. A crisis is, instead, a *turning point*: a change in the expected course – a *revolution*. Revolution is, by definition, the overthrow of a social order or system of governance; it also indicates a circular, cyclical motion. This chapter unpacks these meanings of revolution through some of Pasolini's metaphors of food and eating. Two of his films, *La ricotta* (1963) and *Uccellacci e uccellini* (1966), depict crises through tropes of hunger, predation, and indigestion. In *La ricotta*, Stracci, the protagonist, consumes too much cheese, too quickly. In *Uccellacci e uccellini*, hawks attack sparrows, and protagonists Totò and Ninetto devour a Marxist crow. These three moments of eating reflect the grander-scale socioeconomic and political tensions of the 1960s, but they suggest not definite rupture but, instead, a revolutionary progression. The consumption of these animals and animal products brings life to an end, whether that of the prey or the consumer himself; this change is final and irreversible, signalling a crisis in the alarmist sense. Yet, through those moments of eating and death, society progresses. The results of the predatory, grotesque eating in Pasolini's work are ultimately *absorbed* into the continuum of history, leaving future generations to digest and adapt to the changes that have unfolded. Pasolini positions these food tropes within cultural and religious narratives with which his viewers are very familiar. However, he detours from these stories' usual trajectories, as well as from their norms of eating. These moments, then, will be analysed as changes in direction: movements off course, diverging from the viewers' expectations, but also a circling back towards some simpler time: before conflict, before language, before the story of *History*.

Perversions of Catholicism, Perversions of Narration

Pasolini situated *La ricotta* and *Uccellacci e uccellini* within Christian contexts: respectively, the Passion of Christ and St. Francis of Assisi's interactions with the animal kingdom. Pasolini's Catholicism exerted a constant influence upon his life and oeuvre, but his beliefs diverged from those perpetuated by the Christian Democrats, Italy's foremost political party since it became a Republic in 1948. He identified as Marxist, therefore practising a "dangerous" religiosity: exhibiting Marxist leanings in the Red Scare West, but featuring Christ and Catholic rituals against an atheistic political backdrop. He alluded to Catholic figures and stories that his viewers would readily recognize, but he darkened these narratives, presenting contaminations of the Word of God.[3] These perversions are simultaneously allusions to and detours away from canonical and biblical tales and tenets, as well as from cinematic precedents; rarely would one find the likes of pious Pina (Anna Magnani) from Roberto Rossellini's *Roma città aperta* (1945), or the gullible, innocent Cabiria (Giulietta Masina) from Federico Fellini's *Le notti di Cabiria* (1956). In *La ricotta* and *Uccellacci e uccellini*, Pasolini presents more malicious sides of the Passion of Christ and St. Francis's sermons to animals. St. Francis, along with Jesus Christ and His twelve disciples, are deeply venerated within Catholicism. The viewer is uncomfortable, then, with Pasolini's treatment of these figures: their exploitation, their predation, and how, ultimately, these characters and their virtues not only go unrecognized but are ignored. In *La ricotta*, Pasolini bypasses the paschal Resurrection of Christ, and how He died for one's sins, to create instead a spectacle through the exploitation of Stracci's basic needs – namely, hunger. Similarly, in *Uccellacci e uccellini*, the animals misinterpret God's message of brotherly love and empathy, delivered vicariously by St. Francis, as the hawks kill the smaller, hungrier sparrows. Likewise, Totò and Ninetto ignore the prophecies of the crow, consuming his flesh instead of his reasonings. Thwarting this traditional religious lore with instances of excessive, grotesque eating, Pasolini's protagonists are agents of spiritual crisis. These breaks – from the typical innocence of these tales, as well as from the usual expectations of these narratives – come as an unsettling shock to the viewer.

Stracci: Non aveva altro modo per fare "rivoluzione"

La ricotta is a film set on the outskirts of Rome, where the protagonist, Stracci, plays the Good Thief in a rendition of the *Passion of Christ*, directed diegetically by Orson Welles. Stracci is starving. His work on the film is his meal ticket, as he earns a boxed lunch each day he reports to work, which he in turn delivers to his family. Donning a blonde wig and a dress, Stracci's "double" earns a second lunch, but a dog – belonging to the star of Welles's film (Laura Betti) – finds and eats it. Stracci sells the dog to a visiting journalist for 1,000 lire, and, with that money, he purchases a wheel of ricotta, which he stores in a cave. When there is a break in production, Stracci runs to the cave to eat the cheese, only to be taunted by his fellow cast members with more food: eggs, a whole watermelon, and a banquet table representative of the Last Supper. Immediately following this episode of binge eating, Stracci is bound to the cross for his crucifixion, but dies of indigestion before he delivers the words, "Lord, remember me when thou comest into thy Kingdom." Welles demands that he say his line, ultimately realizing that Stracci is dead; Welles thus concludes, "Poor Stracci. Dying … He had no other way of reminding us that he, too, was alive."[4] Pasolini closes his film by zooming in on the fateful table of plenty, particularly on the cheese, centrally situated.

La ricotta is Pasolini's narration of Jesus Christ's crucifixion and Resurrection: two of the most defining moments of the Christian calendar. The Gospels describe the crucifixion as a spectacle. Jesus was publicly mocked in the hours immediately beforehand, and His death was on very public display;[5] in Luke 23:48–9, it is written: "When the people who had gathered there to watch the *spectacle* saw what happened, they all went back home, beating their breasts in sorrow. All those who knew Jesus personally, including the women who had followed him from Galilee, *stood at a distance to watch*."[6] A spectacular crucifixion is the very premise of *La ricotta*, as Pasolini converts the sacredness of biblical Jerusalem into a filmic production of the *Passion of Christ*. The directors (both Welles and Pasolini) thus capitalize upon one of the holiest moments in Christianity, employing the Gospels in a money-making scheme, cast and crew profiting as viewers pay an admission fee to watch a modern-day crucifixion. Yet the crucifixion is not that of Jesus, and not everyone gains from the spectacle. Pasolini's protagonist is, instead, Stracci, playing the role of the Good Thief. In the Bible, the Good Thief is publicly crucified next to Jesus; in *La ricotta*, Stracci, too, dies on the cross, at the centre of the spectacle. Stracci is also killed by Romans – not the governors of the ancient empire, but the bigwigs of Cinecittà. Film is what both kills Stracci and, in a way, resurrects him, as film commits his death to public memory.

La ricotta is a perversion of the biblical narrative particularly through Stracci's frenzied eating. The Bible does not report what the Good Thief eats in the hours preceding his death; instead, Christians immediately remember the Last Supper that Jesus shared with His disciples the night before the crucifixion – an intimate dinner laden with tension and hints of betrayal. Nevertheless, Jesus gives bread and wine to His disciples; the bread and wine, representing His body and blood, symbolize the forgiveness and compassion Jesus unconditionally extends to His closest confidants and generations of followers, despite the severity of their sins and their culpability in His death.

Pasolini's rendition of the Last Supper, meanwhile, is the "Stracci Show" – a jazzy name that denotes the spectacle of consumption. Jesus is absent, and Stracci consumes an entire table of food for the voyeuristic pleasure of two audiences: the cast of Welles's production, who encourage the binge eating, and Pasolini's viewers. Nor is the "Stracci Show" the initiation of an everlasting covenant with God. The laws governing Stracci's world are, instead, decided and enforced by the film director: not just Welles, but Pasolini, whom Welles represents. As the "Stracci Show" is, indeed, a spectacle, Stracci's access to food and the rate at which he consumes it are conditioned by the demands of film production: both the diegetic film directed by Welles and *La ricotta* itself, with Pasolini at the helm. Stracci must, first, report to work and act in accordance with the script in order to receive a meal. Then, his eating is subject to changes enforced by Welles and the star of his movie, as well as by changes in the weather that impact the shooting schedule; these production aspects betray and kill Stracci. His relationship to food, when impacted by such precarious factors, is hardly stable. Pasolini underscores this instability by manipulating the time at which his narrative unfolds, slowing his frame rate to speed up Stracci's eating – at a speed unnaturally too fast for healthy digestion.

Pasolini engineers a number of constraints – executed through his characters' actions and his directorial choices – which ultimately crucify his protagonist. Stracci's consumption-death is because of the social circumstances under which the eating occurs. "Constraints," a term borrowed from sociologist Anthony Giddens, is one way in which Pasolini manipulates Stracci. In an essay titled "Time, Space, and Regionalisation" (1984), Giddens, writing in response to notions of time-geography established by Swedish geographer Torsten Hägerstrand, underlines five boundaries that limit behaviours within the axes of time and space. Among the boundaries are the laws – the constraints – that govern the spectacle of eating: "The limited 'packing capacity' of time-space. No two human bodies can occupy the same space at the same time; physical objects have the same elemental characteristic. Therefore any zone of time-space can be analyzed in terms of constraints over the two types of objects which can be accommodated within it."[7] Scientifically, this factor is true: A container with a fixed volume can only hold so many molecules, no matter their size. Socially, were we to consider a "container" with fixed dimensions of time and space, a human living and working within such a space would need to make choices with respect to the constraints imposed by other individuals occupying the same space. In Pasolini's films, one sees a similar hierarchy, where everyday choices – in this case, eating – are impacted by industrialized time. In *La ricotta*, it is the tight yet precarious production schedule, and Stracci, the sub-proletariat, exists outside this capitalistic structuring of time. Stracci, who exhibits solely the fundamental need to eat, must obey the tight schedule and the rules of his domain, the film set – but with deleterious consequences. As an extra, he works tirelessly just so he and his family can secure even one meal a day. In this role, he must meet the exorbitant demands of production, particularly those of the film's star, thereby attempting, but failing, to defy the scarcity of time. His biological needs are scheduled according to industrial clock-time, a register that his body does not recognize, so he dies attempting to fulfil them. Ostensibly, he dies of indigestion, but that is a symptom of his inability to adhere to a schedule and the standards by which he is exploited.

In line with the constraints that Giddens puts forth, the underlying tensions of the film surround two opposing entities. *La ricotta* focuses on a single film set, but the opening shots establish two disparate worlds that struggle, and ultimately fail, to coexist in one space. The first world is shot in Technicolor and is embedded with aspects of both popular and mannerist cultures; Pasolini's camera focuses on two men gaily dancing the twist, alongside a banquet table overwhelmed with eggs, grapes, dangling garlic cloves, an enormous cut of prosciutto, bread, and, as the title of the film hints, ricotta cheese. The world of these two men is one of abundance, conviviality, and leisure: a pleasurable break before they reassume their positions within a profoundly colourful *tableau vivant* of Welles's *Passion of Christ*. But their sense of pleasure is by no means universal. Pasolini is quick to juxtapose these colour shots with a second, grimmer world – that of the two protagonists, Stracci (Mario Cipriani) and Welles. Behind the scenes of Technicolor, by way of mostly reverse-zoom but also shot- reverse shots, these two characters gaze into the realm of colour, dance music, and fun from without. Their vantage point remains black and white, the absence of colour portraying a grimmer perspective on the events that unfold. Being behind the scenes, standing opposite the carefree consumerism shown in Technicolor, Stracci and Welles convey not only loneliness but also a sense of unrecognizability and even invisibility. Although Stracci and Welles are consistently shown in black and white, apparently belonging to the same domain, Pasolini's use of low- and high-angled shots separates the two characters so that they are never seen together. This separation accentuates the stakes of working, eating, and starving *alone*. Eating together exudes a social and nutritional wealth, with healthy digestion aided by conversation and intimacy with loved ones; eating alone, meanwhile, reveals an emptiness

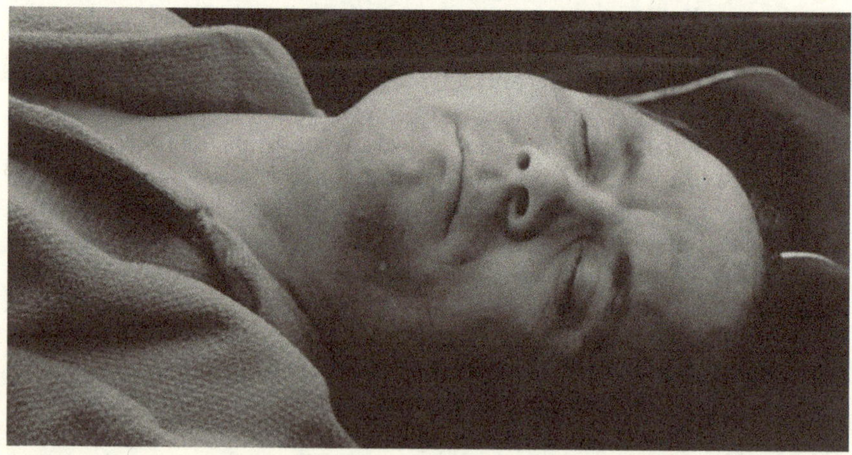

Figure 4.1. A shot-reverse shot of Stracci (Mario Cipriani) and the table of plenty in the establishing shots of *La ricotta* (1963, dir. Pier Paolo Pasolini).

in one's life.[8] The feelings of community and conviviality underlined in previous chapters have shifted, becoming more exclusive. The banquet table, containing the Last Supper prepared for the diegetic Christ and His disciplines, is out in the open, its foods readily available for consumption – but by those principal characters only. Watching a film, viewers see the director's work but not the director himself; the extras, meanwhile, are hired to occupy the background of frames, to blend in, thus contrasting with the easy recognizability of stars in the foreground. As an extra who is denied such recognition, Stracci sees the table of plenty, but he is not invited to eat; the food is rooted in a space to which he does not belong. The extra's mouth is to be closed; there is no talking or eating while the main and supporting actors come forth to deliver their lines. One could connect the silence of the extra to his exclusion from the convivial meal. The mouth and tongue are sites of speech, as well as of eating and taste; if one is restrained from opening his mouth to speak, he is, likewise, forbidden to eat and, consequently, to partake in conversations over a meal, or to express a need for medical attention. Because Stracci's sole job is to be invisible, his fundamental survival needs are refused by those in positions of authority: the star in the Technicolor space, as well as the directors, Welles and Pasolini, both inside and beyond the black-and-white scenes.

The viewer's first glimpse of Stracci – a close-up of him lying on the ground, starving and feverish, as if he were already dead – affirms not merely Stracci's invisibility but also the life- denying constraints imposed upon him by the greater cast and crew.[9] It is precisely this invisibility that kills Stracci, because the two men in Technicolor – and we, the paying viewers – fail to truly *see* Stracci's hunger as a dire physiological need. Unlike the positive correlation between hunger and humour presented in Chapter 1, here, the viewer fails to acknowledge that Stracci is actually dying; assuming his hunger is part of the greater spectacle, an outside viewer's response is to laugh – all the while denying Stracci food and, hence, life. But whereas Totò's exaggerations of hunger were a means of placation, of softening the blows of the recent *dopoguerra*, Stracci's hunger is a matter of capitalist exploitation. Stracci will not be fed because, if he is nourished, the source of laughter dissipates; to ensure the success of the film, his hunger is manipulated to extremes. Referring to Giddens's theory once more, Stracci's deathly exploitation results from a combination of two constraints: capability constraints and coupling constraints. Below are Giddens's findings at length:

The encounters into which individuals enter in the trajectories of daily life are subject to constraints deriving from the list indicated previously.

Hägerstrand acknowledges, of course, that agents are not merely mobile bodies, but intentional beings with purposes or what he calls "projects." The projects which individuals seek to realize, if they are to be actualized, have to utilize the inherently limited resources of time and space to overcome constraints which they confront. "Capability constraints" are those of the sort listed above. Some affect primarily time-distribution – for example, the need for sleep, or for food at regular intervals, ensures certain limits to the structuration of daily activities. "Coupling constraints" refer to those that condition activities undertaken jointly with others. The volume of time-space available to an individual in a day is a prism bounding the pursuance of projects. Prisms of daily conduct are not just geographical or physical boundaries, but have "time-space walls on all sides." The size of such prisms, of course, is also very strongly influenced by the degree of time-space convergence in the means of communication and transformation available to agents.[10]

Regarding *La ricotta*, what is problematic is that Stracci's "project" and primary "capability constraint" are one and the same: He needs to eat and to provide for his family, and he must therefore report to work to earn the boxed lunch available on set; if he does not work, neither he nor his family gets to eat. Paradoxically, he is too starved and feverish – too invisible – to complete his sole job of delivering a single line as the Good Thief. Because of these coupling constraints, no one – neither the cast and crew, nor Pasolini's audience – really notices Stracci until it is too late.

The space in which Stracci works is not necessarily controlled by Welles but, rather, by the film's star. Stracci and the star jointly, but by no means equally, occupy this space; whereas Stracci is dispensable, the show could not go on without the star. As a result, the star establishes the rules, and the cast and crew – including Welles – must concede. Stracci, a mere extra, must conform to all demands and scheduling changes set forth by the star; otherwise, he will lose his job and, thus, his lunch. Without even knowing who Stracci is, the star is responsible for his death. She is the coupling constraint whose symbolic capital and overall presence overshadow and render Stracci invisible, but she – and her dog – commandeer the chain of events that leads to his fatal bout of indigestion. As mentioned, the star's dog discovers and eats the food that Stracci cleverly earned by way of cross-dressing. In order to eat anything at all, then, he must again be creative. Selling the dog to the journalist, he at last has the financial means to eat. There appear to be no legal repercussions for his theft, nor does the star realize that the dog is missing, let alone exhibit any sign of anger or grief; Stracci has truly become the Good Thief. In this evolution, he is still subject to the rules and rhythm of the film set, so he must proceed to purchase and consume his food in tandem with the tempo of the set, and, more specifically, the tempo of the star. In other words, Stracci has no choice but to eat quickly – more quickly than the human body physically allows.

Pasolini's manipulation of Stracci is most clearly manifest through his slowed frame rate, and thus, the noticeable increase in the speeds at which Stracci first abandons the film set, purchases the ricotta, and hides the cheese in a cave for safe-keeping, and, later, rushes to the cave to eat the cheese. The change in tempo could be read as a homage to comic actors, such as Charlie Chaplin, whose films centred on the procurement of food.[11] This comic allusion only feeds into Stracci's exploitation. The increase in tempo is the only way for him to combat the constraints that constrict his time-space; he needs to increase his speed in order to eat – to alleviate his hunger and survive – and to remain employed in order to keep feeding his family. In other words, Stracci's eating must never conflict with the schedule of production. He must defy nature, his own circadian rhythm, in an attempt to both satisfy his hunger and play his role as the Good Thief; hence, these scenes of food procurement unfold with unnatural speed.[12] As the extra with no say in the production, he cannot eat or taste foods at times when he is hungry, or at a tempo at which he could truly enjoy what he is eating.[13] In *La ricotta*, with Stracci's speed, gone is the appreciation of food, and its dance on one's senses, as consumption is squeezed into an industrialized routine. He must wait to eat the ricotta, because the expectations of his role – being bound to a crucifix adjacent to Christ's – supersede his need to eat.

An Interlude on Cheese

With a title like *La ricotta*, one must isolate and better define another constraint impacting Stracci's eating: the ricotta itself. Ricotta cheese, renowned for its sweetness and creamy, buttery texture, is usually a by-product of sheep's milk.[14] Chapter 2 spoke of breast milk and its quality of connectivity between a mother and her child. Indeed, since the Renaissance, milk – not just from one's mother but also from a cow, goat, or sheep – has been praised as a substance of strength and good health. Italian scholar Bartolomeo Sacchi, otherwise known as Platina, wrote on milk in *On Right Pleasure and Good Health* (1465): "It is agreed among all doctors that milk nourishes well, generates much blood (since blood may be drawn from udders and breasts), warms the brain, is good for the stomach and lungs, and increases fertility."[15] If milk, and, by association, cheese so strongly embody qualities of healthfulness and versatility – in other words, if the innumerable varieties of cheese aid digestion and can sustain a worker's long hours – one wonders why Pasolini established cheese as his instrument of death in *La ricotta*.

In addition, ricotta cheese is a whey by-product. Casein, a milk protein, is used to make cheese, and through that process, there remains a precipitate of secondary proteins; these secondary proteins, when acid-fermented and brought to a boil, comprise the whey of ricotta. Metaphorically speaking, Stracci's inferior role in *La ricotta* mirrors the precipitate left behind in creating cheese; Stracci, a word which in cheese terminology refers to "shreds," is himself a by-product in Welles's production. Both by-products, Stracci and the ricotta alike, are on the clock. The process of making ricotta is deeply precarious. As one of the fresher varieties of cheese, ricotta is extremely perishable; the cheese will spoil if it is not either used or consumed immediately, or refrigerated to extend its shelf-life. Likewise, Stracci's indigestion by ricotta – a stark contrast to the delicious versatility and digestive benefits of the cheese – is a question of time. Ricotta is a cheese with urgency, with a rapidly dwindling expiration window; unlike aged cheeses, such as Parmigiano Reggiano or an asiago, ricotta must be eaten *now*. Pasolini's choice of ricotta thus only aggravates Stracci's challenges with time. He will lose his third lunch of the day if he does not quicken his pace. The ricotta is as problematic as his duties on set.

The postponement of eating the ricotta continues as Stracci, the Good Thief, is called to set and must be tied to a cross lying on the ground. This position of immobility and frozenness further foreshadows his death. Although it was published four years after *La ricotta*, Pasolini wrote extensively in *Heretical Empiricism* (1967) on the connections between death and cinematic montage. He explained that, when someone dies, their life is preserved and expressed through a series of curated moments; language gives meaning to the life that was lived. He wrote, "Death effects an instantaneous montage of our lives; that is, it chooses the truly meaningful moments (which are no longer modifiable by other possible contrary or incoherent moments) and puts them in a sequence, transforming an infinite, unstable and uncertain – and therefore linguistically not describable – present into a clear, stable, certain and therefore easily describable past."[16] Film, Pasolini advocated, thus captures events that had once happened in real time, "as if death had already occurred. This means that in cinema time is complete, even if only through a pretence … Time in this context is not that of life when it lives, but of life after death."[17] The existence of film depends on a story that has already run its full course. The entirety of a film, an amalgam of edited frames, is analogous to death: the cessation of corporeal actions, but the attribution of meaning to that completed life. A singular frame, then, signifies stasis – a moment frozen in time, an instance of cessation and paralysis.[18] When Stracci's supernatural quickness is brought to a jarring halt, his movements paralysed by his binding to the cross, Pasolini is accentuating film – both the demands of Welles's *Passion* and the editing of *La ricotta* itself – as the instrument of Stracci's death.[19] Stracci may not eat or move, because that is what film production demands; film first suspends, then terminates, his corporeality.

Stracci's fellow cast members eagerly continue to deny him his basic needs and, thus, his life, particularly while he is forcibly immobilized. It is the star, and the complacent director, who keep Stracci confined to this position, as she insists that the shooting schedule be changed so that her scene may be shot first, or else she will leave for the day.[20] In other words, the star once more reinforces the power dynamic that denies Stracci any food. It is only when clouds cover the sun that production stops, Stracci is freed, and the speedy tempo resumes, but, in the meantime, the cast initiates their fatal taunt of Stracci. While he is bound to the cross, Stracci's very human cravings come to the fore but are teased and ultimately rejected; motionless and horizontal, he struggles against cast members who are all decidedly vertical and free of constraints (physical and otherwise), and who thus feel empowered in their being situated at the winning end of a brutal joke. The cast members make fun of Stracci by dangling a sandwich and a bottle of juice before him, and they test his sexual frustrations by inviting an actress (playing Mary Magdalene) over for a striptease. The more formal qualities of these moments, such as the close-up shots of Stracci licking his lips, underline his impotence and continued hunger – both gastronomic and sexual – as his position on the cross bars him from biting the sandwich or engaging fully with the stripping actress.

In this scene, the viewer is at once in tune with Stracci's jeopardized humanness and reminded of the macrocosm in which this film exists: the gap between the exploitative bourgeoisie, represented by the Hollywoodized film machine, and Stracci, the oppressed subproletariat, amid the broken promises of prosperity for the new consumerist Italy. Stracci, then, represents life at its absolute barest but is thus the emblem of Pasolini's latest political commentary: artistic spectacles starring the rich are built on the hunger of the poor. In fact, while Stracci and the actor playing Christ are still bound to their crosses, Stracci complains of hunger and threatens to act out; the actor responds, jokingly, that if Stracci rebels, he will not take Stracci with him to the Kingdom of Heaven. Despite his voicing a real human concern, Stracci's complaints

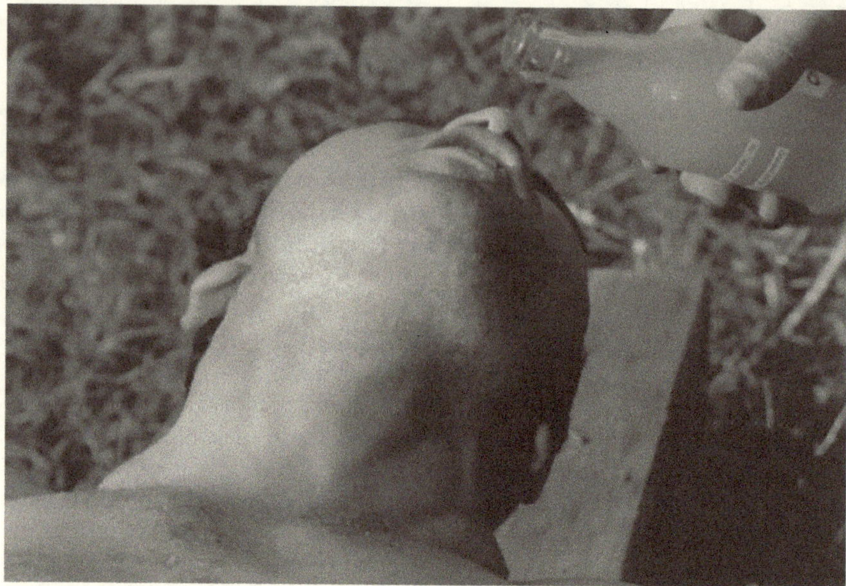

Figure 4.2. Stracci, tortured by his fellow cast members.

are distorted by the filmic spectacle; denied his basic needs, he is rendered sub-human. Such exploitation of Stracci lays the groundwork for revolution.

This idea of the sub-human becomes quite literal when Stracci is at last unchained. Pasolini once again slows the frame rate, increasing Stracci's tempo as he scurries down to the cave, where the ricotta awaits. Despite Stracci's escape to the dark subterranean, the cave is nonetheless initially presented as a safe haven, where he can eat in peace, free of the demanding constraints of the spectacle above. However, essences of the spectacle soon invade his space. Stracci eats alone – he is the sole consumer in the frame – but he eats for two audiences: the diegetic spectators in the cave and the paying viewers in the theatre. The rhythm of the audience(s) is noticeably slower and more relaxed than Stracci's speed, and, based on the chorus of hearty laughter, Stracci's hunger remains a joke to the cast. This time, though, instead of denying Stracci his basic needs of food and water, the cast finds it funny to overwhelm Stracci with a chaotic, excessive, even carnivalesque banquet. This "banquet" is a spectacle which the cast calls the "Stracci Show." Although such a title implies that Stracci is a star with agency, he is, instead, treated like an animal at a zoo, fed at scheduled times for an audience's viewing pleasure.

Figure 4.3. A shot-reverse shot of the "Stracci Show."

In his defence during a trial for public defamation of religion, Pasolini stated, "I do not understand what harm can be seen in the fact that
Stracci goes and hides in a cave so he can eat in peace. I really don't."[21]
Yet, the underground setting of the "Stracci Show" is entirely harmful.
In the Bible, following His crucifixion, the body of Christ was buried
in a cave; here, too, the "Stracci Show" implies a burial, where Stracci
is once again coded as already dead. Indeed, the events in the cave
facilitate his eventual death by indigestion. Stracci retreats to the cave to
hide, seeking an invisibility necessary to eat in peace, but it is in the cave
that the cast notices not only his body but also his hunger, which they
brutally exploit. The cast assumes two roles: They are Stracci's audience, laughing at both the gargantuan amount he eats and the ravenous
rate at which he is eating, and they are also accomplices. This laughter
is decidedly different from the therapeutic tactics of Totò, discussed at
length in Chapter 1. Whereas Totò's humour was a way of engaging
the public, of amassing togetherness as the nation transitioned away
from material hunger, the laughter surrounding Stracci's hunger is,
instead, a divisive tool, separating those who do and do not have easy
access to food. This laughter is criminal. In addition, in the cave, there
is decidedly less accountability for such a crime, as Stracci's invisibility
is only amplified through the underground location; how can one be
held accountable for acts against a person whose existence is unseen?[22]
By contrast, it is only when Stracci gasps his last breath, above ground,
bound to his cross above a throng of publicists, that he is no longer
exploited. Instead, his exploiters – the cast, Welles, Pasolini, and even
the paying viewers – finally see the man hiding behind such intense
hunger.

From the moment Stracci takes his first bite of the ricotta to Pasolini's resumption of shots above ground, the "Stracci Show" lasts only
two minutes and eight seconds. In that time, in addition to the wheel of
ricotta, he is fed two raw eggs, a whole watermelon, a bowl of spaghetti,
and, finally, the entirety of the banquet table, complete with more fruit
(most visibly, grapes and pears) and eggs, which were first introduced in
the establishing shots. This table, once central to the shots in Technicolor,
now pervades Stracci's black-and-white world, thus foreshadowing the
grim, aggressive fate surrounding these foods. In line with Welles's story
of the *Passion of Christ*, the foods that the cast feeds Stracci – namely, the
eggs and the fruit – are paschal symbols, both signifying new life and
rebirth as Jesus is resurrected. But Stracci's unnatural tempo and tunnel vision surrounding his need to eat, in combination with such top-
down feeding by the cast, turn these foods deadly. Stracci's crazed eating
is analogous to Christ's Last Supper; Stracci's final meal takes place in

an intimate setting, but this lunch is, too, peppered with malevolence. He does not enjoy the food because of the time constraint, but instead, viewers relish the spectacle created at his expense; as he must engulf his food at the Pasolinian rate to keep the audiences laughing, in turn, the demands and constraints of film production engulf *him*.[23]

The "Stracci Show" abruptly ends and Pasolini's camera moves above ground, focusing on a new spectacle. Accompanied by jovial marching-band music, publicists, investors, and celebrities have arrived on set to witness the crucifixion of Christ. Welles hinted at their arrival earlier while speaking to the journalist; hopeful that the journalist had a bad heart, Welles claimed if that he did have a bad heart and dropped dead on set, it would be good publicity for the film's release. Welles adds, "You don't exist anyway. Capital acknowledges the existence of labour only insofar as it serves production." This quote, while directed at the journalist, refers to Stracci's non-existence and eventual death by production; with his death, the cogs of the capitalist film machine will at last come to recognize him. Through his Christ-like death, he dies for, and by, our neo-capitalist sins.

Stracci emerges from the cave and is bound to the cross once more, and his cross is elevated to join Christ's. He has been commanded to recite just one line: "Lord, remember me when Thou comest into Thy kingdom." These are Stracci's last words; spoken quietly towards the sky, they go unrecorded. Moments later, with the crowd watching from below, Welles repeats, "Azione!", but Stracci has already passed away. Following a series of close-up shots, alternating between Welles's pensive expression and Stracci's closed eyes and beads of sweat, Welles sombrely concludes that the only way for Stracci to overcome his invisibility is to die.

Like the death of Christ, who too was robbed, mocked, and taunted with drink, and whose cultic following evolved into one of the world's biggest religions, the implications of Stracci's death – thus, of his new visibility – resonate far beyond the fatal moment of indigestion. In fact, Welles's original concluding line was, "Poor Stracci. Dying ... he had no other way of starting a *revolution*."[24] Since it presents an interruption of the work-flow, Stracci's death is a manifestation of a proletarian revolution: the exploited worker throwing a wrench to stop the bourgeois wheel from making more revolutions. His death paralyses the spectacle: The crowd waits for him to deliver his line; the star once domineered the shooting schedule, but now the show cannot continue without Stracci; and, consequently, here is where Pasolini's film draws to a close. Stracci, then, appears to be the new coupling constraint with which the cast and crew must contend.

One might even conclude that Stracci *is* the film: He is rendered visible only by the film, and his death – his story brought to a close – is what brings the film product to fruition, thereby affirming Pasolini's theory of filmic life after death.

Since Welles's line was ultimately revised, one must wonder: *Is Stracci revolutionary?* Yes, he transitioned from the subterranean to the spectacular, and from distant periphery to the centre of the show, by eating from the Technicolor table of plenty. Once taunted while immobile, and once overindulged underground, he is allowed by those acts of consumption to overcome the constraints – hunger and production – that once confined him to invisible powerlessness. But he ate and he died: Does this necessarily mean that he is the pioneer of Pasolini's Marxist revolution? The lumpenproletariat is, after all, marked by lack of interest in revolutionary advancement such as Stracci's.

The discussion, thus, must transition to a revolution of a different kind. Revolution, synonymous with rebellion and uprising, also indicates a turn, a spin, often in the formation of the infinite circle – with no beginning or end, or a clear path set for humankind. The shape of a circle represents everlasting continuity and perfection: a stark contrast to the perversions and ruptures presented in Pasolini's work. To these ends, with Pasolini's *Uccellacci e uccellini* as its case study, the rest of the chapter explores this second definition of "revolution." My reading of *La ricotta* borrowed the theoretical groundwork laid by Giddens, explaining Pasolini's manipulation of linear time as a means of narrating his disturbing rendition of the Passion of Christ. The next section, meanwhile, establishes the contours of Pasolini's circular writing, and in so doing, qualifies to what extent the tropes of eating in *Uccellacci e uccellini* bolster – or break – any continuities in eating and in history.

The Disorientation of *Uccellacci e uccellini*

Uccellacci e uccellini continues the sense of narrative discomfort conjured by *La ricotta*. In *La ricotta*, the focus was mostly on questions of hunger and invisibility, as well as the unnatural tampering with time. The overarching question surrounding *Uccellacci e uccellini*, meanwhile, is not necessarily a question of time, but of "where?" It is not a particular protagonist, but rather the *setting*, which is unrecognizable in *Uccellacci e uccellini*. Pasolini takes leave of the diegetic film set of *La ricotta*, which evokes the memory of Jerusalem, and positions the two protagonists of *Uccellacci e uccellini* within parts unknown, walking along a single road. Despite the presence of road signs that mark distances to real places such as Cuba and Istanbul, and despite street signs that affirm the existence of life and laws – examples include "Private Property" and "Via Antonio Mangiapasta, Scopino" – the viewer is unsure of the film's setting: Where are the protagonists headed?

Likewise, it is more difficult to formulate a synopsis of *Uccellacci e uccellini* than of *La ricotta*. The episodic nature of the film mirrors the wandering protagonists: ambling, directionless, and non-teleological. The film even has the potential to unfold out of Pasolini's intended order: the core tenets of the film would not change if the viewer were to watch the diegetic stories in a different sequence. There are, nevertheless, two key plot points: First, Pasolini offers a disturbing contradiction to the work of St. Francis of Assisi, thereby transporting the viewer to the 1200s. This distorted tale is narrated by a talking Marxist crow who is ultimately eaten: the film's second crisis. With an overarching teleology eliminated, however, these parts are just episodes of a larger work. *Uccellacci e uccellini* is the portrayal of more macrocosmic issues, potentially surprising and upsetting Pasolini's audience and contemporaries: the iconic comedy of Totò, as discussed in Chapter 1, now decidedly darker; the questionable state of Italy's political landscape after the death of Communist leader Palmiro Togliatti; and the clash between Marxist culture, with its traditions growing obsolete, and the saccharine, yet increasingly alluring, "pulp" of Hollywood. These sociocultural moments in themselves reveal the disturbing tumult of 1960s Italy, but the way in which Pasolini narrates them jars the viewer even further. *Uccellacci e uccellini* is a difficult narrative to follow, because it is a project in which Pasolini explores the inefficiency of spoken and written language and experiments with new, more primal, ways of expressing oneself and the history in which Italians were living.

Although "non-linear" could represent a variety of geometries, if the non-linear structure of *Uccellacci e uccellini* embodied a shape, it would be the circle: a shape with no origin or endpoint, and thus, no clear beginning or end. The circle is perfectly disorienting, because where are the protagonists, but similarly, how does the viewer position herself to the story? And what resolution, if any, does Pasolini provide in his filmic carousel? "Going around in circles" does not achieve new ends, but that is, perhaps, Pasolini's objective. He accentuates not only a path towards an unknown future but also a return towards the *past*: a counterclockwise shift towards the archaic, the pre-industrial, and the pre-linguistic.

Circular Writing: Language and Movement

In 1977, film scholar Geoffrey Nowell-Smith introduced a diagram: a binary of value systems prominent throughout Pasolini's oeuvre. Columns A and B, listing archetypal characters and themes, boil Pasolini's storytelling down to digestible components:

A	B
Present	Past
Repression	Freedom
Technology	Nature
Bourgeoisie	Peasantry (and sub-proletariat)
Adult	Child
Father	Mother
Progress	Regression[25]

Nowell-Smith's diagram draws comparisons between "positive" and "negative" axes, parallels between reality and imagination. Column B, focused on the past, nature, the peasant, and freedom, works against the trajectory of History, representing not a linear, teleological path forward but a circling back towards a pre-industrial, pre-modern world that evades the marginalization, exploitation, and lack of recognition prominent in, for example, *La ricotta*. Pasolini's films document a return towards the *positive* values of Column B, an attempt to overcome the negative, exploitative values of Column A. A regression *towards* such a moment, however, reveals a limit concept. Such movement back in time is just that: movement, with the end or destination unattainable. Instead, Pasolini's writing reflects the changing tides of power and the continuity of such ebbs and flows over time. His work not only counters the current of history but is also a current itself: the streams of events and consciousness approaching and retreating from the shoreline *ad infinitum*. This disturbs the viewer, because, as with any story – *history* or otherwise – she expects an ending, a resolution of conflicts. Closing shots and a credit scroll might signal the end of the film, but how does a story end if it has not actually ended – if its focus is not on "progress" or "regression," but on the *towards*?

While not arriving at anything specific, such movement is not meant to be binary: not forwards or backwards, but cyclical. Pasolini's work is revolutionary precisely for this geometry of movement. His parables on language "initiate a return to a time before history and before language where time is eternal," thus assuming the form not of a timeline but of a clock: a circle.[26] Circles do not have a point of origin or an endpoint;

free of lines, circles represent eternity, infinity, wholesomeness, and per-fection. Cycles, frequently designed in circular formation, proceed in continuum, without beginning or end. Circles and cycles, then, are an appropriate depiction of Pasolini's writing as he conveys the continuous push and pull between the values of Columns A and B.

Both literal and figurative manifestations of circles and cycles are prominent across Pasolini's oeuvre, particularly with respect to eating, or, rather, turning points in the *digestive* cycle of history. *Uccellacci e uccellini* exhibits attacks on animals, and it considers the digestion of prey and the absorption of their nutrients and values as parts of Pasolini's filmic digestive cycle: movements by diet. The attacks, in combination with Togliatti's death, may be read as "crises": times of intense difficulty. However, "crisis," or the Greek *krisis*, is a "turning point." A turning point is defined as a decisive change, whether in geographical direction or circumstance. In an interview with Jean Duflot, Pasolini once stated, "We want the crisis of Marxism to be perpetual, because it is only in this way that Marxism will stay in history and will avoid entering the museums as well as being smothered by the Party's conformity."[27] He speaks of perpetuity and permanent "crisis" *towards* the fall of capitalism, because otherwise, the Marxist revolution would remain a frozen frame in History, a museum relic: Reminiscent of the still images of Stracci, it would be immobilized, static, dead. The point is, thus, *not* to end: a mobilization, despite the presumption in *Le ceneri di Gramsci* that our history is finished. A question by Mao Zedong's opens Pasolini's film: Where is humanity headed? Is humanity going anywhere new, or will it circle back to the habits of the past? To Mao, I will counter: So long as there is movement, thereby evading stasis, does the direction matter?

The Shortcomings of Language

In a return to the archaic and pre-industrial, there is also the turn towards pre-language. If the movements towards "the before" are on the premises of eating and being eaten, written language is irrelevant. Thus, Pasolini encourages a return to pre-linguistic communication: a return to the autochthonous and the visceral, away from the syntactic and, thus, the bourgeois. From his early Friulan poetry to *Le ceneri di Gramsci*, from *Ragazzi di vita* (1955) to *Una vita violenta* (1959), and numerous screenplays, including his novel-film hybrid project *Teorema* (1968), Pasolini is, first and foremost, a writer. But in the early 1960s, in creating and directing characters who function outside erudite spaces, he underscores the communicative prowess of *images* over prose.

Pasolini divides the realm of Language into two components: *im-segni*, or cinematic images, and *lin-segni*, or the symbols of written language. He is careful to distinguish between the "symbols" conjured by written text and the "icons" depicted on screen. The primary difference between *im-segni* and *lin-segni* is this: While the written word "mela" and a photograph of an apple, for example, are both associated with the round fruit of autumn, the written requires a mental image of the word to be conjured, whereas the photograph is a sign of real life; the eye does not need to do extra work to transform the image into its signification.[28] And for Pasolini's hungry protagonists, the mode of language must match their visceral needs; their hunger is searingly real, and so, too, should be their way of communicating about it. Stracci, who is very likely illiterate, and the hungry, hopping sparrows of *Uccellacci e uccellini* lack the resources to decipher the rules of *lin-segni*; they do not, and cannot, subscribe to the bourgeois channel of written language. Words are insufficient when describing the needs of the sub-proletariat and animals. Images, meanwhile, depict outright the motions of the life cycle, such as eating, excreting, and sexual intercourse, of which words may only conjure mental visions at best.

Therefore, *Uccellacci e uccellini* – and Pasolini's outlook on the world as narrated by a sage Marxist crow – is ultimately a visually dominant project. Totò and Ninetto grow bored of the crow and his verbose lectures, so they eat him. In their consumption of the crow, Pasolini demonstrates that it is *image*, not word, that endures crises: these revolutions, these turning points, in society. The viscerality of his protagonists outdoes the Word of God and the cultured voice of Marxist wisdom. And to demonstrate the prowess of images over words – and of one's body over one's mind, and of archaic physicality over bourgeois refinement – Pasolini's characters eat not merely food but linguistic and cultural signs. Emblems of Italy's history, religion, and politics are not just perverted but savagely devoured. Pasolini's "linguistic, intellectual, and artistic web"[29] is eaten, absorbed, and excreted by his characters, a process which offers "food for thought" for his viewers to consume anew.

Uccellacci e uccellini is a disjointed compilation of vignettes. Before analysing any of those, however, it is necessary to unpack three sketches originally formulated by Pasolini: the intellectual groundwork he had undertaken to arrive at the aforementioned divide between *lin-segni* and *im-segni*. The three vignettes – *L'Aigle* (The Eagle), *Faucons et Moineaux* (Hawks and Sparrows), and *Le Corbeau* (The Crow) – were published sequentially in 1965 in the weekly magazine *Vie Nuove*. *L'Aigle*, in particular, communicates the shortcomings of language. Pasolini actually adapted *L'Aigle* for the screen before changing course, abandoning its bourgeois, Francophone setting in favour of the feature-length, disorienting, Marxist story of *Uccellacci e uccellini*. *L'Aigle* features Monsieur Cournot (Totò), who attempts to domesticate an eagle for his circus but struggles to make the eagle speak *"una lingua perfetta,"* a refined, bourgeoisified language – likely French, the language of Enlightenment thinking. The eagle remains silent, even amid the rest of Cournot's menagerie, all of whom speak "politely, civilly: the tiger, for example, does not say, 'I am hungry,' but 'I have a bit of an appetite.'"[30] It is only when Cournot's assistant, Ninetto (Ninetto Davoli), addresses the eagle in a dialect "that immediately establishes a pact 'between poor folks'"[31] that the eagle finally elects to speak, driving Cournot into madness.

My use of "pact" is a translation from Pasolini's original *omertà*. *L'omertà* is a code of silence that today is largely associated with the Mafia; if one were to speak out against their power, one would face severe consequences. Pasolini's use of *omertà*, then, constructs a power structure over Cournot by avoiding the "perfect language" that he is enforcing. In using dialect, Ninetto and the eagle "speak out" against the legacy of French – the language of colonizers and the bourgeoisie – and insist on a new code of conduct: one more natural and applicable to their everyday lives. Making a pact that rejects bourgeois language forges a connection between humans (Ninetto) and birds (the eagle), a kinship that Davoli furthers with the crow of *Uccellacci e uccellini*. In an interview with Oswald Stack, Pasolini again uses *omertà* to describe a friendship that formed between Davoli and the crows: When the crow died during post-production, this "upset Ninetto a great deal, so when he went to India and saw all the crows there he felt he was among friends again because a kind of *omertà* had been established between him and the crows."[32] The harmony, this *omertà*, between species was the objective of St. Francis, and it is the mission that Pasolini's monks undertake, but fail to achieve, in *Uccellacci e uccellini*. Why, then, was the premise of *L'Aigle* removed from Pasolini's eventual film?

In an essay titled "Technical Confessions," Pasolini reveals why *Faucons et Moineaux* became the centrepiece of *Uccellacci e uccellini*. Pasolini first blames Totò, who is incapable of playing an "enforcer," and second, the poor quality of production resources available. He writes:

[*L'Aigle*] had lost [that poetic value] for two reasons: the impossibility of Totò acting as a "cognizant character," in "possession of the privileges of Culture." ... He is an "innocent": and he is as "innocent" as he can become poetic. The other reason is the scarcity of resources with which I shot that episode. Not having anything but four white sheets on the walls constricted me to shooting an episode equal to a black-and-white doodle, a kind of do-it-yourself illustration, made with two or three enormously poor factors: the white, the black, some grey (a Léger on the wall), and the faces of the protagonists. Any possibility of expressionism had gone missing in that kind of stylization.[33]

If Pasolini's narrative prioritized nature, then his film needed to exhibit natural surroundings; he abandoned Cournot's *Salon des Lumières* and his "four white sheets," going outdoors. Only a few scenes take place indoors; the main setting is instead a road, on both sides of which are mostly open, overgrown fields, and above which shines a full moon. Buses pass, airplanes occasionally land, and a Cadillac fails to run, but these are largely episodic; Pasolini instead foregrounds mankind's interactions with nature, prioritizing bodily needs and instincts – such as eating, fornicating, and excreting – over technological advances and cultural sublimation. The calls of nature supersede culture, history, and language, hence Cournot's unsuccessful attempts to dominate the eagle. The premise of *Uccellacci e uccellini*, then, is the devouring of all things – and creatures – bourgeois, which sends traditional European intellectualism, as embodied by Cournot, into crisis.

It makes sense, then, that *Uccellacci e uccellini* is a series of perverted narratives – chiefly among them, St. Francis's famous engagement with birds, speaking to creatures of nature and compelling them to acknowledge and love not only God but all of God's creations. Pasolini perverts stories, especially the aforementioned tale of cross-species communication, so as to dismantle the preexisting power dynamics surrounding language: the hold that literacy has over others.[34] A new system of signs is required not only for more effective communication but also to create a sense of harmony: to close the gap between once disparate and miscommunicating parties. There is, hence, an emphasis on what one *does*, not says.[35] Totò and Ninetto, the protagonists of *Uccellacci e uccellini*, thus learn to utilize their bodies to establish a connection with the animals they encounter; they hop, they fornicate, and fundamentally, they eat. They watch predatory birds savagely consume their prey, and they themselves dismember and devour a crow, once their sage travel companion and a loquacious voice of unwanted, misunderstood, Marxist wisdom. Indeed, as the crow touts, "The time of Brecht and Rossellini is over"; the codes of communication by which the crow abides no longer function, as he is eaten, and with him, old ideologies and the irrelevant, obsolete ways of publicizing and perpetuating them.

Figure 4.4. Ninetto (Ninetto Davoli) and the crow. From *Uccellacci e uccellini* (1966, dir. Pier Paolo Pasolini).

A Return to ... Totò?

What are other tactics in which Pasolini upends the status quo? Pasolini's casting choice of Totò is, for one, certainly a change from the Chaplinesque buffoonery illustrated in Chapter 1. Totò's presence was cited as one of the shortcomings of *L'Aigle*, so what makes him necessary for *Uccellacci e uccellini*? Totò functions in tandem with his *maschera*: the holistic transformation of Antonio de Curtis into the scheming, slapstick, Southern-charming Totò. Pasolini, too, insisted on employing Totò specifically for this "type," recognizable among audiences for his credulousness and clownish behaviour; he recounted to Stack, "I chose Totò for what he was – an actor, a recognizable type whom the public already knew. I didn't want him to be anything but what he was … Totò was an actor who had been manipulated by himself and by other people into a type, but I used him precisely as that, as someone who was a type."[36] The cinematic function of Totò is archaic innocence, a continuity to which viewers could latch on – but one which Pasolini tests against historical moments such as Italy's housing boom and

neo-capitalist speculation. Functioning "outside of politics," and existing irrespective of history, Totò is a blank canvas upon which to explore
a world after Togliatti: Italian Marxism without a North Star.[37] Whether
shovelling spaghetti into his pockets in 1954 or wandering the streets in
1966, he remains a point of recognizability for viewers as they navigate
historically uncharted territory.

The casting of Totò is also appropriate because it underscores the
(dis)connections and (dis)continuities between one's expressions and
eating. In Chapter 1, his physicality and harebrained schemes surrounded one objective: procuring food. The cinema of Totò has been
long foregrounded in the search for food to "get by,"[38] to satisfy a
desperate hunger that his audiences of the late 1940s and 1950s, too,
suffered. It makes sense, then, that Pasolini cast such a hungry icon in
his film on the importance of eating and digestion. *Uccellacci e uccellini* is a realization of obsolete, stale techniques of expression, and
the consequent exploration of new communication tactics; language
falls short before the need to eat. Who is more appropriate than Totò,
whose fame is connected to the legacy of material hunger, to star in
such a film?

Totò (both Antonio de Curtis's stage presence and Pasolini's character, aptly named Totò Innocenti) *is* hungering for food, but the hunger
in *Uccellacci e uccellini* is not the same as in earlier decades. Totò –
previously defined as a vehicle of continuity – must now digest new
historical situations. At sixty-eight years old, he had to contend with
a new, youth-oriented market that spent upwards of 250 billion lire
(roughly $140 million US) on non-essentials like drinks, cigarettes,
music, Vespas, comics, and escapist movies.[39] They were most inspired
by American ways of doing things, thereby dashing the objectives of
the Marxists, with Togliatti once at the helm.[40] To contend with these
changes, Totò had to discover new ways of communicating with not
only the animals of *Uccellacci e uccellini* but also his admiring fans across
the peninsula, who recognized the *maschera* and, by extension, his
expressions of material hunger. The harmonious continuity and series
of happy endings that Totò once propagated are jeopardized; in another
act of perversion, Pasolini incorporates Totò into a non-teleological narrative of barriers. Totò's predatory eating in *Uccellacci e uccellini* is, thus,
a predictable strategy amid Pasolini's unknowns. Unable to connect
with any of the birds in Pasolini's story, but continually recognized for
his hunger, Totò eats his way out of predicaments, as he and Ninetto
first witness the hawks' predatory eating and then become predators
themselves, ultimately absorbing the struggles of the Communist subculture. By the end of the film, although the viewer is unsure where

Figure 4.5. Father Ciccillo (Totò) struggles to connect with the hawks in *Uccellacci e uccellini*.

humanity is headed, she at least recognizes hungry Totò – though his hunger is decidedly different this time.

The Hawks "Love" the Sparrows

There are two predicaments in *Uccellacci e uccellini* which involve eating, and more specifically, the consumption of birds. The first is the longest episode of the twelve that comprise the film: Pasolini's perversion of St. Francis of Assisi. St. Francis becomes a saint following his disappearance into a cave; when he emerges, he is unrecognizable, psychologically transformed and bearing mystic qualities: "… he was almost as different as if he were dead, as if he were a ghost or a blessed spirit. And the effects of this on his attitude towards the actual world were really as extravagant as any parallel can make them. He looked at the world as differently from other men as if he had come out of that dark hole walking on his hands."[41] Through this transformation, St. Francis is thus portrayed as "a magician speaking the language of beasts and birds … For a mystic like St. Francis the monsters had a meaning; that is, they had delivered their message. They no longer spoke in an unknown tongue."[42] The language and kinship that connected St. Francis to the animal kingdom was that of love for God.

Children's author Leo Politi romanticizes Francis's relationship with, among other animals, birds:

> One day as Francis was walking through the countryside with two of the brothers, he saw on the trees and on the ground a great number of birds.
>   Wondering at the sight, he said to his companions:
>   "Let us stay here for a while. I wish to preach to my sisters, the birds."
>   And going into the fields he began to preach to the birds. As he walked among them and touched them with his robe, not even one flew away. The birds on the trees flew down to listen to him.[43]

Within the film, meanwhile, Pasolini denotes the cracks in this utopian vision, emphasizing St. Francis's topsy-turvy foolishness: the likeness of St. Francis, and of Totò, to clowns.[44] In what becomes the central story within a story, Totò and Ninetto assume the role of two Franciscan monks, Brother Ciccillo and Brother Ninetto. The lore of St. Francis is narrated but desecrated by a crow: not just a bird, but a black bird, opposite the white dove of the Holy Spirit.[45] As St. Francis is best remembered for his communication with birds, the crow's storytelling to humans is yet another way in which Pasolini upends the traditional narrative; the recipient and emitter of the message have switched roles. The story is further carnivalized when its outcome is far from expected; its ending is by no means one of brotherly love. The crow's narration, as the first experimentation with language in the film, concludes that language alone fails to curb hunger. The content of the diegetic story highlights the inefficacy of language with respect to animals' primal instincts; words are ultimately useless against the birds' predatory tactics for survival. The episode unfolds as follows.

Ciccillo and Ninetto are charged with preaching the love of God to two different classes of birds: arrogant hawks and humble sparrows. Ninetto himself is challenged doubly: His inclination to bypass the Word of God in favour of hunting and eating is immediate. As with Totò, Ninetto's proclivities were, too, autobiographical. Unlike Antonio de Curtis, a man of nobility, Ninetto Davoli had a decidedly poor upbringing, and this stratification was reflected in their differing eating practices. Davoli once recalled an evening in which he and Pasolini dined at de Curtis's house, remembering the exceeding elegance of the dining space – candelabras and flowers adorning the table, and stacks of plates of different sizes and a wide array of silverware to be utilized for different courses – where Davoli, unaccustomed to the decorum of fine dining, was unsure how many people were expected to join them, given the numerous settings. Thus, Davoli ate everything on just one plate. De Curtis's partner, Franca Faldini, later revealed to Davoli that de Curtis was so appalled by his behaviour and the amount that he ate that night, that de Curtis sprayed Davoli's seat with DDT upon his departure.[46] DDT – a powerful insecticide, outlawed for the damage it caused among bird populations – not only reduces Ninetto to vermin but also symbolizes the hierarchies at play in *Uccellacci e uccellini*: hawks over the sparrows, Ninetto and Totò over the crow, but also, as discussed in *L'Aigle*, M. Cournot/Signor Totò pitted against the *omertà* connecting Ninetto to the birds.

Ninetto the monk, staring at a tree with branches full of birds, pulls a slingshot out from under his robes and takes aim at the tree. Once apprehended by Ciccillo, he then suggests that they avoid the task of preaching and instead seek refuge with peasants, "the ones who gave us that really good ricotta," previously established as a food of the *burino*, the rustic lumpenproletariat.[47] Ciccillo responds that they shall take on Francis's task, because although they are not saints, they are human men with God-given brains, with which they can learn how to speak most effectively to the birds. In other words, the monks work to suppress their primal, human instincts to diffuse God's message.

They arrive at a dilapidated castle, upon which the hawks are perched. Questions immediately rise as to how the Brothers will speak to these birds. Ciccillo kneels on the ground and prays to God, asking for strength to remain in that very spot until contact has been made with the hawks. In the shots that immediately follow, amid strong winds, Ciccillo and Ninetto withstand a horde of bullies who taunt Ciccillo, the "mushroom-monk." This follows the precedents of bullying: the ridicule of Stracci and, before that, of Christ – moments in which hunger and thirst also abounded. Indeed, before the bullies roughhouse Ninetto, he once again thinks "hunger first," as he is seen eating from a pot; Pasolini's script alludes to beautiful plums.[48] The bullies flee and the seasons pass, and Ciccillo still yearns to understand the lexicon of the hawks, miserably imitating their shrill squawks; Ninetto meanwhile grows very impatient and, expectedly, hungry.

Before this synopsis continues, a parenthesis must be opened, concerning three, but nonetheless extremely telling, pages of Pasolini's screenplay: "Il Paradiso di Ninetto." "Il Paradiso," omitted from the film, illustrates a dream sequence that emphasizes Ninetto's excessive, harmful love of food. In the film, shortly before initiating contact with the hawks, Ninetto expresses his frustrations to Ciccillo: What is the point of weathering all seasons, continually trying, and failing, to communicate with the birds? Ciccillo regains his voice and responds, "To enter Paradise, my son!"[49] Ninetto appears to ignore Ciccillo's exclamation, asking instead if he may rest in Ciccillo's shade: a mass of plants clinging to the stationary monk. Pasolini's screenplay progresses with the following dream, encapsulating Ninetto's unconscious quest for Paradise.

Pasolini describes the setting of Ninetto's dream as a colourful painting by Giotto, accompanied by angelic chants: "Maybe Ninetto dreams in colour. The blue of Prussia, a bit rumpled and worn, the black horse, the ox blood, the grey mire ... On one side there is a little chorus of boys, in lines, one line after another. On the other, there is a little chorus of girls. Their chant is angelic."[50] Ninetto thus envisions Heaven, the realm of the Father, *il Padre Eterno. Il Padre Eterno* welcomes Ninetto to Paradise, encouraging him, among other activities, to eat from His table of plenty:

> *He first sees a long wooden table covered with a beautiful tablecloth, incredibly white, that falls over the corners. And above, every thing of God's, but as Giotto would have painted it, with great sobriety and almost grandiosity: ricotta, cheeses, loaves of bread, bowls, watermelons ...*
>
> BROTHER NINETTO: (*feeling timid*) Am I hungry!
> PADRE ETERNO: Eat as much as you'd like!
>
> *Ninetto runs to the table and fills his mouth with ricotta, and then, with his mouth full and lips white, looks around, laughing, and sees:*
>   *Against a pristine thirteenth-century wall, a big bed, and surrounding it, as if the Epiphany Witch had put them there, a pile of toys.*[51]

This banquet table is continuous with the Technicolor table of *La ricotta*, once again featuring gross amounts of cheese and watermelons, and again linked to a grotesque act of eating and admission into Heaven. Stracci could not deliver his line as the Good Thief because he was too weighed down by food. In this space, Ninetto is likewise no longer burdened by preaching, or by words in general, as God encourages the young monk instead to embrace tactile, primal, "innocent" activities: eating, followed by sleeping, playing with toys, and sexually engaging a "Neanderthal, merry and nude," in a marvellous botanical garden.[52] The garden is analogous to Eden. In the Book of Genesis, God instructs Adam that he "may eat the fruit of any tree in the garden, except the tree that gives knowledge of what is good and what is bad. You must not eat the fruit of that tree; if you do, you will die that same day" (2:16–17). Shortly thereafter, Eve, a woman formed from Adam's rib, is persuaded by a snake to eat the fruit. The snake says that they will not die; rather, "God said that because he knows that when you eat it, you will be like God and know what is good and what is bad" (3:4–5). Eve considers the prospect of tasting not the fruit – in other words, its sweetness or juiciness – but, instead, the wisdom that the fruit would impart: "She thought how wonderful it would be to become wise. So she took some of the fruit and ate it" (3:6). Although she was not yet formed (2:22) when God warned Adam about the apple (2:16), Eve's blasphemous decision to consume the apple and, by extension, God's knowledge – at once devouring and rejecting His directive – is precisely the premise of *Uccellacci e uccellini*. In this space, and as with the birds outside Ninetto's dreamworld, language is irrelevant; of greater emphasis are physical indulgences and physiological demands for survival – hence, perhaps, why Pasolini contained these heavenly visions to a dream within a sleeping Ninetto. It is extremely curious that Pasolini ultimately omitted this dream sequence from his film, as these few pages contain the message of the entire movie. This may also remind the reader that, in *L'Aigle*, it was Ninetto who so quickly and naturally forged a connection with his fellow *poveraccio*. Ninetto shares the same objective as and therefore speaks the language of the hawks: to eat. Ciccillo's sermons are bypassed in favour of Ninetto's satisfactions through food and copulation.

However, instead of this narrative, Pasolini transitions to Ciccillo's sudden success: He deciphers the language of the hawks. Ninetto and Ciccillo approach the castle to preach, and the birds and monks exchange the following words by way of piercing chirps; the viewer, who does not abide by the same linguistic code as Ciccillo, must read their subtitled conversation:

CICCILLO: Hawks, hawks, come, listen … Come, listen…

THE HAWKS: Who are you? What do you want?

CICCILLO: We are creatures of God, we want to talk with you, creatures of God.

THE HAWKS: God? Who is God?

CICCILLO: The creator of creatures.

THE HAWKS: And why did God create us?

CICCILLO: Why did you create your children?

THE HAWKS: So then all of us are God.

CICCILLO: Too far! There, you cannot consider that they will expand soon.

THE HAWKS: And what does this God want from us?

CICCILLO: Love!

THE HAWKS: LOVE … LOVE!

Fade-out. Brother Ciccillo and Brother Ninetto, joyful, go back down the roads that they had come up full of apprehension and discomfort. Ninetto comes down almost dancing, as in his dream in Paradise, and Brother Ciccillo is decisive, his look proud and honest.[53]

While Ciccillo is able to communicate with the hawks, creating a channel by chirping, it is not clear whether the significance of his message is received. The hawks understand the ritual and power of procreation, blasphemously equating themselves to God through the creation of their offspring, but, despite the repetition of the word, do they grasp the concept of love? What kinesthetic actions might be associated with love? How will the hawks embody a tiny word with such emotional charge? These questions, for the moment, remain unanswered, as the monks abruptly take leave of the hawks to meet with the sparrows.

Ciccillo again makes a vow of immobility to God, affixing himself to the ground and waiting to make contact with the sparrows. Before encountering the birds, Ciccillo withstands new distractions: the sceptical interrogations and singing of three women – Sora Micragna, Sora Gramigna, and Sora Grifagna – who later participate in a bazaar, hawking watermelons and ricotta cheese; one hears the cacophony of other vendors selling cookies, candles, and undergarments. This marketplace thus becomes a site of tension between ascetic, pious life, as embodied by the Franciscan monks of the 1200s, and the neo-capitalist splurges of 1960s Italy. Ciccillo explodes with impatience, and he and Ninetto rise to destroy the vendors' stalls, engaging in acts of violence to expel the vendors from their place of prayer. Despite Pasolini's slowed frame rate, which quickens and adds comedy to the monks' destruction, Ciccillo's anger mirrors that of Jesus, who once expelled moneylenders from the Temple, thereby desecrating a holy place.[54] Curiously, the monks utilize the vendors' own products – the food that the ladies egregiously hawk – as weapons against them: They throw ricotta in Sora Grifagna's face and smash a watermelon on Sora Gramigna's head. As the monks' verbal pleas would have been drowned out by the noise of the market, they must resort to physical violence to clear out the piazza; words do not work, and food is converted into weaponry.

Verbal communication is pointless among the sparrows as well. Ciccillo and Ninetto try chirps and birdcalls to connect to the sparrows, but they do not respond. Once more, Ninetto grows impatient, and he asks Ciccillo if he may play hopscotch. Ninetto's hopping, the monks realize, is what speaks to the sparrows; the sparrows do not speak the same shrill language as the hawks, but, rather, a more kinesthetic language of hops and jumps. The monks approach the sparrows, hopping to get the birds' attention. Their conversation, again translated by way of subtitles, is as follows:

> CICCILLO: Sparrows, come, listen … Come, listen …
> THE SPARROWS: Who are you? What do you want?
> CICCILLO: We are servants of the Lord, we want to bring you good news.
> THE SPARROWS: Oh, finally! It's all that we've been waiting for!
> CICCILLO: This is great! Really?
> THE SPARROWS: Eh, yes, especially in the winter, when the snow covers everything, and you can't see even one crumb of food in the whole field!
> CICCILLO: Um … What kind of good news were you waiting for, friends?
> THE SPARROWS: Beh, the good news where you announce mountains of millet, of wheat, to make us all as fat as thrushes!
> CICCILLO: Ah, how much I endured to bring you true good news!
> THE SPARROWS: What does this true good news want from us?
> CICCILLO: Starvation!
> THE SPARROWS: What? What did you say?
> CICCILLO: Starvation! But not starvation proper … We hardly want you to die of hunger … But sacrifice, love … Oh Lord, love!
> THE SPARROWS: Love … love!
>
> *Fade-out.*[55]

When compared to the hawks, the sparrows appear to be the more inviting, yet more vulnerable, species. The sparrows are more open to conversation with the monks – but not under the premise of God, love, and sacrifice, but because they think that Ciccillo comes bearing food. The sparrows are hungry, and the winter has been a difficult season, and they therefore readily associate preaching with feeding; their hunger preempts any dialogue with Ciccillo. It is implausible, then, that the sparrows would forgo their hunger to accept love through sacrifice; their hunger presents an immediacy that supersedes any understanding of the abstract notion of love.

Because the monks explore alternative, more physical, means of expression, they manage to converse with the birds, but they do not allow either species the time or means to meditate on the vastness and ambiguities of love. Love is multifaceted. Self-help gurus speak of love languages, which span acts of service, quality bonding time, gift giving, words of affirmation, and physical touch.[56] The monks, for one, root themselves to the land and speak of love as an act of service to St. Francis and to God, but the love of the birds is not one of duty. Love may be expressed through words, but love is also the grounds for physical engagement: hungering for and consuming the flesh of another. Acting on their physical needs, the hawks ultimately prey upon the sparrows, killing and eating them. As a result, the hawks uphold their sense of supremacy, and the sparrows no longer face starvation, as they are sacrificed; these are the very hopes and tenets that the monks have just preached. Despite their great efforts, the monks' miscommunications cost the sparrows their lives, as the hawks, not the sparrows, *s'allargano*: they expand their territory, getting fatter in the process.

With the death of the sparrows, the viewer takes leave of the allegorical Ciccillo. Bound by his desire for food, Ninetto was always Ninetto, and remains so throughout the film. Moving on to another vignette, ushered back in is Totò, himself ready to eat.

The Crow, Best Eaten in a Spicy Sauce

Totò and Ninetto are generally politically apathetic, known for their innocence. Nevertheless, across their travels, they encounter various signs and symbols that represent clashes, between past and present, Right and Left, and religiosity and secularity.[57] The aforementioned marketplace is a site of these very tensions. Even more representative of these clashes, however, is the crow, juxtaposed with the double entendre of the moon/Luna. The crow is not just integral to the film but also emblematic of macrocosmic issues that extend far beyond the road in *Uccellacci e uccellini*: chiefly, the crisis of 1950s Marxism.

Who is the crow, and what purpose does he serve in Pasolini's film? He is the narrator, but he *is* the film: He joins Totò and Ninetto at the start, narrating the ill-fated story of the hawks and the sparrows, and the film concludes with his death. He is a road sign of a philosophical kind, intended to guide the two "innocenti" in their meanderings. His teachings are stories reflective of Gramsci and Togliatti, the leaders of 1950s Italian Marxism. As Pasolini exercises his authorial function by way of the crow, is the crow autobiographical, too? In his essay "Le fasi del corvo," Pasolini is careful to distinguish between his Marxism and that of the crow:

The crow was, at this phase, Marxist ideology, at a particular "historical moment" in time – which is to say the Marxist ideology of the Fifties – just when it was about to become obsolete. I had to make this point clear in the contradiction: if the Crow's Marxism coincided with my Marxism, since I am in a state of evolution, and since I am above all conscious of the crisis of Fifties Marxism, his story couldn't end, he clearly couldn't become obsolete – as a simple story would demand – and end up being eaten.[58]

In other words, like Stracci, the crow can come into existence only after being caught on film: a snapshot of a moment in time that has long passed. The crow's messages on 1950s Marxism are perpetuated through Pasolini's work and his evolution as a director. The crow is ultimately eaten by Totò and Ninetto, but it is Pasolini's intention that we, the viewers, consume the story of the Revolution in the process.[59]

Indeed, Pasolini expands upon the crow's purpose specifically with respect to cinema. His narrator is both a product of and antagonist to the film industry, and he is a filmic, irrational image that, paradoxically, attempts to preach rationalism.[60] Pasolini writes, "The philosopher had to explain himself, because without precision, simplification (necessary not as an obligatory element, but as a fascinating prosodic norm) is not possible, for a product whose consumer is the movie-goer, etc., etc."[61] Not only does the crow's elitist intellectual wisdom counter Totò and Ninetto's primitive proclivities for food, drink, and sex, but he also stands in opposition to moviegoers at large, who seek a lighthearted escape (especially with Totò as star) from the gruelling workday and the ennui of a daily routine. The crow is too intellectually committed, too rational, for the simplicity that Pasolini expresses, so he is engulfed by mainstream culture. He is, therefore, the embodiment of the crisis facing Marxism: the Communist struggle against Italians' increasingly conformist mentality, the advent of television, and the growing, internationalizing Hollywood machine. The crow is dismantled and swallowed up ostensibly out of hunger, but primarily out of boredom.

The death of the crow is foreshadowed by a silent newsreel depicting the funeral of Togliatti, who had led Italy's Communist Party from 1927 until his death in 1964. Pasolini edits the newsreel so that it appears that Totò and Ninetto, having missed a bus, must walk directly into the funeral, joining the parade of mourners in their remembrance of Togliatti. Togliatti's death is not only a crisis – a turning point – in Italy's Marxism, but it is also the death of an exceedingly traditional intellectualism: a major challenge that the Communist Party confronted in the 1950s and 1960s, as the stronghold of Marxist culture waned against the modern allure of capitalist Americana. Togliatti embraced and propagated a culture that was unrealistic, too erudite, and closed off from the everyday realities of the Economic Miracle – namely, Italians' increased spending power and newfound propensity for consumer durables, such as the refrigerator, the television, and the Fiat 500.[62] While Marxist cadres encouraged younger generations to read the *Prison Notebooks* of Gramsci and see the neorealist films of Luchino Visconti and Giuseppe De Santis, their vision was archaic; products of popular culture – whether Hollywood movies or Italian photo-romances – were more approachable and seemed harmless. A twenty-three-year-old student, "enrolled in the PCI … admitted preferring westerns and adventure films to Visconti's *La terra trema* (The Earth Trembles, 1948), which was 'too intellectual and difficult.' Another Communist also confessed to finding 'complicated' films empty and sterile. Much preferred were American adventure films that 'even if unlikely, do no harm.'"[63] The crow, then, as an emblem of Togliatti's Communism, is a preachy bore for Totò and Ninetto, as well as for Pasolini's audience. No longer serving his professorial purpose, the crow is eliminated in order to fulfil basic human needs.[64] The crow is not necessarily consumed out of malice, but the men see the crow more for his flesh, of greater priority than his empty message.

Totò and Ninetto's decision to eat the crow is preempted by their interactions with the moon/Luna. The moon, presented two ways in the film, is the symbol *par excellence* of the pre-industrial, of a world grounded in nature – of the primitivity that ultimately devours the crow. Both the establishing and closing shots of the film are of a full moon. The moon is foregrounded in the film for several reasons. It is a force of nature; it stabilizes the earth's rotations and its gravitational pull impacts ocean tides. It is a psychological factor: Totò's first line in the film reads, "Co' la luna nun se prende," which could be interpreted as bad luck in fishing and/or sex; whichever the referent, he elaborates that a high tide – as created by the moon's force of gravity – is necessary for things to turn around. Time also corresponds to the circular moon; one month represents the time between new moons, and nocturnal life proceeds by moonlight. With respect to the 1960s, the moon is also a historical objective, a destination of desire; no astronaut had yet reached the moon by the film's release, but Totò at one point in the film does speak of Yuri Gagarin's travels in space. Encapsulating history, technology, and nature, the moon is a powerful symbol in Pasolini's film of the tensions between nature and industry, and between ideologies and human instinct. With the film bookended by the moon, one may assume that it lasts one lunar cycle, over the course of which Communism, or political credence of any kind, has fallen, and language dies with the crow.[65] The life and death of the crow are juxtaposed with the moon, whose presence on Earth manifests as Luna, a brush-dwelling prostitute. Indeed, the moon – in Italian, *la luna* – is a feminine noun. In *Uccellacci e uccellini*, the moon is not just an astronomical satellite; its forces of sexuality and maternity are embodied by Luna, whom Totò and Ninetto encounter along their walk.

Luna's appearance is brief, just within the last ten minutes, immediately following the Togliatti newsreel. Nevertheless, her existence waxes as the crow's wanes. Her function in the film, though short, depicts the endurance of physicality and natural instincts over the constructions of politics and language. Though Pasolini's screenplay confirms that Luna is a *puttana*,[66] Luna is not the typical prostitute – Federico Fellini's Cabiria, along with Adua and Mamma Roma in the previous chapter – to whom viewers have grown accustomed. For one, Luna has no interest in money, nor does she seek entry or acceptance into the bourgeoisie. In addition, whereas prostitutes typically solicit work while walking the paved streets of the city, Totò and Ninetto walk past Luna, who is perched on a crate, as if rooted to the earth – detached from the city centre and untainted by capitalist transactions.[67] Luna, Totò, and Ninetto rely on their bodies to express themselves, reflecting on their senses of smell, touch, and taste, and utilizing their noses, stomachs, and groins to communicate and satisfy physical needs. Totò feigns stomach pains to enter the grass and engage with Luna; Luna, meanwhile, uninterested in coitus, expresses interest in the aroma of freshly mown hay and comments on her lunch of sliced meat and spinach. When Luna returns to the crate after her time with Totò, Ninetto follows suit, likewise feigning the desperate need to excrete. However, the scene is hardly "uncontaminated." Despite Luna's excitement over the smell of hay, and despite the tall grasses that enclose her and her suitors, capitalist noise drowns out the possibility of conversation, both before and after coitus. Pasolini taints Luna's verdant world with machines.[68] Indeed, Luna performs her acts of sex in the vicinity of an airport, where planes roar overhead and land in the background. Planes appear not to belong in such natural, primitive surroundings. The industriousness and modernity of the plane are similar, then, to the crow, in that their objectives – flight, closing gaps between people – do not fit into the autochthonous world of Luna and her suitors. The crow announces that "il viaggio è finito" – his journey is complete, his preaching stale and obsolete. Luna's presence, however, instils a sense of hope, rebirth, and, potentially, a revival of revolutionary spirit in an otherwise uproarious time in history, amid all the noise. The tides thus shift; "le fasi del corvo" are complete, allowing the moon to shine.

Totò and Ninetto resume their journey, recharged from their escapades with Luna. The crow, meanwhile, blabbers on, recognizing that his time is up: "I'm done … My time is up … My words fall into the void."[69] Totò and Ninetto are bored and exhausted by the crow, nor do they understand his message; Pasolini transitions from verbal to visual cues as the film progresses, so the crow – a verbal pedagogue – is useless in the second half of the film, which exhibits more visual experiences and physical pleasures, such as food and sex.[70] To this end, Totò

Figure 4.6. A before-and-after shot sequence towards the end of *Uccellacci e uccellini*.

announces to Ninetto that they will eat the crow, because Totò starts to think the crow is truly crazy.[71] The crow's words are incompatible with the men post-coitus, hungrier than ever before. In the shot-reverse shots that immediately follow, Totò grabs the crow's neck; Totò's eyes manically widen; there is a lengthy pause as the camera continues focused on his eyes; and the crow is completely dismembered, smoke emanating from his remains. Totò and Ninetto continue walking, their backs to the camera in an extreme long shot. The voice of Domenico Modugno, singer of the transatlantic hit "Nel blu dipinto di blu (Volare)," permeates the closing shot, as he chants, "Dear friends, / as always, / it ends this way, it starts this way, it closes this way, it continues this way! / this story of *Uccellacci e uccellini*."[72]

Modugno's verses refer to the continuation of the men's journey, as well as to the cyclical nature of history: the changing political tides, the death of Togliatti and the upsurge of the Left amid the longstanding dominance of the Christian Democrats. In a certain sense, the verses also refer to the digestive cycle, the after-effects of eating the crow, who exclaims, "Professors get eaten in spicy sauce, but whoever digests them becomes a bit of a professor himself!"[73] In his interview with Oswald Stack, Pasolini elaborates on the crow's exclamation, insisting that we read the consumption of the crow as "what Catholics call communion: they swallow the body of Togliatti (or of the Marxists) and assimilate it; after they have assimilated it they carry on along the road, so that even though you don't know where the road is going, it is obvious that they have assimilated Marxism."[74] In assimilating Marxism, Pasolini's "communion" is analogous to the act of "absorption" in Gramsci's passive revolution. In order to maintain control, the dominant class requires the active collaboration of the masses over which it rules; in so doing, the hegemony resolves and *absorbs* any prospect of conflict and, by extension, the praxes and values of the subcultures.[75]

Yet, with the camera resting on Totò's eyes, it is unclear how, if at all, the crow was consumed, which leads to a bigger dilemma: Was the crow actually eaten, for his flesh or for his representations of Culture and Language? What digesting is to be done? The body metabolizes macronutrients – fats, carbohydrates, and proteins – in accordance with what is most useful at a specific moment in time. For example, if the body is undergoing immense physical strain, it will first digest simpler carbohydrates for their immediate release of energy, whereas proteins are more useful in the long run, helping to maintain muscle mass that breaks down during exercise. The body prioritizes what to digest based on the external demands imposed upon it in specific situations. What part of the crow, then, is useful for Totò and Ninetto in

1966? What will be absorbed and what will turn into waste? To this end, we return to Pasolini's interview with Stack: "Before being eaten, the crow says: 'Teachers are made to be eaten in spicy sauce.' They must be eaten and overcome, but *if their teaching has any value, it will stay with the consumer.*"[76] Pasolini thus leaves the viewer unsettled with the *caso ipotetico*, unsure *if* the teachings of the crow, or of his contemporaries, are of any value, and whether those "nutrients" will be digested by his audience. What is certain is that he has to be eaten to be overcome.

Conclusion

In both Pasolini films analysed in this chapter, the protagonists are killed, ostensibly, by acts of consumption. In *La ricotta*, Stracci dies of indigestion from eating too much cheese, too quickly; and at the end of *Uccellacci e uccellini*, Totò and Ninetto savagely devour their travel companion, the talking Marxist crow. Whether killed by food or treated as food itself, neither Stracci nor the crow continues on in Pasolini's world of material excess and spiritual deprivation. Food, however, is but an alibi in these films. The production of film – its exploitative nature and its frenzied schedule, all to create a profitable commodity for public consumption – is what kills Stracci. Likewise, the crow's exceedingly elaborate speeches – and the boredom they arouse within Totò and Ninetto – kill the messenger. Through these deaths, Pasolini paves a return towards the pre-industrial, the pre-capitalistic, and the pre-Hollywood, and in so doing, he subverts traditions of narration and the bourgeois codes of language. Pasolini distorts sacred and popular tales that once bound Italian Catholics together, and he underscores the insufficiencies of *lin-segni* and the visceral prowess of *im-segni*, to exhibit the revolution, the crisis – the *turning point* – of the lumpenproletariat's struggle to fulfil basic survival needs. These moments of "unfinished business" disorient the viewer, because any sense of continuity appears to have vanished. Indeed, we are far from the wholesomeness and easy points of recognizability underlined in my earlier chapters. Instead, as encapsulated by the directionless yet violence-filled road along which Totò, Ninetto, and the 1960s viewer meander, we are on a path of not only great uncertainty but also annihilation.

Yet, despite the disorientation and destruction that Pasolini's work embodies, within this tumultuous, ominous period is the notion of hope and renewal. Given the likeness of his death to the crucifixion of Christ, through Stracci, we anticipate a second resurrection. Similarly, at the end of *Uccellacci e uccellini*, the viewer seeks solace in the moon: the feminine, the maternal, the bearer of life. In Pasolini's *Teorema*

(1968), too, there are continued connections between femininity and the earth, as well as the removal of bourgeois, capitalist codifications in the search for an authentic self. As he recounted in an interview with Jean Duflot, "Bourgeois society has lost this sense [of the sacred, rooted in the heart of human life] and replaced it with an ideology of wealth and power."[77] The premise of both *Teorema* and *La grande abbuffata* (1973) – the basis of my next and final chapter – is precisely this loss of sense: the crises that unfold when the protagonists realize the ennui of the affluent society. Thus, this chapter would be remiss without some discussion of *Teorema*, which affirms the ideas underscored in *La ricotta* and *Uccellacci e uccellini*, but also introduces the themes central to *La grande abbuffata*.

Teorema, a novel and a filmic adaptation both authored by Pasolini and released in the same year, depicts a wealthy Milanese family sent into existential crisis after the arrival and abrupt departure of an unnamed houseguest. The guest extracted the family's vulnerabilities, curiosities, and desires, sexual and otherwise; in his absence, each of the family members recognizes the emptiness in their life, as their self-image has until that moment consisted exclusively of skewed ideas on life – *idee sbagliate*[78] – and luxury materials: cars, tasteful clothing and furniture, and dinner parties. Indeed, the early shots of the film are muted in two ways. Pasolini shoots scenes of city life in sepia, juxtaposing these urbane moments with shots of a rocky, barren desert, thereby forming a monochromatic montage which reveals the ennui and emptiness impacting the family. In addition, the characters are muted; they are captured walking and dancing with friends, moving their lips and calling for others' attention, but their words and laughter are inaudible. These formal qualities convey that, before the arrival of the guest, the family is only superficially going through the motions of life. By contrast, the viewer is jarred by the abrupt changes in colour and audio in the first scene in which the guest is present. The sepia has been replaced by navy blue and olive-green couches, Chinese vases, and bright floral arrangements, and there is the din of lively party conversations. The clearest line of dialogue amid all the noise acknowledges the guest in English, a language foreign to most of the guests, thereby rendering the guest as otherworldly. "A boy," as daughter Odetta names him, revolutionizes the family, breaking up the humdrum of their lives.

The guest could thus be interpreted as a vehicle of complete rupture. He is the impetus by which the family unearths all that they have long repressed; they realize that they have attempted, but failed, to *buy* happiness, filling their emotional and spiritual voids with material possessions. The guest's departure, then, has great consequences for each of the family members. The repercussions for two people in particular –

Paolo, the father, and Emilia, the housekeeper – offer a segue into the themes discussed at length in the next and final chapter.

Paolo (Massimo Girotti), a factory owner and the sole financial provider for his family, experiences one of the more major identity crises. In the novel, a poetic monologue titled "The Destruction of the Idea of Oneself" – in which Paolo laments the absence of the guest – is laden with diction of destruction and uncertainty. This diction, written in the simple preterit, and which is combined with his discontinued feelings described in the imperfect tense, affirms the rupture left in the guest's wake. Paolo questions:

> So you came into this house to destroy?
> What did you destroy in me?
> You simply destroyed –
> along with all my past life –
> the idea I have always had of myself.
> So if for a long time
> I had assumed the form I had to assume
> and my figure was in some way perfect,
> what now remains for me?
> I can see nothing that can reintegrate me
> in my identity.[79]

Following the guest's departure, Paolo's malaise is both physical and psychological. The sepia desert of the establishing shots is, in fact, the locus of Paolo's unravelling; over the course of the film, Paolo abandons his factory and employees, any sense of intimacy with his family, and even his clothes. Indeed, Pasolini takes a rather literal approach to the unravelling, focusing on the removal of clothing, offering close-ups of items that the family discards throughout the film. The act of stripping down to the naked body enables the family to shed layers of repressed thoughts and interests; it is a gesture that reveals their true selves, free of the markers of their bourgeois identity, to the guest and to the outside viewer. The most striking decloaking is Paolo's, who strips down in the middle of Milan's central train station. What unfolds in the station in 1968 is extremely different from Totò's experience in *Totò, Peppino e ... la malafemmina* twelve years earlier. Whereas Totò and Peppino arrive in Milan overdressed in fur coats and hats, as if to protect themselves from the cold and foreignness of the northern city, Paolo instead removes his suit, tie, and undergarments, completely and very publicly exposing himself. Captured in an extreme long shot, Paolo's naked body is dwarfed by the large, overarching billboards advertising products such

Figure 4.7. Paolo (Massimo Girotti) (centre left) undresses in the middle of Milan's central train station. From *Teorema* (1968, dir. Pier Paolo Pasolini).

as San Pellegrino water and Baci chocolates. Whereas the billboards encourage commuters to purchase goods, to add these foods and drinks to their diet, Paolo, in an act of *subtraction*, removes material possessions from himself. This gesture initiates his transition to the complete barrenness of the desert; the closing shots are of Paolo, naked and small among the dunes, where his scream – a final, cathartic release – penetrates the frame of "Fine." In the next and final chapter, *La grande abbuffata*, too, recuperates this process of subtraction, as increased quantities of food lose their significance, and the consumers' bodies are gradually destroyed by such grotesque eating.

La grande abbuffata also depicts a continuation, a feminine rebirth, at the end of the world. The function of Andréa in *La grande abbuffata* is similar to that of Luna in *Uccellacci e uccellini*, as well as Emilia (Laura Betti), the maid in *Teorema*. Emilia's response to the guest is strikingly different from Paolo's; her transition is more ethereal. Whereas Paolo exhibits a mental descent into the desert, Emilia assumes the qualities of an earth goddess. Shortly after the guest's departure, Emilia, too, leaves the house, taking the bus to a small farming village – presumably her hometown, as people young and old already know her name. In the rest of her scenes, Emilia is always captured outdoors. She enters the village and sits on a bench, remaining there for an indefinite amount of time.

Indeed, the construct – or, as previously discussed, the constraint – of time appears to have lost its meaning through Emilia's immobility; there is no forward, teleological movement. Being rooted to the ground, Emilia is reconnecting with the earth, separating herself from house-keeping and, by extension, her salary, her interactions with domestic appliances and household furniture, and even the food she once prepared for the family. In fact, she rejects a neighbour's platter of fresh tomatoes, bread, sausage, and *pastasciutta*, asking instead for boiled nettles. Nettles, a plant growing freely along the side of the farmhouse and the road, have been a staple in herbal medicine since ancient times. The medicinal quality of nettles is deeply telling, as Emilia both heals others and is in need of healing herself. Indeed, the nettles supplement Emilia's growing divinity: Prior to her consumption of the nettles, Emilia, still rooted to the bench, miraculously heals sores on a child's face, earning her a cult following among the villagers. And shortly after eating the nettles, Emilia is found levitating over the house. This ability and necessity to heal culminates in her burial at a nearby construction site, in which her body becomes enveloped in the earth. A neighbour joins Emilia at the site, burying everything but Emilia's eyes, because Emilia has not come to die, but to weep; indeed, the final shot of Emilia is a pair of eyes protruding from the mountain of soil, and beside the mound is a puddle of tears. Emilia's buried body – voluntarily implanted in a hole over which new buildings will be constructed – may thus be read as a seed. Much as a seed needs water to germinate and flower, providing food and oxygen for the world above, Emilia's tears are a source of hope and survival – for the world to heal and to continue to exist, despite the looming ennui and unknowns ahead.[80]

In *La grande abbuffata*, we encounter Andréa, a character with a similarly regenerative purpose. When four men convene to eat themselves to death – thereby eradicating a world that no longer makes any sense – Andréa survives their gorging, standing alone amid the half-eaten platters of greasy, indulgent delicacies and the pools of abject waste. Despite the chaos that surrounds and prompts the self-annihilating act of eating, and within the void hiding behind material excess, Andréa represents a beacon of hope: a clean, blank slate; the chance for the world to start anew.

Chapter Five

La grande abbuffata, or the Reawakening at the End of the World

Thus far, Italy's filmic foodscape has been outlined across material deprivation, the influx of American products and Hollywood values, and, as Pier Paolo Pasolini exhibited in the previous chapters, the contention of the natural and the archaic against constructions of culture and industrialized time. Central to my analysis of Pasolini's work was the image of a circle, a shape of continuum and of cycles – of death and, of particular importance to this chapter, of rebirth. While Paolo of Pasolini's *Teorema* (1968) bares his body, venturing naked across the desert, Emilia exudes an autochthonous divinity; she is voluntarily buried so that she can weep, her tears being the source of new life. This final chapter continues to examine active, grotesque breaks, this time away from the affluent society and the increased standardization of eating, while still reprising Pasolini's "cyclical" ideas, depicting rebirth at the end of the world. Ultimately, Marco Ferreri's *La grande abbuffata* (1973), the most prominent film of this final chapter, documents a return to origins: to neorealism, a point of origin in Italy's postwar cinematic canon, and to the apex of authenticity, before symbols and cultural capital detract from the purity of one's existence.

In *La grande abbuffata,* four well-established men – a chef (Ugo Tognazzi), a pilot (Marcello Mastroianni), a television personality (Michel Piccoli), and an attorney (Philippe Noiret) – come together for a "gastronomic seminar": a weekend dedicated entirely to food, with the ultimate objective of committing suicide by way of excessive consumption. Fatty, creamy, protein-rich food fills the frames. Yet, the prospect of death, not of satiation or conviviality, greatly excites the men, as Ugo states matter-of-factly, "Se non mangi, non puoi morire. / If you can't eat, you can't die." As this very brief description shows, some ways to describe Ferreri's French-Italian co-production are "bourgeois," "apocalyptic," "carnivalesque," and "grotesque." Absent from the list are "neorealist," harking back to a point of origin in Italian cinema, and, in the vein of neorealism, "optimistic." This chapter compares and contrasts Ferreri's film to the neorealist tradition of the 1940s, taking into account casting choices, the *mise en scène* and the significations of quotidian objects, and the notion of origin. An effect of late-state capitalism, food became so abundant that its value depreciated, dissociated from its previous connotations of joy and comfort, approaching meaninglessness altogether. *La grande abbuffata* underscores that the world in 1973 had lost its sense, and accordingly, the filmic foodscape needed to be wiped clean, down to its kernels of filmic and gastronomic originality. A return to neorealism, thus, recuperates a moment of filmic recognizability – in other words, the idea that we have lived through world war, and this, too, shall pass – along with a feeling of resumption, even at the end of the world. Although *La grande abbuffata* is aesthetically by no means in the same category as, for example, Roberto Rossellini's *Roma città aperta* (1945) and Vittorio De Sica's *Ladri di biciclette* (1947), nor does it decry the social injustices particular to the 1940s, its apocalyptic, self-destructive eating signals a return to a *tabula rasa*: a chance to start anew from total destruction.

From Having Everything to Desiring Nothing: A Brief History of Industrialized Eating

The backdrops of Ferreri's and 1940s neorealist cinema are starkly different. In the 1970s, what was missing was not food itself, as it had been in the 1940s; instead, a societal ennui overpowered the food. *La grande abbuffata* is Ferreri's documentation of what economist J.K. Galbraith deemed the "affluent society." The affluent society, defined by a marked rise in privately owned possessions, sparked not only a surge in competition among neighbours but also a decline in sensible consumption. Basic needs were over-fulfilled to a point of exceeding, diminishing returns. Consumers went past the point at which pleasure outweighed the cost of an object; as the consumer's body expanded by overindulgence, psychological connections to the food, meanwhile, began to dissolve. Guy Debord maintained that everything had turned into one giant spectacle; consumption was the mechanism by which to exercise power in contemporary society. Jean Baudrillard elaborated that the experiences deriving from consumer culture were more satisfying than real ones, simulacra supplanting reality; the pretences conjured by merchandise lessened the ability to distinguish between what was real and what was false.[1] In functioning amid too much stuff, people failed to recognize not only the point of such objects but also their own sense of *self* amid those material goods. Indeed, Galbraith warned that the affluent society was "unsustainable, financially, psychologically, and environmentally," leaving people "barren and lost at the same time they were 'stockpiling' consumer goods."[2] Ferreri's film, then, focuses on the unsustainability, the mortality, of the affluent society.

How did Italy get to this moment over the course of thirty years, transitioning from desperate hunger to painful excess? What exactly did the 1970s foodscape look like, and how does it inform Ferreri's film, prompting him to eradicate a complicated web of food symbols? The gastronomic portraits of the previous chapters, the depictions put forth by Totò and Sophia Loren of family togetherness over lavish meals (whether real or imagined), do not match historians' illustrations of the increasingly anonymous, rote experiences of shopping and eating in the 1970s. For example, Andy Warhol's Campbell's soup cans, an image of repetitive, limitless consumption, were deeply *dis*continuous with Totò's extravagant *spaghettata* or the multiplicity of pleasures derived from Sofia's pizzas.[3] By 1973, the foodscape was, instead, one of anonymity and of *rupture*: in Ferreri's world, the testing and outdoing of one's bodily limits under the premise of affluence.

Italy was then home to labyrinthine supermarkets, where pre-prepared and frozen products were designed and advertised to streamline food preparation for working families with, increasingly, two working parents. Though I refer to the supermarket space as a looking glass into consumers' stockpiling of goods, Italy's reception of such an arena was mixed. On one hand, it represented the end of poverty and the dream of a life of well-being, rich with stuff, yet on the other it reflected the fears of such a well-off society: homogenization, anonymity, depersonalization.[4] For its efficiency, technology, and modernity, it was "reminiscent of a factory – but a factory dressed up for a party. The generally sober profile is in deliberate contrast to the bright colours and variety of packages on display. There is background music and a pleasing atmosphere."[5] Luciano Bianciardi's *Vita agra* (1962) offers biting criticism of the sensory "appeals" of the supermarket: "The customers go around, eyes bulging due to the bright lights and pounding music. They have forgotten how to blink. They can't see you."[6] This all said, Italy did not subscribe fully to supermarketing: In 1971, whereas Britain was home to over 3,500 supermarkets, there were only 600 in Italy, mainly in the northern regions. In the 1980s, Italians still bought only 3 per cent of their food from supermarkets; the French, only 14 per cent.[7] Nevertheless, as rationalization progressed and the consumption of private goods increased, an unsustainable system of favouring "tenuous wants" over "solid needs" evolved.[8] A cornerstone of this chapter, then, is the loss of good sense: Bianciardi's "blindness," the disappearance of smells and flavours, mirroring a fatalistic ennui towards food and the establishments where it was sold, prepared, and eaten.

Eating in an age when food was in (over)abundance and standardized in its preparation and presentation thus converted the Ferrerian consumer. Capitulating to an insatiable desire to fill himself with gross quantities of food, but disconnected from the physical sensation of fullness, he overeats. More concerned with filling, rather than satiating, himself, he tests the limits of his body and governing psyche. Eating towards a point of rupture, he is fattened; the expansion of his waistline signals an overextension of bodily boundaries. This act deterritorializes him, as he is unable to distinguish body from food or set boundaries from desire.[9] Such deterritorialized consumption would align with the *schizo* of one's social milieu. A term borrowed from Gilles Deleuze and Félix Guattari, the schizo is a subject that strays from the norms set by capitalist production, and, thus, "plunges further and further into the realm of deterritorialization," seeking out the limits of the social structure and claiming a new identity in the process.[10] The four men of *La grande abbuffata* are precisely such schizo consumers: In search of an existence (or, indeed, non-existence) separate from the norms and practices of the affluent society, the men push and exceed their bodily limits. Grotesque consumption desensitizes the protagonists, rendering them something other than conscious humans, within whom all five senses are typically activated. The sensory register of the viewer, meanwhile, goes into shock.[11]

Through its newfound portability, since the consumer is able to eat in transit, food is also no longer necessarily associated with a particular place or, by extension, the traditions therein. The contours of a consumer's relationship with food are greatly reduced without that *patria alimentare*: ties to the homeland. Eating in such non-places, a term coined by Marc Augé, cuts into the slowness, conviviality, and healthfulness of food, thereby contributing to the deterritorialized "*gastro-anomia*" of the affluent society.[12]

Deterritorialization is a defining characteristic of the production of *La grande abbuffata* itself. My discussions of the affluent society and supermarketing should not be limited to Italy, as the film is a co-production with France, its dialogue is in French and the cast is a mix of French and Italians. France is a country of empire, of high culture – and, by extension, high cuisine – exported throughout the world. One wonders, then, if Ferreri's film could be read as a crisis of the rich, the "Old World": foods of the higher social classes presented and commented upon as works of art, as a defence mechanism against what George Ritzer classified as the McDonaldization of society. In his work, McDonald's is a model for efficiency, predictability, calculability, standardization, and control – customers taking great comfort in that the franchise offers no surprises. Though it is a product of America, "a culture which honours individualism above all," it is an emblem of a world in which there are few surprises.[13] French restaurants had once offered a taste of the high cuisine and culture of European empires. McDonald's – half of whose profits come from outside the United States – exposes consumers to America's national meal: "the burger, with its beef and bread, fries, and shake ... eaten by people of all ages, occupations, and classes, alone or with friends and family."[14] It is everywhere, it is *gastro-anomia*: a founding model by which, as economist Max Weber had feared, "Society would eventually become nothing more than a seamless web of rationalized structures; there would be no escape."[15] Hence, whether in Italy or France, the four men of *La grande abbuffata* opt for suicide as their way out – a "solution" that Ritzer names in his conclusion.[16]

In line with McDonald's drive-thru culture, *gastro-anomia* is conveyed most poignantly through scenes where vehicles and food are presented simultaneously. When the viewer first sees the pilot, Marcello, he is ordering flight attendants to unload his cargo from the plane. These are all nondescript boxes, with the exception of an enormous wheel of Parmigiano-Reggiano; despite its striking size, and its position at the centre of the frame, more jarring is the nonchalance with which Marcello acknowledges the cheese. Later, when the four men are seen together for the first time, they are driving to the villa, the site of their gastronomic seminar; all the while, they are sharing a pizza. Once more, the camera's focus is not on the warmth or the sensory qualities of the pizza, and it is certainly not on the pleasure that the pizza gives its consumers. Ferreri accentuates the drive itself, conducted in relative silence; conviviality is dead. Through these frontal shots, the pizza is given very little attention, as Marcello sits in the backseat, holding a nondescript white box, which is continually obstructed by the glare on the windshield. Food is no longer, for example, the steamy, saucy spaghetti that the Sciosciammocca family frenetically stuffed into their mouths and pockets in Chapter 1. Likewise, gone is the visceral *desire*, the physical hunger, that prompted Totò's multi-sensory, hallucinatory *spaghettata*. The steam emanating from Totò's spaghetti, the bright red of the tomato sauce, the *al dente* texture of the pasta, and the starchy, acidic flavours lose their appeal, because these ingredients – the bases of his exaggerated sensory responses – are readily available at every market. Material hunger, and the conviviality surrounding food, have vanished.

Likewise, the opening shots of *La grande abbuffata* comprise formal contrasts which both entice and subvert the viewer, delineating at once the warmth and the fatalistic qualities of food in excess. Ferreri opens his film with a still image of a relatively empty commercial street on a grey day in Paris; the viewer is primarily focused on the line of black, dusty cars parked along the sidewalk. "Grey" and "dusty" is diction that characterizes the bleakness of both Ferreri's narrative and the affluent society at large; all outdoor shots are of grey days, and the cinematography of these scenes is foggy – as if to offer an aesthetic rendering of such unrecognizability and of the loss of sense. And yet, returning to the image of the street, now a moving image, the camera pans to "Le Biscuit à Soupe," a grocery store that Ugo frequents. The differences in colour between the grey street and Le Biscuit à Soupe are striking: We escape the grey and cold of the outside and enter the store, which, with soft lighting and a backdrop of brown and gold, appears inviting and warm. Chains of red sausage links cascade above Ugo and the grocer, and the walls of the store are adorned with loaves of bread. This presentation, with freshly baked bread at its centre, conjures an atmosphere that is warm and nurturing, but there is also an air of wastefulness, in that the bread is not the alimentary staple of life but, rather, a wall decoration. What the viewer experiences, then, is a feast for the eyes, not the stomach. The camera – and, by extension, the viewer – gravitates towards the fullness, the colour, and the warmth of the grocery store; the foodscape is inviting, but Ferreri upends these sensations. Then, unbeknownst to the viewer, the excesses of food are heightened so much that food becomes lethal. Food overwhelms and intoxicates Ferreri's four protagonists, denying them any pleasure from eating. He roots his work in the experiences that arise within Italy's modernized consumer culture: the thrill of having "stuff" soars to such an extreme degree that the objects lose their value. People own stuff, but they fail to recognize the essences and the purpose of those things, and, by extension, what connections – sensory and otherwise – exist between the consumer and the consumed. In so doing, Ferreri is lamenting the loss of taste – the perception of any gastronomic pleasure – to the mass production and standardization of food.

Consequently, in moving from such a phenomenon to a mundane, rote experience, the sensory joy of food has dissipated. In the brain, there are neural pathways, such as the pleasure centre and reward system; with the introduction of certain foods, which engage one's senses of smell, sight, and taste, these zones "light up," generating feelings of euphoria within the consumer.[17] This chapter focuses on the converse of this reaction: With an excess of food, this joy diminishes; the potential of these neural zones is weakened. When considering rows of identical

Figure 5.1. The storefront of "Le Biscuit à Soupe" in the opening shots of *La grande abbuffata* (1973, dir. Marco Ferreri).

soup cans at the supermarket, standardized to appear indistinguishable from one another, the consumer's sense of sight is dulled. Similarly, gone is the sense of taste; any differences between salty, sweet, bitter, sour, and umami vanish. The five senses lose their function, and the consumer, in turn, cannot make sense of what she is eating. Historians and anthropologists have reported such lamentations, both generally and microcosmically. In the supermarket space,

> Compared to the old larder, here there are various industrial, trademarked foods … This transition led to more standardized products where shape, color, and taste are concerned. Biscuits are invariably all the same (cooked the same way, with the same shape and color, and all with an identical taste). The same is true for fresh produce (cheese no longer has the old crust, malodorous creamy center and the mold that appeared as soon as it was opened.) In fact, it could be said that all strong smells have disappeared.[18]

On a more individual level, Renzo, one of anthropologist Carole Counihan's Tuscan interviewees, spoke of the decline of desire and food quality as time wore on:

> Today we eat much better, with more variety. However, in the old days, the food was more desired – Sunday, because we ate better; holidays,

because we ate capon. In contrast, today every day is Sunday. Then we longed for things. Today, instead, pretty much every day, we have everything we want, but the taste of food is much worse. Today the food has no taste. Today, if you eat, let's say spinach, or Swiss chard, or beet greens – everything tastes the same.[19]

La grande abbuffata, too, underscores a sensory shutdown. Without the honed senses of taste or sight, the men over the course of the weekend lose their ability to recognize foods, even confusing them with inedible or abject objects: Paté is the building material for an edible cupola; hot chocolate assumes a disturbing likeness to diarrhea; *la tarte Andréa* and nondescript pink mounds, both described later, simultaneously signify sweet, fruity cake and a woman's flesh. These confusions are a symptom of the men's excessive consumption; without recognizing the feeling of fullness, the brain is the first organ of many to be deactivated during the "gastronomic seminar." The connections between food and consumer are therefore severed, with food catalysing death, not sustaining life.

Through *La grande abbuffata*, Ferreri recognizes the philosophy that entire truckloads of food make no sense; the more that is added to the frame, the less room there is for meaningful connections to be built between the consumer and the food. Of particular interest, then, is the nihilist agency that Ferreri assigns to his protagonists; in making food together, the four men create the end of the world as they know it, because they will not have the sense to perceive the world any longer. Food is automated, yet it is the means to intentional self-destruction in Ferreri's film. Until this point, food was a part of a system of symbols that dictated moments of happiness, duties, and desires in one's daily life; daily life as a whole was considered possible thanks to "symbolic institutions" that brought pleasure – and stability – through repeatable actions. These symbols governed sexual legitimacy, human interactions, and the conviviality and rituals of eating, but they also represented the self with respect to external forces.[20]

The idea of "I think, therefore I am" involves a conscious recognition of the self as a body, mind, and soul functioning in tandem with the outside world. Given my ongoing discussion of food, let us reframe this decree as "I *eat*, therefore I am"; eating is a ritual that sustains the survival of humankind, but one that has become automated. The symbols of food have come to signify less. Ferreri, in turn, underscores eating as an *active* verb, an action of choices: to eat or not to eat, and how much; what, when, and where to eat; and with whom, if anyone, to eat.[21] Ferreri's protagonists choose not only to eat, but to eat such a gross amount that they invert the revised Cartesian principle into "I eat, therefore I am *not*." Ferreri's oeuvre is, indeed, situated at this end of the world, as he converts automated routines into acts of wilful nihilism.

For these reasons, critics view Ferreri's work as apocalyptic; many of his films culminate in explosions, murder, and suicides. However, while "apocalypse" does refer to the end of the world, in this case it is more the process of unravelling and re-ravelling sense; in response to meaninglessness, extinction is necessary for the world to start anew, to make sense again.[22] In other words, what follows ultimate rupture – "apocalypse," as it is usually defined – is a reawakening: the *rebirth* of sense. Jean-Luc Nancy emphasizes that sense will be recuperated only through complete abandonment: the negation of "sense" as well as of "being." The two verbs comprising "I think, therefore I am" must be negated to become "I do *not* think, so I am *not*," thus signalling the end, but also a call to return to the opening, of the world.[23]

In other words, Ferreri's films suggest a return, albeit violent, to a realm preceding significations, to a place that simply "is": a precursor for the things of the world to resume their sense. The return is reminiscent of 1940s neorealism, or "cinema year zero": a film movement that captured both the voids of the *dopoguerra* and a nation starting anew out of total rubble. My analysis of *La grande abbuffata* considers Ferreri's connections to and detachment from traditional neorealism, and, in recuperating the neorealist motif of rebirth, how his work may offer viewers a taste of continuity in revisiting the hope embedded in the filmscape of the past.

Ferreri the Neorealist?

There is significant debate about whether Ferreri belongs to the neorealist tradition. In particular, one must assess what from 1940s neorealism Ferreri perpetuated and discarded in order to sculpt his vision of the end of the world. In an interview with Spanish film scholar Esteve Riambau, the director himself toyed with the creation of "new realities," the grand-scale stories erupting from a singular moment, a quotidian image, of one's day:

RIAMBAU: *One of the aspects of your movies that most interests me is your ability to create new spaces out of older real spaces, as if it were a puzzle.*

FERRERI: This is a matter related to the question of, Where does cinema come from? It always has to be born from a small story, because cinema follows the images of a small story.

RIAMBAU: *When you talk about a "small story," are you referring to cartoons?*

FERRERI: No, to short stories. Afterwards, a whole relationship is formed with an image that keeps changing. I think the image is very important:

its structure, how it changes and constructs new realities. Every story has its own image. America is an image. There's my own daily discourse, one that's internal, with respect to all this.

Nevertheless, the most important result that comes out of this is the anecdote, the small story. Producers only want that.

RIAMBAU: *Nevertheless, your movies continuously insist on the creation of new realities, like the use of the hole of Les Halles for the shooting of* Touche pas la femme blanche *(1974).*

FERRERI: Cinema is cinema. It's a visual force. The force of the image should be at least equal to the force of a text. This for me is much less important, but – and I can't say why – everyone now is asking for text.[24]

In this vein, neorealist screenwriter Cesare Zavattini was a major influence on Ferreri's work: The Zavattinian pursuit of truths – which Italian scholars name *pedinamento* or *film-inchiesta*; the Spanish, *el acecho de la realidad*, or the "staking out of realities" – greatly appealed to Ferreri and shaped his career. In searching for a story, Zavattini followed the slow, tired steps of the worker, or a woman's day of shopping for shoes; Ferreri adopted a similar practice.[25] In the early 1950s, as well as upon his return from Spain in the early 1960s, Ferreri, too, put his cinema into direct contact with everyday objects, people, and places, with the intent of extracting truths from them. These positionalities define his early journalistic, documentarian projects: *Documento mensile* (1951), the omnibus film *L'amore in città* (1953), and *Le italiane e l'amore* (1962). In "Paradiso per tre ore," the twelve-minute vignette of *L'amore in città* on which Zavattini and Ferreri collaborated, the premise is, at face value, couplings of men and women, young and old, meek and bold, while at the Astoria Dance Hall on Sunday evenings for three hours. Through the long shots of the crowded dance hall and zooms into enamoured and bored facial expressions, Ferreri and Zavattini underline the twists and turns of courtship and gender roles in urban, postwar Italy. Although this is just one example of Ferreri's documentary work, one must ask: After a thorough investigation (hence the notion of the *film-inchiesta*), what could one learn about the self and the surrounding world from interacting with all this "stuff"? Returning to René Descartes and the axiom of "I think, therefore I am," my knowledge of the self – my life as I know it – is developed and upheld with respect to the objects and bodies of the world among which I function; the "stuff" makes sense of the self. But one must consider the varying kinds of stories – the kinds of selves – that develop after uncovering multiple quotidian truths. Whereas Zavattini stressed the importance of filling empty spaces with human life, to maximize the potential of every minute – "to take any moment of a human life and show how 'striking' that moment is: to excavate and identify it, to send its echo vibrating into other parts of the world"[26] – Ferreri appeared to do the exact opposite with his truths. When the "stuff" that comprises one's day no longer makes sense, the self, too, loses its definition.

To accentuate these existentialist perspectives, let us zoom into two of their respective films. In 1952, Zavattini created Umberto D., a wizened pensioner who, with his dog, faces eviction and homelessness, and thus debates ending his life; five years earlier, in *Ladri di biciclette*, Zavattini illustrates the massive stakes of a single bicycle, a vehicle required for Antonio to make a living and support his family, including his infant child. Meanwhile, in *El cochecito* (1961), don Anselmo, Ferreri's rendition of the retiree, cons his family into buying him a motorized wheelchair – a purchase he does not actually need, as he is healthy and mobile, but one he wants in order to be like his disabled friends. Don Anselmo, a middle-class member of Spanish society, is trying to "keep up with the Joneses," thereby engaging in irrational consumption, emblematic of the affluent society: purchasing something for which there is no real need.

The works of these filmmakers are situated within periods of great historical and sociopolitical rupture: for Zavattini, the totalizing devastations of world war; for Ferreri, the anxieties accompanying the "Brave New World" of neo-capitalism, the global energy crisis, and the terrorist violence by political extremists. Thus, Zavattini and Ferreri differ in their treatment of survival; as with the dire absence and oppressive presence of food, the meaning of survival, too, changed between 1943 and 1973. Indeed, Ferreri focuses on the quotidian, as did Zavattini, but Ferreri's films concern survival in a new light: the struggle for individuality, and knowledge of the self, against objects; a clash between human subjectivity and objectification. Ferreri's early work was focused on capturing not the slow, tired steps of the worker, as Zavattini had done in the 1940s, but humans' interactions amid the electric velocity of Italy's boom: the arrival of the supermarket and its big-brand goods, the dream of the sparkling American kitchen, and the debut of television in Italy's bars. But just because Ferreri's protagonist has "stuff" does not mean that he is content. Through the frenzied stockpiling of goods and purchasing of consumer durables, the individual's world was increasingly automated, at the expense of his own human agency – indeed, of his individuality, of his selfhood. Proceeding further, don Anselmo actively chooses to fuse his able body with wheels: an exhibition of man and machine becoming one entity, as the wheelchair supplants the voids of the self. The Ferrerian struggle, then, is not survival by its fundamental definition – that is to say, the procurement of food, water, and shelter – but contention with the ennui, the tastelessness, of consumerist Italy; how does one define herself in a world of standardized sameness? The self regressed into a passive, even anonymous, bystander as Italy modernized and globalized; as Ferreri demonstrated across his work, while society grew increasingly affluent, the self was blinded and, ultimately, dismantled. The questions remain, then, of what such dismantling looks like, and how life proceeds at a zero-point origin.

Dismantling, Ferreri-Style

Unmasking the Star

Ferreri most poignantly illustrates the feelings of malaise and regression, the ennui of existing within a world of excess, through the formal qualities of *La grande abbuffata*. This chapter considers, first, Ferreri's cast – his mix of French and Italian comedic stars and frequent collaborators – and second, the *mise en scène*: what key frames contain and where these frames are shot. These formal choices demonstrate the ways in which Ferreri underscores the ineptitudes of 1973, all the while hinting at rebirth, replete with optimism: a fresh chance to redo the world that has been undone.

Previous chapters focused heavily on stardom: stars' iconic recognizability, as well as their exemption from the greater population's hardships, such as hunger and poverty. As discussed in Chapter 1, Totò, played by the noble Antonio de Curtis, did not communicate an authentic suffering, as he did not partake in the collective experience; because he was too much of a star, and de Curtis was too wealthy, Totò's hunger remained entirely farcical. Likewise, Sophia Loren's cosmopolitanism and travel anecdotes of avocados and exotic fruits were not a direct reflection of 1960s domesticity. Ferreri, too, incorporates the star into his narrative. His casting choices include Ugo Tognazzi, Marcello Mastroianni, Michel Piccoli, and Philippe Noiret – all of whom had established acting careers of great acclaim well before 1973.

Ferreri had stated that he did not care whether his cast was comprised of amateur or professional actors; what mattered instead was the actor's likeness to the character he played.[27] However, his employment of the star in *La grande abbuffata* underscores the philosophy of subtraction. In his dissolution of sociocultural symbols, as he documents the end of the world in 1973, Ferreri cast stars because the stakes of subtraction are much greater when someone has attained an iconicity through certain costumes, gestures, and bodies of work; there is significantly more to lose. The star thus becomes the focal point in Ferreri's dismantling of the world, as the star's body is stripped of the costumes, makeup, and elaborate hairdos that once enabled the transformation from man to star. Ferreri disables and reverses the rise to stardom, reducing the star to flesh, food, and feces. He removes the *maschera* of his four stars, thereby eliminating any distance between the actors and their characters. The actors of *La grande abbuffata* even share the same name as their characters – Marcello Mastroianni plays Marcello, Philippe Noiret plays Philippe – further blurring the distinction between the character and its interpreter. With the star stripped of his own distinctive traits and "undressed," bare-naked[28] before the world, the character's tics and manias become those of the actor, thus exposing the actor's existential vulnerabilities when he realizes there is nothing – no role, no mask – left to hide behind.[29] Ferreri, then, capitalizes on the *maschera* in a much different way from what Mario Mattoli, Camillo Mastrocinque, and even Pasolini did with Totò, as seen in Chapters 1 and 4, respectively. Through his four protagonists, Ferreri emphasizes that the star is not exempt from the end of the world; he is not only as vulnerable as anyone else, but also, returning once more to the Warholian soup cans, he is yet another fixture in a standardized world. Indeed, in this film, the viewer does not admire Mastroianni, for example, for his star qualities, but instead witnesses the distortion of Marcello's bodily limits. Though I analyse Tognazzi and Mastroianni in the upcoming sections, the focus is, ultimately, on bodies in peril, jeopardized by an excess of food.

Ugo Tognazzi, the Seven-Time Veteran of Ferreri's Duress

Tognazzi is a peculiar case study because his oeuvre is an exhibition of mediocrity. "Mediocrity" is defined as ordinary, as far from remarkable as possible: anti-stardom. Tognazzi's stardom is grounded in the *un*spectacular; he did not have the glamour or sex appeal of Sophia Loren or the absurd excesses of Totò, but, instead, a sense of humour and outlook grounded in the everyday, in the average. And yet, this averageness is the very cornerstone of Tognazzi's stardom, his only means of being *above* average. In Tognazzi, viewers paid to see a not particularly handsome, not particularly tall man with a wry sense of humour, delivered in a calm, monotonous voice; he was also frequently dressed in shades of brown. There are negligible differences between, for example, Ugo in *La grande abbuffata* and *l'anarchico* in Nanni Loy's *Il padre di famiglia* (1967). Viewers expected Tognazzi to embody the same archetype – never mind that he replaced the original *l'anarchico*, played, of all people, by Totò, who died during production; his scenes had to be redone using the second-choice Tognazzi.

Roberto Buffagni records Tognazzi declaring his intentions "di costruire un personaggio identico a tutti ma che, nello stesso tempo, è Tognazzi."[30] The stakes of being "identical to all, but at the same time, Tognazzi himself" are crucial to my discussions on standardization and the annihilated star-sign; what does it mean to somehow stand out among strikingly similar objects, and what are the consequences when those distinctions are removed? Across their collaborations, Ferreri emphasizes Tognazzi as part of a homogeneous series and renders him, in the words of film scholar Casimiro Torreiro, "little more than a monkey trapped in the insurmountable pits of his own impotence."[31]

How does Tognazzi transition – or, rather, descend – from a star to this trapped, powerless monkey, where he is no different from his countrymen and no more refined? Ugo is positioned most frequently in the background, dressed in brown so that he even occasionally blends in with the villa's wooden panels, so the viewer's attention does not gravitate towards him; there is nothing spectacular about his presence, nothing "unique." In so doing, Ferreri positions Tognazzi as a pawn in the greater historical picture. Tognazzi's performances are consonant with the historical events and sociocultural phenomena of Italy in the 1960s and 1970s,[32] much as the physicality of Totò was a response to the socioeconomic tumult of the 1950s, fostering a connection with his audience by way of the history they shared. Considering that the 1970s experienced crisis by automation, sameness was the name of the game: The increasingly standardized production of goods was the backdrop with which Tognazzi had to contend.

In addition, film production is quite similar to the industrialized, systematic, repetitive standardization of Western supermarketing. Tognazzi was an actor embedded within Italy's star system: a network of people who became icons only through the repeated mass production and distribution of films – yet another product consumed ritualistically by the public, just like food. And in many of these films, as their *maschere* took shape, the stars were repeatedly hired to play the same character archetype, thus becoming standardized products, marketed as such for the benefit of the film and their careers. We can return momentarily to the example of Sophia Loren. Starring in photo-romances in her early career, Loren was repeatedly cast as the "foreign temptress or slave girl, usually of Arab or Gypsy origin" on account of her olive complexion and "exotic air"; her persona was fabricated in this fashion so as to sell her body and sexuality through film.[33] Conversely, Tognazzi's archetype is that of mediocrity. These instances of repetition are very much like those of developing and advertising products on grocery shelves; with increased availability comes a depreciation in value – a trend that speaks even further to Tognazzi's mediocrity. In *La grande abbuffata*, signs lose their meaning, and the star-sign is no exception; the actor's *maschera* is but a façade. The sparkling veneer of stardom fades to reveal human shortcomings, missteps, and neuroses.[34] Thus, whereas de Curtis was able to hide and thrive behind the *maschera* of Totò, this could no longer happen in the 1970s. Through his seven collaborations with Ferreri, Tognazzi partook in the repeated dissolution of systemic markers that bolstered him as a star positioned above his fellow citizens. With the removal of the *maschera*, Tognazzi was more clearly connected to his audience through the history they shared: a questioning of the world and where, if anywhere, they fit in: where can the self exist free of any industrialized series.

Out of this mediocrity, it is jarring to the viewer that Tognazzi not only accepted Ferreri's grotesque experiments but that in *La grande abbuffata* he *creates* the grotesque. Ferreri cast Tognazzi as the chef, the head and mastermind of the "gastronomic seminar." Ugo/Tognazzi is not just a part of the background; he is an agent of destruction, as he converts these standardized foods into the meals that kill all four protagonists. Indeed, when Ugo is handling food, these are the few moments when he is captured in the foreground and commands the viewers' attention. In one close-up shot, in which he is smelling a wedge of Parmigiano-Reggiano, he is so close that it just might be possible to smell the hard cheese and taste its pungency and saltiness through the screen. Even then, though, we do not desire Ugo or the food he manipulates, but really, we imagine what that food can do to the consumer. In being given agency and leadership over food, Ugo/Tognazzi is the crux upon which automated consumption is converted into the intentional act of grotesque eating. The mass quantities of food combine with his serial mediocrity to form a weapon of destruction, a means of rupture; by making Ugo the chef of the group, Ferreri has doubled down on the stakes of eating repeatedly and with resignation.

Ferreri's choice was partly personal, even autobiographical. Tognazzi, himself an author of four cookbooks, claimed that while acting was "a hobby," eating was in his blood, "which, besides red and white blood cells, also includes a fair amount of tomato sauce."[35] In the preface of his first cookbook, *L'abbuffone: Storie da ridere e ricette da morire/The Pig: Stories to Laugh At and Recipes to Die From* (1974), he goes as far as likening his refrigerator to a religious idol, assigning himself martyrdom around food – thereby acknowledging the paradoxical combination of death with the pleasures of convivial eating. He writes:

This fridge is my family's chapel. Some mornings, my wife might be surprised to find me kneeling before the idol, this totem of human adventure.

> I am there, gathering my thoughts, waiting for some inspiration for lunch.
> This image ... gives you the idea of how ascetic my attachment is to the
> banal pleasures of the table and, thus, of life; and how I could be consid-
> ered a martyr of the hearth – even though on the fiery embers I am not
> arranging my own body, but instead, with endless care, veal chops.[36]

Food was Tognazzi's lifeblood: an expression of pleasure and conviviality, but one with lethal consequences if overused.

Given their repeated collaborations, Ferreri and Tognazzi were
close friends; thus, Ferreri was among the "twelve apostles" invited to
Tognazzi's compound for dinner parties.[37] The meals themselves report-
edly "had nothing to them, just the pleasure of being together, of pure
conviviality."[38] Yet, not only did these occasions run from "'extraordinary' to 'total shitshow' – with tickets placed into a silver basin," but the
richness and large quantities of the food also caused Ferreri significant
digestive problems, resulting in his admission into a Swiss clinic.[39] His
hospitalization was in fact the impetus for *La grande abbuffata*, as Ferreri
denoted the close connections between eating and death: not just that
starvation, or not eating, could lead to death, but that overeating could
be just as fatal. In his biography of Mastroianni, Donald Dewey writes:

> As Tognazzi was to recount it, *La Grande Bouffe* (Blowout) arose from the
> elaborate meals that he and Ferreri had once devoured in the actor's Rome
> apartment. "When everything was out on the table, all of it seasoned to
> a turn, we would survey it very carefully, then say to each other almost
> ritualistically, 'This is going to kill us.' Then we would dig in." When the
> director had dug in once too often and had to be admitted to a Swiss clinic,
> he has acknowledged, "I began thinking about death." No sooner had he
> gotten back on his feet than he wrote the script for *La Grande Bouffe* ...[40]

Since Tognazzi was so intimately involved in the moments of consumption that both damaged and inspired Ferreri, it makes sense that he
was chosen to coordinate such grotesque feasts on screen. Although
haute cuisine – the extraordinary, the silver basins, food presented as
art – appeared to be a more refined, classier contrast to the aforementioned grocery shelves, these elaborate meals, served every Friday
night, became routine, one no more special than the other. The routine
of feasting, then, matches Tognazzi's mediocrity: engaging in the same
experience, time and time again.

Yet, one might question to what extent Ugo orchestrates the feast.
Ultimately, *Ferreri* directed his cast to the grotesque – which further
supports Ugo's mediocrity, as one man among many. Indeed, Tognazzi

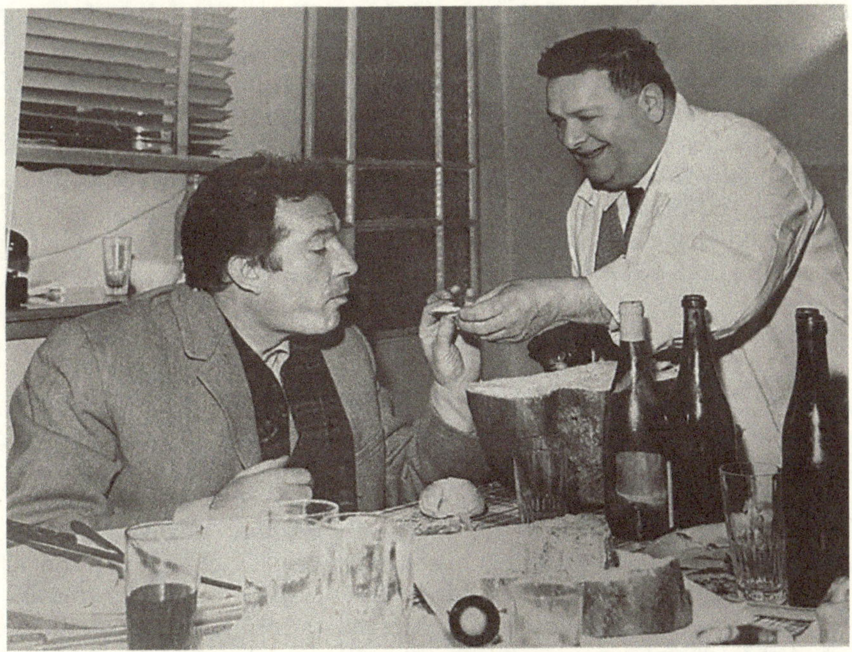

Figure 5.2. "The 1960s: Ugo Tognazzi (left) and Parmigiano-Reggiano. The chef is one of the Stoppani brothers, owners of the Salumerie Peck (Milan)." ("Anni 60. Ugo Tognazzi e il Parmigiano Reggiano: lo chef è uno dei fratelli Stoppani, propietari delle Salumerie Peck.") Archivio Storico Peck, Milan. This caption and photograph are derived from Coop's collection *Occhio al cibo: immagini per un secolo di consumi alimentari in Italia*, ed. Alberto Capatti and Cesare Colombo (1991).

was not alone in his mass consumption. In *La grande abbuffata*, Ferreri subjected his protagonists to an onslaught of food. In becoming one with their characters, the entire cast, too, was forcibly overwhelmed by food. For example, Ferreri demanded that Andréa Ferréol, playing a schoolteacher who joins the men in their eating frenzy, gain twenty-five kilograms for the role, forcing her to have five square meals per day.[41] In anticipation of the stoic automatism of their consumption, Ferreri had excessive amounts of food regularly delivered to the studio, so that his cast would be weighed down both physically and mentally by all the fat, sugar, and calories; in this process, weakened by food, they came to accept grotesque eating and defecation as unquestioned routines, mirroring precisely the automation of the 1970s foodscape.[42]

In other words, although Tognazzi assumed the role of chef, he is but the head of these feasts. The consumers are just as invested as the preparer; indeed, the notion of "suicide by consumption" implies that the *consumers* kill *themselves*. Another such consumer is Marcello (Mastroianni), the pilot at the "gastronomic seminar," and who off screen is traditionally hailed as the "Latin Lover" of Italian cinema. Since Marcello is the first of the four to die, this virile archetype must now be debunked – especially considering that men are no longer, in the Edenic sense, the first sex; *Andréa* is the first to exist in Ferreri's reborn world.

Marcello Mastroianni, or Debunking the "Latin Lover"

Despite Mastroianni's reputation as Italy's "Latin Lover," Ferreri stripped the star of his sex symbolism, likening him to an *inetto*: a physically impotent and, thus, socially powerless man. I mentioned the *inetto* in Chapter 2, in which I discussed Mastroianni's filmic relationship – and indeed, impotence – with Sophia Loren, the "unruly woman." The *inetto*, in conflict with this unsettling, radically changing political environment, as well as with shifting gender roles, continued to transpire on the silver screen through Mastroianni.[43] Indeed, Mastroianni exuded a powerlessness with respect to the social and political turbulence impacting Italy amid waves of revolution and on the eve of the Years of Lead. In *La grande abbuffata*, despite his gluttony for the flesh of women and animals alike, Marcello's masculinity is challenged by the men's weekend of competitive eating. Not only is Marcello the first to lose this test of *machismo* but, in the end, he is outdone by a woman.

At the film's onset, Marcello embodies a virility that mirrors Italy's futurism of fifty years earlier. I reference futurism because of his deep-seated attachment to technologies, and because of his ability to soar and travel to faraway places at inhuman speeds. He is the pilot of the foursome, regularly flying commercial jets across Europe's airspace; later, at Philippe's villa, he expresses great fondness for and tinkers with a blue Bugatti. The car's blue colour, the enormity of the plane, and the speed and power at which these machines function are all meant to resonate with Marcello's masculinity. And yet, Ferreri combined Marcello's proclivities with the softness, warmth, and fragility of Ugo's dishes. When Marcello is the first of the four to die, viewers immediately blame the car; the metallic machine offers no warmth or protection from the frigid air, so Marcello, who ventures outside to take the car for a drive, freezes to death overnight. However, cars have been previously described as *non-luoghi*, non-places: sites of mechanized, absent-minded eating. The absent-mindedness associated with the car extends to Marcello; the richness and grotesque quantity of the food weigh him down, inhibiting his senses and his ability to gauge his body temperature accurately. It makes sense, then, that Marcello would be found dead in the car; Ferreri upends the sign of futurist virility, exposing the man to the extremes of temperature and food, with the car – perhaps a *maschera* itself – offering no protection.

Although Mastroianni claimed that his death was first in the series simply because he and Catherine Deneuve, his lover, had planned a trip to Jamaica, Ferreri's choice to kill the "Latin Lover" quickly is a means of underlining Marcello's impotence.[44] Unable to respond accordingly, Marcello dies in the driver's seat, frozen, immobile, and exceedingly full. While the car and the plane are traditional symbols of masculinity that Ferreri inverts in his narrative on food – which, too, has its life-sustaining quality inverted – how else does Ferreri weaken the prowess of the "Latin Lover"? How does Marcello – both the actor and the character – engage with the gastronomic seminar: a feast from which women are largely absent, thereby emphasizing the rapport between the male participants?

Like Tognazzi, Mastroianni always had a strong penchant for food, of which Ferreri – among other directors – was aware. Film scholar Pascal Schembri records comments made by Ferreri and Mario Monicelli, director of *I soliti ignoti* (1958) and *La mortadella* (1971), both of which provide some rationale for why Mastroianni loved food, and for how Ferreri alluded to this obsession in *La grande abbuffata*. Monicelli, for one, cited Mastroianni's obsessive pursuit of food as analogous to the pursuit of a lover. Whereas women often fawned over him, Mastroianni was attracted by the difficult "chase" of food; a delicious plate of food, not a beautiful woman, was a successful conquest:

> Mastroianni was a man with an innate humorism. Super-pleasant despite his fixation on food. He would spend the work day thinking about where we were going to eat after shooting. At night, after dinner, he would down an entire bottle of grappa … His love of life went hand-in-hand with his love of food and love of women. Mario Monicelli initially seems to compare the two, when he maintains that all the women on set were in love with him [Mastroianni], but he thought of nothing but food. Maybe because they offered themselves up to him, but food, meanwhile, he had to look for, with great intention, even seeking out particular restaurants that were not always easy to get to.[45]

And yet, when women *abandoned* Mastroianni, food provided an almost motherly solace in such difficult, lonely times. It offered a consolatory pleasure, a means of continuity despite the loss of a lover. For example, Schembri reports that following the filming of *Non toccare la donna bianca* (1974), when Deneuve and Mastroianni ended their relationship of three years, Mastroianni cried to Ferreri, "'I want to die, I want to die, it's best to end it all,' only to throw himself on a plate of freshly served pasta."[46] Food gave Mastroianni a strong centre of gravity in such moments of turbulence, pleasuring him when a woman could not – giving him self-assurance and peace of mind when there was no woman fawning over him. As his *mangiate* with Tognazzi formed the premise of *La grande abbuffata*, here, too, Ferreri incorporated components of Mastroianni's biography into his feast.

For his close connections to food, combined with the widespread acknowledgment of his sexuality and manhood, Mastroianni provides a clear lens through which to consider questions of gender in *La grande abbuffata*, a film in which strikingly few women are present. With the exception of Andréa, who will be discussed in greater detail in an upcoming section, the "gastronomic seminar" is organized, prepared, and executed by men. Although Ugo is at the helm, all four men play a role in ordering the trucks of food, acting as Ugo's sous-chefs and preparing the *mise en place*, and feeding each other forkfuls and fingertips of meats, pastas, cake, and sauces. Such feasts are a means of demonstrating one's manhood: a test of endurance, just like injuries sustained from contact sports or "winning" a bar fight. These injuries are meant to be worn as badges marking one's strength, endurance, prowess, and masculinity. Despite such immense physical exertion, the men do not wish to lose face in front of their peers and surrender to the feminine cakes and purées, so they willingly undergo force-feeding, eating while prostrate, and excessive consumption against the warning signs of gas, nausea, and diarrhea.[47]

The pleasures that the men seek from the food – the "consolation," "peace," and "naturalness" that Mastroianni sought so feverishly – are won at the expense of outdoing and, in this case, eliminating male rivals. Ferreri's feast is not a pleasurable pause from the daily humdrum but instead an exhibition of rivalry: of violently negating the conviviality and wholesomeness of food by becoming the man who consumes the most food, lasting longer than the weaker, "lesser" men. Thus, whatever the actual reason might have been, when Marcello is the first to die, we may read his death as a blow to Mastroianni's masculinity, emphasizing the *inetto* once more. The "Latin Lover" persona fades as Mastroianni's sex symbol is emasculated and erased by the pleasure/pain dynamics of the feast. But even as meek, anxious Philippe endures the longest, eating after his friends are dead, the manly competition ultimately

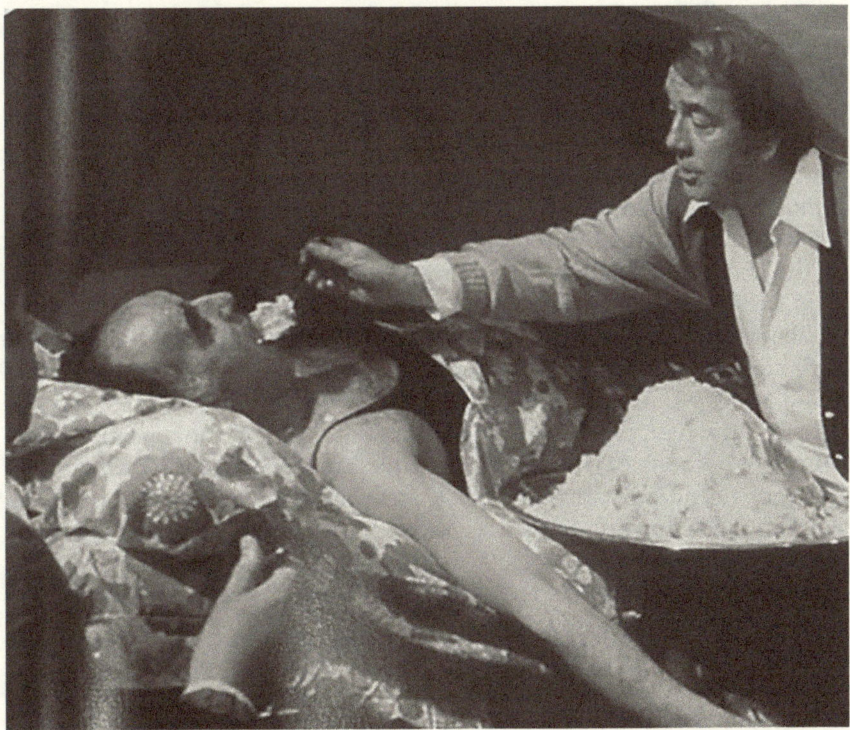

Figure 5.3. Ugo (standing, right) and Michel in *La grande abbuffata*.

ends with a woman as the supreme victor, alone with the overwhelming amount of food, the men's foe and weapon of mass destruction in Ferreri's film.

Dismantling the World with Food and Feces

Quotidian Objects, Historical Artifacts

The objects that are part of Ferreri's *mise en scène* recuperate and comment on the historical moment in which his films are set; *La grande abbuffata* is just one case in which Ferreri employed seemingly banal objects to comment on the spiritual and moral voids present in society. Central to his oeuvre is the relic, the object with museum quality, intended to commemorate and educate contemporary viewers on a specific moment in history, or on a particular aspect of one's culture. In his *Dillinger è morto* (1969), Glauco (played by Michel Piccoli), a designer of gas masks, unwraps a bundle of old newspaper and uncovers a revolver that once belonged to John Dillinger; the newspapers from the past inform Glauco's discovery of the present, and the object guides his transition from passivity/defence (the gas masks) to activity/attack (the gun). After giving the gun a modern, feminine look, transforming the phallus-shaped weapon by painting it red with white polka dots, Glauco uses this "antique" to kill his sedated wife: a nod to the ubiquity of drugs in the 1960s. Likewise, in *Il seme dell'uomo* (1969), in the days immediately following the apocalypse, Cino and Dora – who survive by driving through a tunnel as the world ends – convert an abandoned house into a museum; Cino meticulously catalogues and classifies household items, informing potential future visitors on what those of the pre-apocalyptic period used in their daily life. The museum project, however, precludes Cino from realizing that the museum exists precisely because of the apocalypse; the "treasures" of the past contain the very decadence and hostility that sparked the end of the world in the first place, turning what was once a house where people lived into a museum of mummified objects.[48] Four years later, in *La grande abbuffata*, it is *food* that communicates parallels between the affluent society and their wealth of problems.

Sublime Cuisine

Ferreri utilizes food as a classist tool, a lens through which to view the "*gastro-anomia*" of the 1970s affluent society. These men are not eating the simple *minestre* of previous decades, or having to "make do" with scarce ingredients, but, instead, they are feasting on paté, roast duck, oysters: displays of their bourgeois status. Situated within the "affluent society," the men's high socioeconomic standing is another means through which they may separate themselves from other creatures of nature. From the class distinction, their eventual fall into savage consumption is all the more shocking for the viewer.

Similar to the star, who rises above his fellow countrymen through his recognizability and iconicity, the treatment of food as "cuisine" elevates the consumer – and humankind at large – above the animal kingdom. In his *Distinction: A Social Critique of the Judgement of Taste* (1979), Pierre Bourdieu describes the direct correlation between one's socioeconomic standing and her consumption preferences. Bourdieu concludes that upper-class members of society have culturally refined tastes. He offers, among others, the example of music: Music by Mozart, Beethoven, Bach, etc. may be defined as "classical" because of the aristocratic patronage assigned to these composers, thereby giving their work an

Figure 5.4. "To be, or not to be!" Michel (centre, holding the cow's head) shouts into the stratosphere. From *La grande abbuffata*.

air of distinction. Rap and rock music, meanwhile, tell stories of work, life, and survival in working-class and, often, urban communities. *La grande abbuffata* is, thus, an exhibition of traditionally upper-class tastes in food, art, and literature, with which only the wealthiest men could engage. Likewise, the coding of the weekend as a "gastronomic seminar" assigns the men's grotesque eating an elevated air of distinction. At the gastronomic seminar, led by Ugo the *chef de cuisine* (labelled as such instead of "cook," which sounds less formal and classy), the table is elaborately set with fine china and floral centrepieces, and the men, elegantly dressed for dinner, not only address each other with heightened formality but also make constant allusions to art and literature. What they choose to eat is just one demonstration of their affluence, as their distinguished tastes are amplified through conversation. The men praise Ugo's ornate creations, such as paté in the shape of a cupola, which itself is a precious work of art, but they also debate artistic trends in tandem with the food they eat: Michel recites *Hamlet* as he dances around with a cow's head, and, over oysters, the men view vintage pornography and comment on the artistic lighting of such images.

Yet, the premise described above is but the beginning of *La grande abbuffata*; the feast quickly loses its markers of order and distinction as it descends into orgiastic turmoil. The men unbutton their shirts, lose their good posture, and trade silverware and plates for each other's hands, as they feed and are fed while lying prostrate on beds, tables, and benches. This transition from upper-class man to savage requires the stripping of the signs of the men's symbolic capitalism; in response to all the excess, Ferreri removes such "non-sense" from the world. Just as Ferreri rips the *maschera* away from the actor, who is suddenly no different from his spectators, the elements of *haute cuisine*, too, turn on the well-dressed, well-to-do protagonists. The excess of food, and Ferreri's gruesome exhibition of the men's flatulence and bowel movements resulting from such extreme consumption, reduce them from white-collar citizens to an animalistic status. The focus is no longer on their occupation or their salary, or even their first names, but rather on overindulgence and the body's physical response to such a process. In other words, we no longer care about Marcello the pilot or Michel the television personality but are instead attuned to mass eating-turned-excretion, a process which reduces human consciousness and lethally attacks the body. Thus, despite its overwhelming presence in every shot, Ferreri's film is not about food but, instead, the inversion of *sublimation*: a violent return from the affluent society back to the world of animalia. All sociocultural elements that once positioned the men as elites – in particular, their power to purchase and enjoy rich foods such as paté, pastry, and expensive game meats – are the very tools that Ferreri employs to kill his protagonists, turning them from distinguished men to their most basic roles as eaters and defecators, no different from the animal carcasses they once consumed.

Artists and psychoanalysts alike consider sublimation as a glue that binds the dichotomy of private perversions and public endeavours, safeguarding artists – among others – from becoming emotionally unbound, encouraging them to convert personal, internalized energies into externalized objects.[49] In his definition of sublimation, Volney P. Gay refers to the powerful example of alchemy, or the science through which the chemical and physical composition of ordinary metals becomes that of gold: the suppression and conversion of the intrinsic qualities of, for example, lead, into something far more precious and powerful.[50] In this vein, let us reconsider the protagonists of *La grande abbuffata* through this transformational, sublime lens – in particular, how the taboos of pornography and masturbation, generally consumed and performed alone, are converted into moments of high culture. In an early scene in Ferreri's film, the men suppress the natural inclination to play with the phallus for orgasmic pleasure and, instead, critique pornography as a vintage aesthetic. Watching porn has been elevated into a group discussion among men dressed in blazers and enjoying aphrodisiac oysters. The base carnality of masturbation is converted into an Enlightenment-style salon, as the phallus is tucked away, porn is bypassed as "taboo," and the lighting of the pornographic slides and the oysters sliding down the men's throats are meanwhile signs of cultural repute. Casting aside the desire to stroke the phallus, and even the anality of masturbating among other men, the men achieve a sublime atmosphere.

Being early on, this scene illustrates a starting point of distinction: the high amount of symbolic capital that Ferreri subtracts over the course of the film as he reverses the process of sublimation, restoring the "base carnality" within his protagonists. Men embedded within such cultural super-structures, humans swathed in so much symbolism that it blocks and represses their "freedom," must undergo the same disembowelment as the routines and industrialized products that, too, no longer make sense. In order to see the men for what they truly are – to view humans "as is," in their most natural state – they must be stripped of the symbols of the sublime. Thus, the oysters and the pornographic slides – the markers of affluence and of cultural institutions with which the men interact, thereby suppressing the body's natural inclinations – comprise some of the tokens of Ferreri's "game" of eradication, of *annientamento*. The question is not who among the men will eat the most or live the longest, but, instead, who will survive the raid of symbols?[51] Ferreri keeps score, marking the loss of symbols and underscoring the men's transition from artificially sublime to naturally primordial beings, through one of the foremost societal taboos: uncontrolled excrement.

The Consumption and Excretion of Symbols: The End of the World?

This section addresses a series of conflations present in the final half-hour of the film, brought together in the same frame: the disturbing closeness between consumption and excretion; the increasing ambiguity about what – or who – may be categorized and recognized as food; and death and rebirth. In turn, as much as the latter scenes of the film exhibit death and destruction, my reading is instead centred on creation, reincarnation – Andréa's culinary transformation from woman into dessert – and rebirth.

With only twenty-seven minutes remaining in the film, Marcello is the only one of the four who has died, having frozen to death outside in the Bugatti. His corpse is stowed in the kitchen closet, positioned behind its glass door like a phantom in the viewers' gaze during the scene's long shots: ominous foreshadowing of what will soon happen to the other three men. The kitchen is, thus, a space at once of joy and of death: the site where Ugo creates rich culinary masterpieces which the consumer decimates, only for his insides to wreak destructive havoc. Two creations – or, rather, fusions – are thus underway. We see Ugo tending to a pot on the stove. Despite the canisters of herbs and spices on the counter, and the egg he drops into the pot, it is not revealed exactly what he is preparing; this shot emphasizes the irrelevance of food itself, as the film underlines instead the systems and physical relationships that govern the process of human digestion. The egg soon becomes a double-entendre, as Andréa fondles Ugo's groin while he examines and pricks the egg with spices; likewise, a man penetrating an egg may also be read as the moment of fertilization, foreshadowing the "rebirth" that culminates in the closing shots of the film. When Andréa asks, "Can I taste it?", it is not clear whether she is referring to the dish or Ugo himself – as if the egg and Ugo's body are one. In the same scene, Ugo gets the idea to create the *tarte Andréa*, fusing her body with food as well, as he literally hoists her bare bottom onto a sheet of pastry dough, kneading her butt-cheeks and the dough in the same motions; as she squeals with glee, Andréa's white rear-end of cellulite becomes one with the doughy pile of flour and yeast.

Meanwhile, juxtaposed with the creation of *la tarte*, Ferreri cuts to Philippe's bedroom, where he and Michel exhibit symptoms of extreme indigestion: malaise, exhaustion, and confusion, their human composure waning as Philippe mistakenly greets Michel as Marcello, and Michel hoots in response like an animal. The four eventually gather in a room to admire the now-complete *tarte Andréa* – in the shape of Andréa's rear, as emphasized by Ugo's hand gestures, and adorned with green grapes and red fruits. When Andréa asks Michel if he would like some, again, it is unclear whether she is asking him to consume the cake or her body; nevertheless, he declines her offer, choosing instead to play the piano: a final sign of his dwindling refinement. The music, however, is overshadowed by his flatulence. Whereas Philippe, with his mouth full of the tart, exclaims, "We've gotten used to it!", Michel's farts are the prelude to his death by diarrhea. Ferreri zooms in on Michel's face – eyes scrunched, beads of sweat along his forehead, and mouth in its own flatulent formation of a Bronx jeer – as he struggles to play classical music against bodily emergency. Wordlessly, Michel gravitates outside to the balcony, where he nearly tips off the ledge. Retrieved by Philippe and Ugo, Michel slides to the ground, dying atop a pool

Figure 5.5. The final shot of Michel in *La grande abbuffata*: much different from when he was reciting *Hamlet*.

of his own diarrhea. What emerges from the anus looks no different from the hot chocolate Philippe was slurping just seconds earlier – only adding to Ferreri's conflations.

In this scene, Ferreri takes the process of symbolic disembowelment almost literally, documenting the men's bowel movements even more attentively than their consumption. The rationale behind this choice is two-pronged. First, whereas the gastronomic seminar was meticulously organized and prepared, excretion – especially when illustrated as wet flatulence and explosive diarrhea – is the antithesis of control. Excretion is a physical act that likens humans to animals, and no work of art or intellectual discussion can prevent the body's conversion of food into waste; figments of the men's bourgeois culture are no shield against natural processes.[52] Excess consumption will, likewise, make for excess waste. It is only natural for viewers to follow the digestive process, no matter how extreme, in its entirety; considering that this is Ferreri's way for humans to return to their most natural state, free of cultured repressions, viewers should see the whole digestive journey through. Echoing the affirmations of Pasolini scholar Sam Rohdie, the sublime is not to be found in vintage slides or museum relics, but in feces.[53]

Shit, as Ferreri advocates, is the vehicle by which humans can shake the markers of their distinction and return to existing on the same plane as the animals they eat and among which they live.

Secondly, defecation is a means of showing the cracks in a world of long-unquestioned routines, of revealing the quirks of the human body that once seamlessly demarcated one's inner psyche and outside surroundings. In line with psychoanalytic readings, the object of feces is itself a product of numerous dimensions. It is at once abject waste and a new development, to which its creator assigns a variety of significations: Feces is an individualized product, formed by the digestive processes occurring in one's own stomach and intestines; it is an object that requires the parent's attention and disposal, and is thus an object connecting baby to mother; and, as illustrated in *La grande abbuffata*, it is a weapon.[54] Except for the butchering of animal carcasses, there are no gaping wounds or blood in this film, nor are there any outward signs of foul play in the men's deaths; the violence inflicted upon the four bodies emerges, instead, from within, as it is manifest through feces. Amid the frenzied stockpiling of goods, feces, which the self creates by ejection, is a new object through which to consider the decadence, the literal waste, of the world; the feces, then, catalyses the process from passive automation to active nihilism, upon our realizing that the world has lost its sense.

Defecation is the ultimate acknowledgment of, and way of bursting through, the world's numerous cracks. Thus, the body turns on itself as a final, albeit failed, attempt to make sense of the self – as if the expulsion of feces equalled the expulsion of life, or our sense of it, from the body.[55] Yet, diarrhea – among other social taboos that exhibit humans' physicality – is the means of not only contemplating one's physical existence but also of liberating oneself, of breaking free, from the cultural institutions and historical moments that have long repressed humans.[56] Thus, in being stripped of the symbols that both define humans and suppress their natural instincts – in other words, expelling an index of moral concerns and acknowledging that the world has turned to shit – humans are demystified and cleansed, and the world as *tabula rasa* may, perhaps, begin to start anew. This notion of starting anew is the foremost commonality between Ferreri's work and 1940s neorealism. The end of the world appears barren and bleak, but these are precisely the grounds upon which the survivors – of the war, of the feast – rebuild and reinstil sense into new beginnings. Andréa, the survivor of *La grande abbuffata*, embodies precisely such newness.

The Reawakening at the End of the World

Andréa and the Survivors of Neorealism

Women are, at least initially, the glaringly missing component from the feast; promiscuous Marcello threatens to leave because of his overwhelming desire to fornicate. The men invite three whores to the feast, all of whom are too crass for and too bored by the formalities of the gastronomic seminar. Because of their socioeconomic status, but also as a means of foreshadowing what will ultimately happen to the men, the three women cannot access the "rich" arena of the seminar and therefore behave in sloppy, unrefined ways: One of the whores spits her gum out right on Ugo's cake, and then cuts that cake not with a knife, but a karate chop, proceeding to feed Ugo the slice by hand. Lacking the decorum and, thus, the symbolic capital to participate meaningfully in the weekend, these three women grow bored and leave. However, enter Andréa, who partakes fully in the feast. For her survival, she is key in connecting this film to neorealist tenets.

In neorealism, the precarious boundaries of life and death are frequently tested. In films by Roberto Rossellini, children are those who both survive and, provoked by the war and harmful personal relationships, are driven to suicide. In *Roma città aperta* (1944), in a powerful closing scene, the children – having witnessed the execution of Don Pietro, the neighbourhood priest – walk together towards the horizon, backs to the camera but eyes on St. Peter's Basilica. Likewise, in Vittorio De Sica's *Umberto D.* (1952), the old pensioner Umberto, facing eviction from his apartment and with nowhere else to turn, nearly commits suicide, hesitating on the tramway, but he ultimately decides against it; the closing shot is of Umberto with his dog, Flike, frolicking towards the horizon. While the closing shot of *La grande abbuffata* is aesthetically different, Andréa stands in as a Ferrerian horizon: She persists amid the suicides by consumption, nevertheless venturing forth into unknown territory.

In continuing to exist despite a senseless world, Andréa must be defined: She must be assigned meaning within Ferreri's arena of increasing meaninglessness. The definition of Andréa – the lone female protagonist of the film, and the only one to survive the consumerist ennui – through a neorealist lens would necessitate a recollection of Fascist gender codifications. In neorealism, viewers were presented with a binary of female characters, *donna madre* versus *donna crisi*, thereby reflecting heavily on the Fascists' treatments of women. *Donne madri*, or "mother-women," were an archetype defined solely by societal expectations of motherhood: round, soft, fecund, and devoted to both their growing families and the Fascist cause. *Donne crisi*, or "crisis women," meanwhile relished the diversions of the expanding consumer society of the 1920s and 1930s: smoking cigarettes, going to the movies, reading photo-romances – in other words, enjoying personal pastimes instead of assuming family responsibilities. Constructed and promoted by the Fascists, these archetypes attempted to define femininity in Italy after the First World War: celebrating women (and manifestations thereof) who fulfilled the expectations of their husbands, *patria*, and God, meanwhile villainizing those who rejected motherhood in favour of self-centred, capitalist pleasures.[57]

In neorealist cinema, viewers see both archetypes at play. On one hand, Pina (Anna Magnani), the fallen Resistance heroine of *Roma città aperta*, oversees the looting of a neighbourhood bakery, scrambling for even the tiniest morsels to feed her son and unborn child; later, in pursuit of her fiancé, she is brutally gunned down by Nazis in the street. Likewise, in De Sica's *Ladri di biciclette* (1948), it is Maria who secures her husband's employment and her family's well-being, pawning their matrimonial sheets to finance his bicycle. On the other hand, Marina of *Roma città aperta*, who easily reveals Manfredi's secrets to Ingrid, a Nazi, in exchange for drugs, starkly contrasts with Pina. However, fifty years removed from the Fascist regime, thirty years distanced from neorealist representations, and with Italy's gender norms in flux by the 1970s, where would Andréa fit within such a dichotomy? In *La grande abbuffata*, Ferreri does not perpetuate the archetypes of women in neorealism and, by extension, in Fascism. Instead, Andréa is a teacher who works at the school adjacent to the villa, tasked with educating and ensuring the well-being of young children, and yet she relishes all elements of the feast: the overwhelming mountains of food, the all-male group of diners, and the repeated sexualization of her body as they treat her as yet another object for their consumption. What connects Andréa most profoundly to neorealism, then, is her survival: her inheritance of the end of the world, and her existence in a world of new beginnings. With the closing shot of the film, Andréa, alone but alive amid the greyness of the villa, *is*.

Andréa first encounters the four men when she brings her class into the villa's courtyard for a field trip. Their visit to the villa adds to the collegiate atmosphere that the men seek to attain with their gastronomic seminar, where, even if only momentarily, they may impart some wisdom on the connections between food and society to a younger generation. Exhibited in different shots, some students view and discuss the linden tree of M. Boileau, a French poet of the Enlightenment period; others join Michel at the pond to catch fish, to gain the understanding of the food chain that "mean" humans kill and eat the fish, thereby concretizing the hierarchical distance between mankind and animals; a small handful of children gather in the garage to listen to Marcello's lecture on Bugatti; and, in the kitchen, more than a dozen children sit around the table and enjoy some stuffing that Ugo has prepared, along with a platter of brioche buns and fruit for the taking from an overflowing basket. Though this is the only time children are present in the film, in these brief scenes, they strongly resemble the children of neorealism thirty years earlier in that they, too, bear witness to a world of doom and impending destruction. In the 1970s, the destruction is not that of world war but of material wealth, which we see through this hyper-bourgeois education that the men impart to the children. While there is no scene analogous to the closing shots of *Roma città aperta* – where a group of children, having just witnessed the execution of Don Pietro, marches forth toward the horizon – the notions of survival and of optimism conclude *La grande abbuffata* as well. These neorealist essences are embodied most strongly by the children's teacher, Andréa.

Throughout the field trip, Andréa is refined, demonstrating restraint around the feast, viewing the class's day at the villa as little more than an educational experience; cup in hand, she waves away Ugo's steaming skillet of kidneys *à la bordelaise,* stating, "It smells very good, but I'm drinking hot chocolate." But then the food hits her tongue, the catalyst sparking great change in Andréa's behaviour, as if the rich flavours transcended the stuffy professionalism of the seminar, provoking a sensuality that neither poems, nor fishing, nor cars could achieve. In a close-up, the viewer notes Andréa's slowly blinking eyes and the orgiastic moans emerging from her throat; she is immediately hypnotized, even erotically charged, by the gastronomy of the seminar. Through strategic editing, the viewer is unsure how much time has lapsed, or how much other food she has consumed since the close-up shot, for in the following frame, Andréa is now seated in a different room, away from the children (though we still hear their chatter in the background). With her mug of hot chocolate nowhere in view, Andréa's hands now hold a plate of yellow, flambéed, indistinguishable food. She then puts the plate down and begins to dance, twirling and humming, hardly resisting Ugo's invitation to join them for "a party" that night. The convivial, joyous connotations of a party starkly contrast with the morbidity and cruel intentions behind the seminar, and Andréa's blithe, happy-go-lucky comportment – versus the men's fatigue and malaise – hints at their differing fates: She will join the men in eating and fondling, but she will survive. The food has overtaken Andréa, but for her, food is not grotesque or murderous; instead, food is an innocent aphrodisiac. She is not involved in a suicide mission, but, rather, in an orgy; she shares the men's desire to consume large quantities of delicious foods and flesh, and allows herself to be desired and consumed in the process. She both eats and is *la carne* – blurring the likeness between humans and animals, particularly when markers of Culture have been removed.

Scholars are divided in their assessment of Andréa: Is she a harmful presence? What is her role in the men's deaths and the end of the world at large? On one hand, because Andréa survives and demonstrates a cheery naïveté around the men's suicides, complaining of hunger despite seeing them die at the hands of food, there is condemnation: She is an "angel of death," an accomplice as lethally provocative as the food.[58] Indeed, being a teacher by profession, this may be yet another seminar – like those conducted at school – whose proceedings she facilitates.

Other scholars, meanwhile, refer to Andréa's maternity: her ability to give birth, unique among the predominately male cast. It is jarring, then, to juxtapose her with grotesque eating and death; this maternity is similar to the typically life-sustaining and nurturing qualities of food, which Ferreri inverts. This sort of character juxtaposition is present throughout Ferreri's oeuvre. Dora of *Il seme dell'uomo* refuses pregnancy, because the idea of welcoming a child into the apocalypse terrifies her, and it is only when Cino drugs and rapes her that she is with child. Later, in *La carne* (1991), Ferreri defines Francesca, his female protagonist, by three aspects: her relationship with a spiritual guru, her profession as a prostitute, and her decision to have an abortion – all of which exoticize her and frame her as deviant and otherworldly. While there is no mention of pregnancy or babies or abortion in *La grande abbuffata*, Andréa is positioned among these women who reject motherhood on a more clinical basis, as she helps to destroy life, not create it.

Yet, despite the death and malaise surrounding Andréa, she continues to care for those around her, offering food and respite in times of uncertainty and danger. Although Andréa has no children of her own, her students and the four men are like surrogate children whom she is charged with nurturing.[59] As a surrogate mother, Andréa represents a point of origin and of return: that from which men depart at their birth and to which they return after contending with life's challenges – in this case, automated, senseless eating. In the final scene, Andréa and Philippe are the only two remaining diners. Philippe is sitting outside on a bench, where Andréa greets him with a "sweet and good" dish in the shape of breasts: two pink mounds topped with olive-green "nipples." Philippe eats, and shortly thereafter, he collapses, dying in Andréa's arms, his final resting place being her breasts. The camera

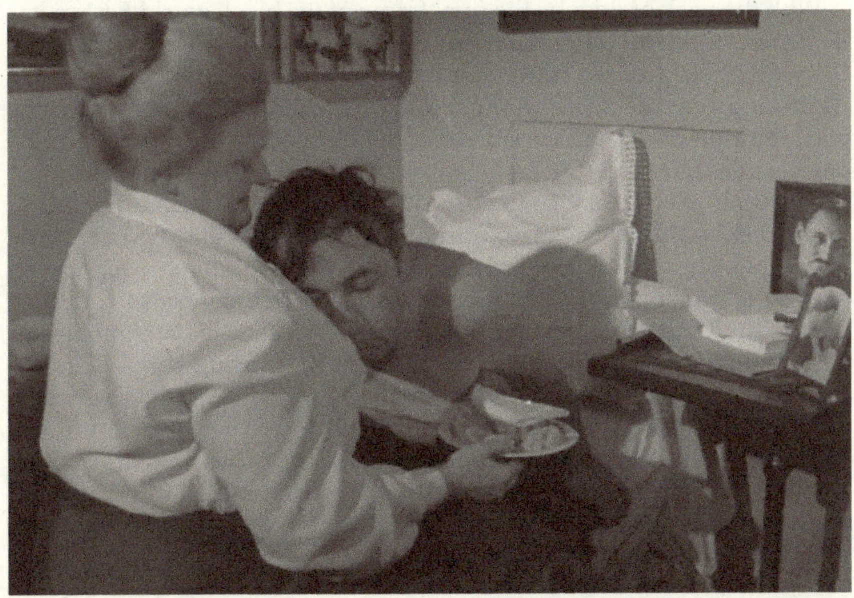

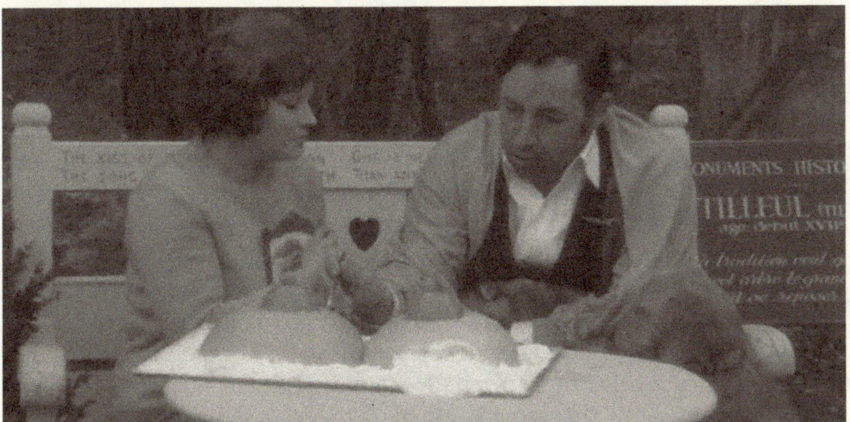

Figure 5.6. Philippe's trajectory in *La grande abbuffata*, from breast to breast.

zooms out as Andréa casts his body aside and rises up, retreating inside the house; the credits roll as a pack of dogs roams the yard, howling and feasting on the newest truckload of meat.

With the pack of dogs as the final frame of the bleak world Ferreri has designed, and with all the humans either dead or out of view, certainly the world that Andréa has assumed is one overwhelmed by humans' death and now decidedly animals' domain. Philippe's last bites, the consumption of the pink mounds at the moment of his death, are the closing of a circle, the conclusion of one life cycle. Indeed, Philippe's last time on camera mirrors his first: At the beginning of the film, Philippe's housekeeper and former wet nurse wakes him up, and he rises from his pillow, only to fall forward onto her breasts. Philippe's progression across the film, then, is from one surrogate mother's breasts to another, coupled with the consumption of surrogate breasts: his wet nurse's as a baby, and the pink mounds presented in the closing shots. This circularity hints at the notion of the return to birth, or rebirth. The end of the world appears grey, empty, and rife with savage intentions – but all the while, the world is opening up to the "new": to new life, to new sense. Andréa is the vehicle for continuity, surviving all four men and the destruction left in their wake, thus bridging the worlds before and after the big feast.

The Neorealist Reawakening of the Affluent Society

Philippe's death is the end of sense: The moment in which the men's ability to make sense of the world, in terms of both taste and conscious thought, is over. By contrast, Andréa's survival represents the continued existence of the world, its intactness, despite destructive forces of change. Ferreri's exposure of the world's end and the acknowledgment of its continuity – in other words, the coexistence of death and rebirth in the same time-space – is precisely the essence of neorealism. Neorealist scholarship is rich with the diction of "springtime": of an awakening, of resurrection, following the privations and struggles of a long, harsh winter. The horrors of the war, and, thus, the metaphor of winter, come to a close, and what ensues is a youthful energy, a feverish urge to communicate all that happened, even an Edenic virginity restored to the world – as if the world returned to its first week of existence. The neorealist movement wields a utopian purity, where the filmmaker may be read, indeed, as God; in his *Neorealismo, ecc.* (1979), Zavattini bestows divine qualities on the creators of the filmic postwar world, conjuring animals and objects into existence: "It was the least contaminated and promising moment in cinema. Reality, buried under myths, was slowly blooming. Cinema was beginning its creation of the world: Here's a tree, here's an old man, here's a house, a man who's eating, a man who's sleeping, a man who's crying."[60] Characters of neorealist film, navigating the prospects and obstacles presented by this new world, seek to fulfil fundamental objectives: procuring food, securing employment, keeping a roof over one's head. Similarly, the world that Ferreri bequeaths to Andréa at the end of *La grande abbuffata* is one surrounded by death but also the promise of new beginnings. Immediately following Philippe's death, Andréa – perhaps reminding the viewer of a phoenix from the ashes – rises from the bench and walks away from his corpse. Where Andréa goes next is uncertain, because the closing credits obstruct her movement, but her kinesthesis is, nevertheless, evidence of continued existence in the world.

Andréa, thus, occupies a space where, echoing Zavattini, the minutes and days and the affluent society of 1973 no longer matter; Andréa just is. Citing the works of Zavattini and André Bazin, Daniele Rugo notes:

> … The world must survive the force of change exercised on it by the film. At the end of the film, there must still be a world out there, which the former cannot totally encompass, overwhelm, or exhaust … As C. Zavattini invoked, cinema "should never look back … it should look at life not from the point of view of the plot, *but from that of existence*" (1952: 14). Bazin's argument could therefore be translated as follows: "*the world is, quite simply*, even after it has been condemned."[61]

Andréa is a surviving emblem of the world from which the men have eliminated themselves. As a woman who "is, quite simply," she demonstrates a fertile ground upon which to start anew: a world of "revolutionary promise" where, as Rugo underscores, "everything becomes possible, but nothing is possible yet."[62] This commentary celebrates the fertility – even divine miraculousness – of neorealism, in that the movement represents the blossoming of new life and significations.

The four suicides of *La grande abbuffata* suggest a return to a zeropoint origin: a time before life, before thought, and, as Nancy would posit, before sense, thus marking the end (or rather, in line with my neorealist reading of the film, a new beginning) of the world. Yet, through Andréa's survival, the world persists; the viewer recognizes Andréa and the visible objects that comprise Ferreri's *mise en scène*: the villa, the dogs, and the food they devour. Likewise, Andréa will continue to assign meaning not only to the objects surrounding her, but also to the history informing her lived experiences. So long as humans seek to make sense of the world in which they live, assigning significations to the objects and creatures among which they exist, the world can never simply "be." And, over time, the wealth of symbols builds up once more, confounding the sense of self and reducing the sensory connections once felt so viscerally with objects, in particular with food. Like Paolo in Pasolini's *Teorema* (1968), naked and roaming the desert, we remain in search of that purity, of an authentic self perhaps never to be fully recognized. Uncertainty abounds, as the question thus repeats: What is the point – the point of roaming the desert, the point of functioning on "auto-pilot," the point of living? This vicious cycle persists into parts unknown.

Conclusion

Throughout Italy's postwar reconstruction, actors and directors of the Italian film industry grappled with the notion of continuity. In particular, this book explored continuities by way of food, or lack thereof, as presented in film. Through the work of Totò and Sophia Loren, viewers remembered not only hunger but also the feelings of imaginative creativity and conviviality that placated the absence of food. The wholesomeness discussed in the first half of the book was tested against the onslaught of changes impacting Italy during the Economic Miracle. In the 1950s, Italy encountered material abundance for the first time, and thus, physical hunger was converted into desire of a deeper kind. The food tropes in the latter half of the book, decidedly more violent than those in earlier chapters, indicated a hungering for what was. As food grew to excess, and as these instances of consumption became increasingly grotesque, there was the desire to circle back to a time before sociopolitical and geographic stratifications, capitalist exploitation, and the bourgeoisification of language. By 1973, the men of *La grande abbuffata* navigated unrecognizable territory, ultimately choosing death over a life that made no sense; these protagonists chose not to continue at all. This book, thus, discussed the digestion of food and, by extension, the changes and continuations informing that very filmic foodscape.

The first two chapters demonstrated a continuity between the past and the tumult of the postwar period. Chapters 1 and 2 both discussed the utilization of the body to portray moments of starvation and satiation. These chapters depicted a transition in gastronomy between the hunger pangs of the *dopoguerra* and the new products and practices of the West – and, as demonstrated through these two Neapolitan stars, the unrecognizable ways of the Italian North. In Chapter 1, Antonio de Curtis's *maschera* of Totò forged a connection between not only material deprivation and the "exotic," luxurious foods of the affluent North but also between Europe's comic traditions of old and new. There is comic relief for viewers in Totò's physicality, his exaggerated facial expressions and gesticulations, his journeys away from hunger – even on a polar expedition to the faraway land of Milan – and his insistence on eating foods that reminded him, and the viewer, of home: stuffing his pockets with spaghetti, hanging salami along clotheslines across his hotel room, but also, when his budget allowed, dining at a restaurant and ordering bottles of champagne and "otherworldly" dishes like turtle soup. This series of food tropes illustrated the continuance of consumption habits but also the effects of increased spending power, where one's traditional diet opened up to new dining experiences and delicacies.

Chapter 2, meanwhile, analysed the corpus of Sophia Loren. This chapter discussed her body of work, from films to cookbooks and beauty manuals, as well as her body as an object for consumption. Loren interacted with a wide array of food, and these tropes – the usage of pizza, fruit, and milk – define her as a Southerner, sultry seductress and, in time, mother. The viewer, in turn, engaged with Loren's body, portrayed as supple and enticing as sticky pizza dough and bright red cherries. Through these very interactions, Loren secured her stardom. She was inscribed within a nexus of Italy's cultural networks and phenomena, as represented by the 1960s spectator: the urban poor; the Left; increasingly ubiquitous Americana and the Hollywoodization of Italy's film industry; and the Catholic heteropatriarchy, which issued its seal of approval only when Loren gave birth in 1968. Although Loren's stardom goes unquestioned today, her acceptance among these circles reflects waves of societal changes and, initially, the friction against such moments, and shows how Loren successfully negotiated sociopolitical tensions with an element of the past: foods as iconic and recognizable as, ultimately, herself. In employing these foods, Loren, like Totò, acted as a bridge between past and present; she managed to compromise her massive sex appeal and liberal behaviour (at least for the 1950s and 1960s) with Italy's longstanding food traditions, which celebrate and perpetuate the values of motherhood and family life, as well as the expectation that women, as food providers *par excellence*, should be the signposts of the home-space.

And yet, the work of Antonio Pietrangeli and Pier Paolo Pasolini *subverts* that very notion. Two sets of women, linked by their former tenure but continued registration as prostitutes, seek to exit their sex work, *wanting* to provide food for others: Adua and her friends, in a restaurant setting; Mamma Roma, selling vegetables from her own cart. These women faced the limitations set by the patriarchy *outside* the home. Language, and misconstructions thereof, inscribed them as prostitutes in the city's orders of operation, thereby severing their ties to traditional domesticity, compelling them to face a lifelong containment of a new, life-threatening kind. This precarity set the stage for my final chapters.

Chapters 4 and 5 were set in a more violent period, given the oncoming waves of political protests, culminating in the Years of Lead and the rise of the affluent society: premises for rupture and fatalistic endings. Material hunger was no longer the major concern, but instead, nearing the other end of the spectrum, gone was the tradition of *conviviality*, of eating and coexisting in a lively, friendly way. In these films, one does not eat to live; one dies eating. Because the ties to a harmonious and convivial past appeared severed, in the works of Pasolini and Marco Ferreri, food was a weapon: a means of exhibiting dominance over weaker, powerless entities – of annihilating one's prey – as well as a way of killing the Self.

A segue from *Mamma Roma* (1962), Chapter 4 continued Pasolini's commentaries on language, in which food and predatory eating remained metaphors for exploitation. Through his early films, he alluded to religious lore as a way of conveying the immoralities of exploiting fellow human beings. In so doing, in his condemnation of the capitalist bourgeoisie, Pasolini's work prioritized the visual over the verbal, as he explored the irrationality of cinematic images and, ultimately, rejected the linguistic codes reserved for the upper classes. Whereas the Passion of Christ is one of the holiest moments in Christianity, in *La ricotta* (1963), Pasolini's short film depicting the Last Supper and the crucifixion of Jesus Christ, he killed his *sottoproletario* protagonist through the manipulation of frame rates: a statement affirming that time is money, and also that the (film) industry is exploitative, denying workers even the fundamental right to eat. So as to conform to the demands of his director and foremost cast members, and having consumed cheese at Pasolini's inhuman speed, Stracci was unable to deliver his lines as the Good Thief because he died of indigestion. Stracci was killed by food but also by the regulations of cinema. Three years later, in *Uccellacci e uccellini*, birds were eaten – by bigger birds and humans alike – because preexisting codes of communication no longer functioned. Animals do not follow the rationality of verbal language; they express themselves through hops, chirps, and adherence to the food chain: Big, carnivorous animals eat smaller, weaker creatures. As a result, despite the valiant attempts of Franciscan monks – played by Ninetto Davoli and Totò, who, indeed, was no longer portrayed as the wholesome figure of the past decade – to unite hawks and sparrows by preaching the compassion of God, the hawks ate the sparrows. Likewise, the Marxist ideology of the crow died with Palmiro Togliatti, and thus, unable to connect with the bird's cryptic, hyper-intellectual commentary, Totò and Ninetto savagely devoured him. In these two Pasolini films, eating was a means of destruction, but also of revolution.

In this regard, despite these ruptures, a sense of optimism was to be found in circles and cycles. The circle is a shape that promotes unity, wholesomeness, and perfection. Cycles, often drawn in circular formation, insist on perpetuation – in this case, the resumption of a world destroyed by conflicts, world war, and the signs that comprise the world itself. This explains Pasolini's intense focus on the moon/Luna throughout *Uccellacci e uccellini*; the cycles of the moon dictate changing tides, and the ebb and flow of sociopolitical forces were precisely the premise of Pasolini's film. As Domenico Modugno chants at the end of the film, "Amici cari, / come sempre, / finisce così, comincia così, si chiude così, continua così!" Togliatti might have died in 1966, but the world did not come to an end; the natural rhythms of the world continued on. Likewise, Emilia in Pasolini's *Teorema* (1968) also reminded the viewer that, out of trauma, one's tears could be a source of renewal.

The circularity of *Uccellacci e uccellini*, as well as Emilia's objective of regeneration, offered a segue into Marco Ferreri's oeuvre – chiefly, *La grande abbuffata* (1973), the case study of my final chapter. Ferreri's work was analysed in part through the lens of traditional neorealism to indicate a strategy of returning to a world that simply "is." Ferreri cast major stars, only to strip away all markers of their symbolic capital. His frames were overwhelmed by mountains of food, contrasting the stark deprivations of the *dopoguerra*, only for his protagonists to kill themselves with such excess. However, Andréa's survival, juxtaposed with the four suicides, underscored the motif of rebirth present throughout neorealist films. Amid death and destruction, the viewer diverted her attention instead to new life existing in a world rich with possibilities: a clean slate, where the great potentials of the world begin again.

Since this is a project of continuities, readers might ask: Why does the book stop precisely at a moment of rebirth, of new beginnings, as the world persists with Andréa's survival? What happens to Italy's foodscape, both inside and out of the theatre, after *La grande abbuffata*? Historically and cinematically, 1973 is the end of an era. Inflation, reduced productivity, and the global energy crisis marked the end of an economic upswing.[1] In addition, scandals and corruption undermined the public's confidence in the government. To that end, the gross quantity and the richness of food, reminiscent of that exhibited in *La grande abbuffata*, were viewed as signs of success – that Italy had "arrived" economically – but they also symbolized the corruption and greed of the 1970s and 1980s. Travelogues of the Sicilian Mafia (also known as Cosa Nostra) detailed how certain foods were associated with the big deals made between *mafiosi*, businessmen, and politicians. Historian Carol Helstosky describes a 1979 banquet hosted by Nino Salvo, an intermediary between the Christian Democrats and Cosa Nostra: "One eyewitness account ... provided a partial list of food for special guest Giulio Andreotti and others: canapes of caviar and smoked salmon, Russian salad, *pasticcio*, lobsters, jumbo shrimp, suckling pig, wild boar, pheasant, veal, grilled fish, ricotta and whipped cream cakes, *profiteroles*, fresh fruit, and wine from Salvo's estates."[2] This extensive list might remind the reader of Totò and Peppino's evening at the Gran Milan restaurant, in which they spent hundreds of thousands of lire on turtle soup and champagne. Though depicted as luxurious, otherworldly delicacies in 1956, twenty-five years later, these foods were recognized as the standard fare for celebrating wealth and success – but they also represented the dark, violent measures taken to get to that point. Yet, in response to such excess, there was once again the turn back to simplicity: to healthier, more abstemious eating habits. Helstosky even recuperates the word "austere," a buzzword of Italy's gastronomic and Fascist pasts, to describe the diets of contemporary leaders like Umberto Bossi and the late Silvio Berlusconi.[3] A circling back to simpler times, to simpler eating, is presented anew.

The 1970s were a bleak period for Italian cinema, too. Italy's top directors began to die: Vittorio De Sica and Pietro Germi in 1974; Pasolini in 1975; Luchino Visconti in 1976; and Roberto Rossellini in 1977. Michelangelo Antonioni and Federico Fellini, meanwhile, seemed to be past the peak of their creativity.[4] Film scholars of the time placed little hope in the newer generations of directors,[5] citing, among other reasons, their inclination to work in television, a decidedly more stable industry than domestic film production. Indeed, in 1968, 294 films were produced in Italy, but in 1978, this dropped to a low of only 98 films, while American imports remained high (201).[6] Pasolini's lamentations of Chapter 4, in which hard intellectual endeavours were abandoned in favour of escapist entertainment, were increasingly valid.

In addition, as this book focused heavily on comedic stars, by the mid-1970s, these great actors were also at an impasse. Totò died in 1967; Loren acted in fewer films, prioritizing quality time with her two sons; and as for the comic performances of stars Marcello Mastroianni, Vittorio Gassman, Ugo Tognazzi, and Nino Manfredi, they functioned in a world that was no longer funny or "rosy." At the premiere of Ettore Scola's *C'eravamo tanto amati* (1974), starring Gassman and Manfredi, women described them as "has-beens, washed-out shadows of their former greatness: 'It's not true that men grow old more gracefully than women,' one remarks; another makes the even more damning comment, echoing the theme of *We All Loved Each Other So Much*, 'if only you could have seen them during the Resistance ...'"[7] Whereas this book began with the notion of laughter as a kind of collective therapy – not only alleviating, but remembering, the hunger pangs of the recent past – by the 1970s, comedy seemed to have lost that therapeutic force.

This is not to say, however, that food tropes in Italian cinema simply end with Marco Ferreri. Numerous films recuperate issues and themes described throughout this book. For example, in 1974, the year after *La grande abbuffata* was released, Franco Brusati's *Pane e cioccolata* revisits the North-South stratifications depicted in *Totò, Peppino e ... la malafemmina* (1956), as viewers follow a displaced Southerner even farther north than Milan – to Switzerland. The opening shots of the film immediately remind us of Totò's behaviour and tastes, which ran counter to "refined" Milan: The protagonist, Nino (Manfredi), enjoys lunch in a park, but the obnoxiously loud crunch of his bread interrupts the diegetic classical music of a nearby orchestra; his tastes are too crass for the tranquillity of the park, and this sets the tone for the rest of the film: Nino does not belong.

Suicide by food is also a gesture repeated in Italy's filmic foodscape. Fast-forwarding to Ferzan Özpetek's *Mine vaganti* (2010), *la nonna* reflects silently on her own lost love within Özpetek's narrative on homosexuality, family values, and southern Catholic traditions and norms. Instead of openly acknowledging her extramarital feelings, *la nonna* retires to her bedroom; on the table are piles of chocolates and sweet treats. As she is diabetic, the sugar is forbidden – just like her love. Allowing herself a pleasure that is socially, but not physiologically, acceptable, *la nonna* chooses death by sweets over the misery of living under the exclusive norms of romance.

Even more recently, Guido Barilla, CEO of Barilla, was under fire for comments he made in September 2013 against the LGBTQ+ community, stating that he "would never do an advert with a homosexual family."[8] In turn, Italian LGBTQ+ groups called for a boycott of his company, which comprises over twenty brands. In an unexpected change of events, in October 2019, Barilla partnered with clothing brand GCDS to release a commercial in which women – white, cis women; women of colour; and transgender women – were invited to a *spaghettata*. Shot in colours and exhibiting fashions that transport the viewer to the 1960s, the commercial includes close-ups of men's and women's feet upon a sidewalk, loafers and high heels alike. There is a woman, her eyes hiding behind sunglasses, who rides the subway unaccompanied; the neighbouring passenger, an older man reading the newspaper, breaks the fourth wall and exclaims to the camera, "Dinner's ready!" Next, a trans woman takes a telephone call while under a hairdryer. Later, two bespectacled women of colour are driving in a top-down convertible, listening to the

Figure C.1. "E' pronto!" Sophia Loren (centre) exclaims to a wide spectrum of dinner guests. From Nadia Lee Cohen's "Dinner's Ready," https://www.youtube.com/watch?v=0fdHLN6G9Hc.

sounds of "Radio Barilla." The medley of shoes, the sunglasses, the trans woman's masculine-sounding voice, and the older man's exclamation that dinner is ready (versus, traditionally, a woman stating this) – these are all instances of gender ambiguities which subvert heteronormative expectations of femininity and of food preparation. These women are not hidden in the kitchen, slaving away over a hot stove, but instead en route to a dinner party to which they were invited. The beginning of the commercial is, thus, hardly continuous with Barilla's vision of a "classic family where the woman plays a fundamental role" – that is, until, the host of the party is revealed: Who is more appropriate than Sophia Loren, then eighty-five years old, to lay down the vat of pasta for these women, announcing with a smile, "E' pronto!" The casting of Loren indicates her continued centrality within changing social arenas; she continues to invite women to "eat with her." At the same time, though this appears to be Barilla's apology, showcasing a family of a different kind, their "classic" vision is upheld by way of Loren, a woman who still plays that "fundamental role" of domestic servant.[9]

Even today, tropes of food consumption and preparation continue to inform viewers of the social, political, and economic changes unfolding beyond the theatre, and of the anxieties that are digested simultaneously with food. Yet, as much as this book considered continuities within the filmic foodscape, it also spoke of finitude: of endings brought about by food and of closing shots. My discussion, thus, stops here.

Notes

Introducing the Filmic Foodscape of the *Boom*

1 Victoria de Grazia, *Irresistible Empire*.
2 Richard Kuisel, *Seducing the French*, 52.
3 Rachel Laudan, *Cuisine & Empire*, 252.
4 de Grazia, *Irresistible Empire*, 454–5.
5 Carol Helstosky, *Garlic and Oil*, 4.
6 Helstosky, *Garlic and Oil*, 66.
7 Alberto Capatti and Massimo Montanari, *Italian Cuisine*, 270.
8 Cf. Olindo Guerrini, *L'arte di utilizzare gli avanzi della mensa* (1918).
9 Capatti and Montanari, *Italian Cuisine*, 270.
10 Helstosky, *Garlic and Oil*, 84.
11 Carmela D'Apice, *L'arcipelago dei consumi*, 100.
12 Emanuela Scarpellini, *Material Nation*, 130.
13 Laudan, *Cuisine & Empire*, 252.
14 Helstosky, *Garlic and Oil*, 145.
15 Scarpellini, *Material Nation*, 129.
16 Kaeten Mistry, *The United States, Italy, and the Origins of Cold War*, 65–6.
17 Data extracted from Martin Schain, ed., *The Marshall Plan*.
18 James Dunn, letter to George C. Marshall, 17 September 1947.
19 Vera Zamagni, *The Economic History of Italy, 1860–1990*, 332.
20 Loredana Pellè, *Mezzogiorno e il piano Marshall*, 110–12.
21 Pellè, *Mezzogiorno e il piano Marshall*, 86–7.
22 de Grazia, *Irresistible Empire*, 346.
23 Maria Paola Moroni Salvatori, "Ragguaglio bibliografico sui ricettari del primo Novecento," 924.
24 Jonathan Rees, *Refrigeration Nation*, 169.
25 Rees, *Refrigeration Nation*, 179. Cf. "Refrigerator a Luxury in British Homes."

26 Franco Momigliano and Alessandro Pizzorno, "Consumi in Italia," 56.
27 Mario Centorrino, Introduction to *Consumi sociali e sviluppo economico in Italia, 1960–1975*, 7.
28 Scarpellini, *Material Nation*, 125.
29 Victoria de Grazia, "American Supermarkets versus European Small Shops."
30 John Brewer, "Il tempo minimo," 12.
31 "Io non mangio maccheroni! Io sono *americano*! Il vino rosso ... io non bevo il vino rosso! Gli americani mangiano marmellata. Questa è roba da americani! Gli americani non bevono vino rosso, bevono il latte! Per questo non si ubriacano! Avete mai visto un americano ubriaco? Io non l'ho mai visto. Gli americani sono forti. Non puoi combattere contro gli americani! Mangiano marmellata! Maccherone, io ti distruggo! ... Mi sembri un verme, maccherone. Questa è roba da americani! Yogurt, marmellata, mostarda ... un po' di latte [*which he pours directly onto a slice of bread*]. Questa è la roba che mangiano gli americani. Roba sana, sostanziosa. [*eats the jelly, mustard, and milk "sandwich," but he looks repulsed, and spits it out*]. Che zozzeria! [*exchanges for the plate of macaroni*]. Maccherone, mi hai provocato e ora ti distruggo. Io ti mangio! ... Verme, io ti mangio!" Do note his use of the *voi*, the "you guys," in his monologue; in so doing, he is speaking not to his food, but to Italy. Unless otherwise noted, all translations are mine.
32 Giancarlo Governi, *Alberto Sordi*, 52.
33 For further commentary on "Tammuriata Nera" in *Ladri di biciclette*, cf. Nelson Moe, "Naples '44 / 'Tammuriata Nera' / *Ladri di biciclette*," *Italy and America, 1943–44*.
34 Found in Mira Liehm, *Passion and Defiance*, 138.
35 Sophia Loren, *In cucina con amore*, 133.
36 Andrea Dworkin, "Prostitution and Male Supremacy."

1. Totò and the Continuity of Hunger

1 Cf. Karl Schoonover, *Brutal Vision: The Neorealist Body in Postwar Italian Cinema* (2012).
2 For a comprehensive historicization of Italy's austerity, see Carol Helstosky's *Garlic and Oil*.
3 David E. Sutton, *Remembrance of Repasts*.
4 Salvatore Gelsi, *Lo schermo in tavola*, 116.
5 Frank Chandler, *Romances of Roguery*, 45–6.
6 Ana V. Perez de Arlucea, "Cervantes y sus personajes eran lo que comían."
7 Georgia Lawrence-Doyle, "From Arlecchino to Wertmuller," 277.
8 Maria Park Bobroff, "Gluttonous Pleasures," 38.

9 Bobroff cites notes to *Le Baron allemande* (1667): "Trivelin leaves Arlequin to take care of matters. He returns and knocks at the door. Arlequin asks him what is in the little jar next to the fireplace. Trivelin responds that it is an enema for one of the sick maids. Oh no! cries Arlequin, I drank it, thinking it was broth. And that white thing that was on the mantel? That's soap, responds Trivelin. Well, says Arlequin, I thought it was cheese and I ate it." Bobroff, "Gluttonous Pleasures," 35.

10 Emanuela Patriarca, *Totò nel cinema di poesia di Pier Paolo Pasolini*, 22.

11 Gordon Poole, "Totò's Talking Body," 241.

12 Cf. Massimiliano Scuriatti, *E io lo nacqui*, 126.

13 Glenda Mottura, "Totò," 11.

14 Ennio Bìspuri, *Totò Principe Clown*, 17.

15 Poole, "Totò's Talking Body," 245.

16 "Totò potrà impersonare qualunque personaggio, sulla scena, sullo schermo, e noi ne ricaveremo l'impressione che egli lo smàscheri socialmente, che ne riveli l'essenza di maschera fittizia: fittizia nella società, non sulla scena, sullo schermo; insomma, che essere poveri è assurdo, che è assurdo essere ricchi, che è assurdo fare il ladro, come la guardia, l'impiegato, o lo scienziato. Egli fa tutto ciò restando miracolosamente se stesso, con la levità d'un Mandrake anarchico." Elio Petri, "Volonté Totò ecc."

17 Dario Fo, *Manuale dell'attor comico*, 12. See also Goffredo Fofi, "Totò e Pulcinella," 83–4.

18 Charles-Victor de Bonstetten, *The Man of the North and the Man of the South*. Excerpted from Nelson Moe's *The View from Vesuvius*, 28–9.

19 In an entry of his *Prison Notebooks*, titled "The Problem of Political Leadership in the Formation and Development of the Nation and the Modern State in Italy," Antonio Gramsci describes the North's misguided views of the South – and, in particular, their fraught justifications for the poverty of the *Mezzogiorno*. Gramsci states that, in the North, the *Mezzogiorno* was believed to be a "ball and chain" for Italy; without this burden, the "modern industrial civilization of Northern Italy would have made greater progress." Gramsci, however, underscores the fact that Italian unity had not taken place on the basis of equality, but as hegemony of the North achieved through an exploitative town-country relationship with the South. He writes poignantly, "the North concretely was an 'octopus' which enriched itself at the expense of the South, and … its economic-industrial increment was in direct proportion to the impoverishment of the economy and the agriculture of the South." This entry may be found in *Selections from the Prison Notebooks*, 3.3.

20 William Nassau Sr, *Journals Kept in France and Italy from 1848 to 1852, with a Sketch of the Revolution of 1848*, 2:2–3.

21 Augustin Creuzé de Lesser, *Voyage en Italie et Sicilie* (1806), 96. Cf. Moe, *The View from Vesuvius*, 37.

22 Tomasso Campanella, *Del senso delle cose e della magia*, Book 4, ch. 14; excerpted in Ernesto De Martino, *Magic*, 135–6.

23 Valletta, civil law instructor and disciple of Genovesi and Giuseppe Pasquale Cirillo, penned *Cicalata sul fascino, volgarmente detto jettatura* (1787). In this work, Valletta comments on binding, and the idea of "untrue truths," as it was manifest in literary works, and as discussed at salons hosted by the Marquis of Villarosa. Cf. De Martino, *Magic*, 144.

24 Sergio Arecco, "Il cinema e il suo doppio," 52.

25 Alberto Anile, *I film di Totò, 1946–1967*, 175.

26 "Mi basta di sapere che il pubblico è contento."

27 "Totò continuò a lavorare nel cinema come a teatro, andava a braccio, si rifiutava di doppiarsi; replicava malvolentieri … e aveva bisogno dell'applauso delle maestranze; osservava perfino gli orari del teatro, imponendo di girare di pomeriggio (non si può far ridere della mattina, diceva)." Masolino d'Amico, *La commedia all'italiana*, 51.

28 Arecco, "Il cinema e il suo doppio," 52.

29 "la miglior commedia di Scarpetta."

30 "Il lungomare da qualche anno è diventato una passeggiata gastronomica. Qui la dieta mediterranea è servita per tutte le tasche. Pizze, spaghetti ai frutti di mare, zeppole di alghe fritte, pezzogne all'acqua pazza, alici fritte. Verdure ripassate, saltate, *'mbuttunate*, parmigianizzate. Nelle mani dei napoletani melanzane e peperoni, *friarielli* (cime di broccolo) e *ciurilli* (fiori di zucchina), zucchine e carciofi abbandonano il loro corpo vegetale per diventare leccornie. Così buone da far socchiudere gli occhi, perché il principio di piacere per questo popolo refrattario all'idea del peccato, diventa una filosofia di vita." Elisabetta Moro and Marino Niola, *Andare per i luoghi della dieta mediterranea*, 40.

31 Alfredo Niceforo, *Italiani del Nord e italiani del Sud*, 203.

32 Pietro Albertoni and Felice Rossi, "Bilancio nutritivo del contadino abruzzese e sue condizioni fisiologiche, psichologiche ed economiche," 152.

33 Antonio Gramsci, "The Problem of Political Leadership in the Formation and Development of the Nation and the Modern State in Italy," *Selections from the Prison Notebooks*.

34 Sutton, *Remembrance of Repasts*, 81.

35 Eduardo Scarpetta, *Miseria e nobiltà* (1887), 213. I have translated this line from the original Neapolitan: "I' tengo famma, i' tengo famma!"

36 Domenico Cammarota, *Il cinema di Totò*, 128.

37 "Magari non ho fame, ma l'abitudine è tanta che devo mangiare lo stesso."

38 "Lei, la signora, quando arriva quest'ora *deve* mangiare." The italics are mine.

39   NADIA: E poi, non sono ancora abituata alla vostra cucina.

FELICE: Alla nostra cucina?

PASQUALE: E come vi potete abituare?

FELICE: Non siamo abituati neanche noi!

NADIA: No, ma io dicevo quella napoletana. Qui a Napoli, si cucina tutto quanto con l'olio, mentre su da noi, nel nord, si fa tutto con il burro.

FELICE: Ah sì? Fate *tutto* col burro? [The italics are mine.]

NADIA: Tutto!

FELICE: Noi invece facciamo tutto con l'olio. Consumiamo *damigiane* d'olio. Lo mettiamo persino sull'insalata! Le macchie, ci macchiamo con l'olio!

PASQUALE: E da loro …?

FELICE: Sono macchie di burro!

NADIA: Oh no, magari questo no, ma certo che ne consumiamo molto, né? Mettiamo il burro persino nel caffellatte! (*pours coffee from a porcelain kettle into a cup, with Felice looking on*)

PASQUALE: Noi nel caffellatte non mettiamo niente.

FELICE: Né latte, né caffè.

NADIA: (*smiling, laughing*) Oh, Signur! Non ci mettono niente!

PASQUALE: Ma parliamo d'altro.

FELICE: Il latte e caffè non ti piace? (*His eyes widen, eyebrows are raised, and his lips begin to pout*) Preferisci una tazza di cioccolata? (*Smiling wide*) Con i brioches, maritozzi? [*Maritozzi* are a sweet Roman pastry, typically served with whipped cream.]

40 "Se reciterete bene, sarete ben ricompensati."

41 "Se stiamo lavorando, ci guadagniamo la minestra!"

42 The "he"/"his" pronouns are left as such to further blur the distinction between il Principe and Felice and, by extension, de Curtis and Totò.

43 "*Scambio d'ingiurie e d'invettive a soggetto e volontà dell'attore. Questa scena deve essere eseguita con molto calore. Poi tutti seggono. Dalla porta in fondo a dritta, si avanzano uno sguattero ed un facchino che portano una grande stufa. Senza parlare, si avvicinano alla tavola e posano a terra, ai piedi di Felice, la stufa. Il facchino va via, poi torna con due fiaschi di vino. Lo sguattero scopre la stufa, tira fuori una grossa zuppiera di maccheroni, poi dei polli, del pesce, due grossi pezzi di pane, tovaglioli e posate, mentre il facchino pone in tavola i due fiaschi di vino. Egli e lo sguattero riprendono poi la stufa vuota, arrivano sotto la porta in fondo, si voltano, salutando con un cenno della testa, e vanno via. Pasquale, Concetta, Pupella, Luisella e Felice si avvicinano alla tavola. Poi si alzano di botto e, tutti in piedi vicino alla tavola, si slanciano con grande avidità sui maccheroni fumiganti, divorandoli e abbrancandoli con le mani. Cala la tela.*" Scarpetta, *Miseria e nobiltà*, 247.

44 "Qua si mangia solo veleno!"

45 "Un miraggio."

46 "Io ho sognato del padre della ballerina, il cuoco."

47 "Il regista ci aveva spiegato che l'avvicinamento delle sedie doveva essere
fatto un po' per volta e che poi dovevamo buttarci tutti sopra la pasta;
è chiaro che poi tutte le scene andavano *ad libitum*, non era detto che si
dovesse smettere finite le battute, perché Totò ne inventava di tutti i colori
e Mattoli lasciava andare … Alzo lo sguardo e vedo che Totò si era alzato,
era salito sopra il tavolo e s'era inventato di mettersi gli spaghetti nelle
tasche. Chissà la scena quanto sarebbe andata avanti, e invece il regista fu
costretto a dare lo stop perché mentre infilava questi spaghetti dentro le
tasche, Totò aveva preso anche uno zampirone messo dentro la pasta per
fare del fumo, e questo zampirone gli stava bruciando la tasca." Anile, *I
film di Totò, 1946–1967*, 184.

48 Dan Sperber, *Rethinking Symbolism*, 117.

49 Sutton, *Remembrance of Repasts*, 87. See also Sperber, *Rethinking Symbolism*,
122.

50 Patriarca, *Totò nel cinema di poesia di Pier Paolo Pasolini*, 21.

51 "Le lave rosseggianti degli spaghetti che guizzano dalle mani di un
Pulcinella che accoglie i visitatori che entrano nelle imponenti scuderie
sotterranee di Palazzo Sansevero …" Moro and Niola, *Andare per i luoghi
della dieta mediterranea*, 44.

52 The four films are as follows, released in this order: *Totò, Peppino e … la
malafemmina* (1956); *Totò, Peppino e … i fuorilegge* (1956); *Totò, Peppino e
… le fanatiche* (1958); and *Totò, Peppino e … la dolce vita* (1961). A possible
fifth film in the series is *Totò e Peppino divisi a Berlino* (1962), although this
film – despite gags and sketches similar to two comics' earlier work – not
only bears a different title but also, more importantly, marks a decisive
end to their years of collaboration, which grew increasingly tense over
time.

53 "L'accostamento ad un grande attore come Salvatore De Muto fu per me
'sangue e pane' per le mie tendenze artistiche. De Muto fu una maschera
pulcinellesca di grandissima risonanza nel mondo del nostro teatro …
Negli anni che gli fui vicino, da giovane, appresi molto dell'arte spontanea
e improvvisata di De Muto studiandolo e imitandolo nella impostazione di
ogni mio personaggio a carattere farsesco." Giuliana Prestipino, "Il comico
popolare nel cinema," 41–3. The quote from Peppino was excerpted from
Antonella Ottai's edited volume, *Peppino De Filippo: Vita è arte*.

54 Stefano De Stefano, "Peppino attore del futuro," 138–9.

55 "Nostro padre lasciò giustamente anche a te una parte di eredità, e tu l'hai
consumata in bagordi, nel vizio, nella brutta vita, nella lussuria! Io no, io
invece, grazie a Dio, ho fatto fruttare la mia parte e oggi sono un signor
sarto!"

56 Prestipino, "Il comico popolare," 93–4.

57 "Te voglio ancora bene, / ma tu nun saje pecchè … / pecchè ll'unico
    ammore / si' stato tu pe' me! … / E tu, *pe' nu capriccio*, / tutto hè
    distrutto oje nè'… / Ma Dio nun t'o pperdona / chello ch'hè fatto a me."
    "Malafemmena," lyrics written by Totò, 1951. The italics are mine.

58 "Ricchissimo! Possedeva un'intera caciotta!"

59 "Un carro armato."

60 "Un gioiello di … meccanica."

61 "Per andare a Milano perlomeno ci vogliono quattro giorni di mare!"

62 Film scholar Ornella Petraroli writes, "Il viaggio compiuto da Napoli
    a Milano dei fratelli Capone e il distacco dalla campagna alla città
    mise in luce soprattutto la lontananza geografica e la distanza sociale,
    economica e culturale tra il Nord e il Sud dell'Italia. Cinquant'anni fa
    per un napoletano, ma in generale per un meridionale, sembrava infinita
    la distanza che separava il Sud da Milano, dalla Lombardia e da tutto
    il Nord, tanto che per Totò avere fatto per tre anni il militare a Cuneo
    significava essere, per estensione, conoscitore del mondo." Petraroli, "Totò
    e Peppino come Arena e Troisi," 324.

63 Gianpaolo Fissore, "Gli italiani e il cibo sul grande schermo dal secondo
    dopoguerra a oggi," 174.

64 "A Milano ci sono persone educate."

65 "Due. Siamo due. Siamo i fratelli Caponi. Ca-po-ni. Io sono il primogenio,
    e lui … il secondo primogenio."

66 "A tavola! Si mangia! Zuppa di verdura! Zuppa di tartaruga! Tartine di
    pesce! Pesce d'Africa! Champagne! Champagne!"

67 Pierre Bourdieu, *Distinction*, 535.

68 Stephen Gundle, "Sophia Loren," 381.

69 Ennio Bìspuri, *Vita di Totò*, 125.

70 Totò, *Fegato qua, fegato là, fegato fritto e baccalà*, 10. This book is a compilation
    of recipes developed by Totò, but the introductory pages are written by
    Liliana de Curtis. The original Italian is as follows: "Ogni cibo, secondo Totò,
    andava curato nella sua semplicità. Se si decideva di mangiare pane ed olio,
    entrambi gli ingredienti dovevano essere di prima scelta e consumati ad una
    tavola bene apparecchiata perché l'occhio e lo stomaco hanno eguali diritti."

**2. From *Pizzaiola* to Phenom: Sophia Loren,
the Nexus of Networks**

1 *L'Espresso*, 7 August 1960.

2 Sophia Loren, *Yesterday, Today, Tomorrow*, xi.

3 In 1957, at age only twenty-three, Loren reported an income of 16 million
   lire, a sum which was heavily contested. Lawyers doubted that she earned

that much, since she was in only one film in 1956, yet the outrage might be more due to her income ranking as high as that of older men. She was positioned fourth after Vittorio De Sica (74 million), Alberto Sordi (34 million), and Totò (20 million). *Il Giorno* and *Il Corriere Lombardo*, both 23 June 1957.

4 *Gente*, 12 March 1964. Loren stated, "The day I'm truly sure I'm going to be a mother, I would distance myself, disappear, hole myself up in a secure and calm place where no one would be able to come near me. That day I would not open [up] to anyone, for any reason, with the exception of Carlo, my mother, and my sister. And all of you will be excluded, working tirelessly to get a crumb of news ..." / "Il giorno in cui fossi davvero sicura di diventare madre, mi allontanerei, sparirei, mi rinchiuderei in un rifugio sicuro e tranquillo dove nessuno potrebbe avvicinarmi. Quel giorno non aprirei a nessuno, per nessuna ragione, fatta eccezione per Carlo, per mia madre e per mia sorella, s'intende. E voi tutti, giornalisti e fotografi, rimarrete esclusi, dovrete affaticarvi per ottenere un briciolo di notizia ..."

5 Loren writes in her memoir, "Because I was very dark and also really skinny, everyone called me Toothpick" (*Yesterday, Today, Tomorrow*, 10). Writer and director Garson Kanin, meanwhile, described a 1950 screen test that Loren failed miserably: "Her hair was too short, and she was still extremely thin. [Carlo] Ponti told her to give up any thought of becoming a film actress because she did not photograph well ... The war-starved adolescent's skin and bones made her difficult to photograph. When she fleshed out – and with *what* flesh! – she became a classic beauty. There are, one observes, advantages in being well-fed." Kanin, *Together Again!*, 204.

6 "Altezza 1,72, seno 95, vita 58, fianchi 95, peso 60 chili, il tutto assicurato per un milione di dollari, oltre 600 milioni di lire, cioè 10 milioni al chilo." *La Notte*, 10 April 1962. These measurements convert to 5'6", 37.5", 22.8", 37.5", and 132 lbs, respectively.

7 "Non avere più fame, questa è la soddisfazione maggiore che debbo al cinema, la maggiore della mia vita. A voi può sembrare poco, ma io sono stata affamata tanto tempo che ho sempre creduto non si potesse vivere in un'altra maniera." *Stasera*, 4 September 1962. The article cites an interview that Loren had given in 1953.

8 "Ed è una Sophia nuova quella che ci appare attraverso le descrizioni dei suoi familiari. Una ragazza coi capelli spioventi, molto studiosa, che ha frequentato con disciplina e profitto la scuola, e che a sedici anni, prima di partire per Roma, ha ottenuto il diploma di maestra." G. Rosi Bernardini, *Fotosei*, 7 June 1957.

9 In an interview with Ugo Naldi of *Corriere d'Informazione*, 7 June 1961, Loren stated, "Personalmente, desidero sentirmi donna, debole, protetta da un uomo. Le donne possono essere independenti, ma entro certi limiti."

10 *Corriere d'Informazione* and *Il Corriere Lombardo*, 21–2 August 1957. Both periodicals wrote that, upon arriving at an event thrown in her honour by the Italian Embassy in Washington, DC (following her work on *Houseboat* [1956]), Loren sneezed, undoing some of her dress's stitches. *Il Corriere Lombardo* reports: "'I can't eat anything tonight,' the brunette Italian beauty said, refusing a sweet that had been offered to her. 'Coming to the Embassy, I sneezed … and my dress came undone. Now I'm afraid to eat for fear it might happen again.'" / "'Non posso mangiare niente stasera,' ha detto la bruna bellezza italiana rifiutando il dolce che le era stato offerto. 'Nel venire all'Ambasciata ho fatto uno starnuto … e mi si è scucito il vestito. Adesso temo di mangiare per timore che possa accadere di nuovo.'"

11 Cf. Stephen Gundle, "Sophia Loren," 368.

12 Gundle, "Sophia Loren," 376.

13 To this end, Nelson Moe records Madame de Staël's thoughts on Naples in *Corinne*: "Naples's hybridity, the coexistence of an 'uncivilized state side by side with civilization,' is 'very original'; all those 'tanned faces … give a picturesque quality to the rabble.'" Moe, *The View from Vesuvius*, 57.

14 Giovanni Verga, *Cavalleria Rusticana and Other Stories*, 39–40.

15 Gundle, "Sophia Loren," 370.

16 Loren, *Yesterday, Today, Tomorrow*, 55–6. Likewise, Morando Morandini of *La Notte* shared one of Loren's encounters with a fan, confused about her name: "'Did you know that in Naples a little boy stopped me to say, Oh, Sofi! Why did you change your name? How do we go about calling you *Sopì*?'" / "'Sa che a Napoli mi fermò un ragazzino per dirmi: oh, Sofi! perchè ti sei cambiata il nome? Come se fà a chiamarte *Sopì*?'" Morandini, *La Notte*, 18 December 1957. The italics are mine.

17 "Ora il suo nome occupa i giornali: non c'è più pericolo che debba mutarlo. Con *l'acca*, o senza *l'acca*, è registrato, ormai, nella storia del cinema." Americo Sala, *Corriere d'Informazione*, 11 April 1962. The italics on *acca* are Sala's.

18 It should be noted that Loren starred in eight of De Sica's films, but they acted together in four additional films – one of which was *L'oro di Napoli*.

19 Loren, *Yesterday, Today, Tomorrow*, 63.

20 A.E. Hotchner, *Sophia*, 96.

21 Carol Helstosky, *Pizza*, 23.

22 Elisabetta Moro and Marino Niola, *Andare per i luoghi della dieta mediterranea*, 48–9.

23 Paolo Jovane, *Corriere d'Informazione*, 11 September 1957.

24 Hotchner, *Sophia*, 95–6.

25 La "piccola capitale del divorzio." *Il Giorno*, 28 September 1957.

26 Loren, *Yesterday, Today, Tomorrow*, 125.

27 "Ma lei – le abbiamo chiesto – quando ha saputo che Sofia era sposata?" "Ieri, poco prima che la notizia arrivasse ai giornali. Sofia mi ha telefonato da Hollywood e me l'ha detto, pregandomi però di non dire niente a nessuno. 'Lascia che lo si venga a sapere dai giornali,' ha detto e così io sono stata zitta." *Il Giorno*, 28 September 1957.

28 *Il Giorno*, 11 September 1957.

29 Réka Buckley, "Marriage, Motherhood, and the Italian Film Stars of the 1950s," 39.

30 Gundle, "Sophia Loren," 377.

31 "… indimenticabile, ma dolcissimo, di certi maccheroni ripieni di mozzarella o di certi spaghetti con peperoni e acciughe che si preparava nel suo cottage prima di coricarsi." *L'Espresso*, 7 August 1960.

32 "Le ho sognate per tanto tempo, fritte e dorate, disposte su uno strato di mozzarella e pomodoro, uno spicchio d'aglio, un pezzetto di pepperoncino, appena uscite dal forno, calde e fragranti." *L'Espresso*, 7 August 1960.

33 "Così se a Hollywood ha scoperto il conformismo, in Inghilterra il piacere di passeggiare per i boschi e a Parigi il gusto d'andare a teatro, ognuno di questi posti è rimasto vivo nel cuore di Sophia per un'invenzione culinaria." *L'Espresso*, 7 August 1960.

34 "'Hollywood mi rende nervosa,' ha detto Sofia Loren durante la sua prima intervista in terra americana. 'Ho paura di diventar matta, questa è veramente una città pazza, addirittura impossibile …'" *Il Giorno*, 11 April 1957.

35 "'Sophia ha conquistato Hollywood che è ai suoi piedi sin dal primo istante,' ha detto guardandosi attorno, non senza una punta di invidia Janet Leigh, la moglie di Tony Curtis, che è legata da buona amicizia con la Loren in seguito a un viaggio a Roma compiuto due anni fa." Vieter Darnantier, *La Notte*, 9 April 1957.

36 "… fra tre mesi Hollywood si chiamerà 'Lorentown,' ha dichiarato il regista De Mille." *Il Giorno*, 11 April 1957.

37 "Voglio, ora, che giudichino come recito. Ho quasi finito il film con Holden e la regia di Carol Reed. Se vi apparirò 'sexy,' non l'ho fatto apposta: vuol dire che sono così. Ma ora adopero il cervello e spero di recitare tanto bene da vincere un Oscar." *Il Giorno*, 15 December 1957.

38 Hotchner, *Sophia*, 146.

39 In the Introduction, neorealism was defined as a film movement which, through non-professional actors, on-location shooting, and recycled film stock, underscored the material and spiritual deprivations of the war and the *dopoguerra*: hunger, unemployment, poverty, and the absence of solidarity. De Sica directed the following neorealist classics: *I bambini ci guardano* (1943), *Sciuscià* (1946), *Ladri di biciclette* (1948), *Miracolo a Milano* (1951), and *Umberto D.* (1952).

40 Viviana Lapertosa, *Dalla fame all'abbondanza*, 108.

41 Hotchner, *Sophia*, 144.

42 "'Da quando Ponti ha scoperto che i personaggi che ho sempre fatto io li può fare anche Sophia Loren, per me non c'è posto nel cinema,' ha affermato Anna Magnani in un'intervista concessa a un noto settimanale." *Giornale del Mattino*, 7 May 1961.

43 "'Per non fare "La ciociara" … ho perduto trecentomila dollari. Ma come potevo? Avrei dovuto fare la madre di Sophia. Per indurmi ad accettare mi dissero che quando sarei apparsa accanto alla Loren mi avrebbero messo sotto i piedi uno sgabello. Non feci una questione di altezza ma trovavo assurda l'idea di metterci insieme come madre e figlia. E non ero la sola a pensarlo … Non aver fatto "La ciociara" mi ha dato un dolore che è durato anni. Quando De Sica insisteva gli risposi di smetterla che mi faceva star male. Malgrado tutto gli suggerii di dare il personaggio della madre a Sophia. E debbo dire che la Loren non va affatto male in quel film.'" *Giornale del Mattino*, 7 May 1961.

44 "Insomma, si era già formata in quelle poche ore l'atmosfera che, in seguito ebbi modo di osservare a Roma per tutto il periodo che durò l'occupazione alleata: gli italiani chiedevano la roba per fare piacere agli americani e gli americani davano la roba per far piacere agli italiani; e nessuno dei due si rendeva conto di non far alcun piacere all'altro. E io penso che queste cose nessuno le vuole e avvengono da sé, come per tacito accordo. Gli americano erano i vincitori e gli italiani vinti e questo bastava." Alberto Moravia, *La ciociara*, 235.

45 For further reading on propaganda and the Marshall Plan – in other words, how the Plan is represented as analogous to Italy's life-blood – cf. Paola Bonifazio's *Schooling in Modernity: The Politics of Sponsored Films in Postwar Italy* (2014).

46 Angelo Fàvaro, "'Mamma quando si parte?'… Cesira o della madre colpevole," 76.

47 "Il mercato era lì a pochi passi da casa, e io giravo tra le bancarelle, per più di un'ora, non tanto per comprare, perché gran parte della roba ce l'avevamo al negozio, ma per guardare. Giravo tra le bancarelle e guardavo tutto, la frutta, le verdure, la carne, il pesce, le uova: me ne intendevo e mi piaceva calcolare i prezzi e i guadagni, valutare la qualità, scoprir gli imbrogli e i trucchi dei venditori. Mi piaceva pure discutere, soppesare la roba, lasciarla lì e poi ritornare a discutere ancora e alla fine non prendere nulla." Moravia, *La ciociara*, 6.

48 "L'acchiappai per un braccio allora, ripetendo la domanda; e lei, sottovoce: 'Se te lo dico, tu poi non vai a raccontare dove tengo le provviste?' Rimasi a bocca aperta di fronte a queste parole, perché erano al tempo stesso intonate alle circostanze e completamente assurde. Dissi: 'Ma che dici? Che c'entrano

le provviste?' E lei, scuotendo il capo: 'Vengono e prendono … vengono e prendono … sono tedeschi, si sa … ma sai che gli ho detto l'ultima volta che sono venuti? Io non ci ho nulla, gli ho detto, non ci ho farina, non ci ho fagioli, non ci ho strutto, non ci ho nulla… ci ho soltanto il latte per il mio bambino … se lo volete prendetelo … ecco.'" Moravia, *La ciociara*, 269.

49 Mauro Lirani, *La Settimana Incom*, 4 May 1957.

50 "… ci vorrà perdonare se mettiamo un po' di amaro nella sua coppa di *champagne*." Guido Aristarco, *La Stampa*, 11 April 1962.

51 "L'Academy finge di segnalare un'attrice italiana. I nostri giornali mettono in risalto il fatto che per la prima volta viene premiata la protagonista di un film in lingua non inglese. Ma ad Hollywood interessa, nascondendo i propri fini, creare il mito Loren, che da qualche tempo fa anche parte della produzione americana." Aristarco, *La Stampa*, 11 April 1962.

52 Howard Curle and Stephen Snyder, eds., *Vittorio De Sica*. De Sica's lamentations can be found in a 1972 interview with Charles Thomas Samuels, excerpts of which are in this edited volume.

53 For a more profound reading of GI crimes in the South, cf. Isobel Williams, *Allies and Italians Under Occupation: Sicily and Southern Italy, 1943–1945* (2013).

54 Stephen Snyder, "Hiding in the Light," 235.

55 *Tenta ancora di leggere; alla fine ci riesce.*

    PASQUALE: … Sra, sga … sgravata … Ah, sgravata! Il 20 ottobre. Io vendevo i fichi d'India …

    Smette di leggere, si fa i conti con le dita.

    PASQUALE: Sei mesi d'allattamento: novembre, dicembre, gennaio, febbraio, marzo, aprile … Aprile, maggio, quando escono le prime primizie delle ciliegie, scade l'impunità.

    CARMINE (*sicuro di sé*): E mo' stammo a gennaio. Il tempo ci sta …

    PASQUALE (*scherzoso*): Se vuoi un aiuto, senza offesa.

    CARMINE: Pasquà, se ti serve un figlio, t'o vengo a ffà a domicilio …

Cesare Zavattini et al., Sceneggiatura di *Ieri, oggi, domani*. Excerpted from Gualtiero De Santi and Manuel De Sica, *Ieri oggi domani di Vittorio De Sica*, 142. I leave "sgravata" untranslated to allow for the double entendre of "pregnant" and "unburdened."

56 *Seguiamo Elvira, la quale raggiunge la bancarella del marito.*

    ELVIRA (*concitata*): So arrivate 'e guardie into' basso 'Mellino. Carminello sta solo, Adelina nun ce sta. Ma 'e guardie hanno detto che l'aspettano, che non se ne vanno.

    PASQUALE: Mannaggia 'o diavolo … Guardame 'e cerase …

Zavattini et al., Sceneggiatura di *Ieri, oggi, domani*, 143.

57 Jacqueline Reich, *Beyond the Latin Lover*, 105.

58 Reich, *Beyond the Latin Lover*, 1–2.

59 La stanza è interamente rivestita di *boiseries* e di vetrine che racchiudono gli innumerevoli premi ricevuta dalla Loren durante la sua carriera. I Bambi d'oro, le statuine del Donatello, le medaglie, l'Oscar formano intorno a lei una trionfale cornice. Adattissima a una campionessa dello schermo. Ora, però, ciò che più importa a Sofia è che il salotto in cui ci troviamo sia a pochi passi di distanza a suo figlio. Ha bisogno di andarlo a vedere continuamente, di sentirlo respirare se dorme, di accarezzargli, se è sveglio, la peluria tenue, scura ("sembra un uccellino," mi dice) sulla testina rotunda … Come per assicurarsi che non è svanito, che non era un miraggio.

    "Eppure c'è," le assicuro. "È una realtà ben precisa. Esiste: l'ho anche toccato."

    Sorride. "Me ne rendo conto un po' per volta, ma non riesco ancora," confessa, "a convincermi completamente. Diciamo che sono persuasa all'ottanta per cento." Anita Pensotti, *Le italiane*, 180.

60 "Darei tutto per avere un figlio e se dovessi scegliere fra la possibilità di continuare a lavorare come attrice e quella di essere madre sceglierei quest'ultima senza esitazione." *La Gazzetta del Mezzogiorno*, 15 March 1966.

61 "Ci si sente bellissime solo quando si aspetta un bambino." Anita Pensotti, *Oggi*, 22 December 1966.

62 *Newsweek*, 23 January 1967.

63 "Per l'episodio di Adelina, Sofia si allacciava dietro la schiena una grossa pancia di gommapiuma, di varie misure a seconda dei mesi di gravidanza, e ogni volta che ripeteva quel gesto, gli occhi brillavano di soddisfatto orgoglio. Fu proprio in quel periodo che la Loren si accorse di aspettare davvero un bambino. Nessuno lo seppe, nemmeno De Sica. E siccome il film era in piena lavorazione e non si poteva interromperlo, Sofia continuò a girare davanti alla macchina da presa, ad alzarsi all'alba, a sottoporsi a ogni genere di strapazzi e di rischi (c'era perfino uno scontro automobilistico, nel terzo episodio), seguendo la voce della sua coscienza professionale. Finché, purtroppo, perdette il bambino." Pensotti, *Oggi*, 22 December 1966.

64 Loren, *Yesterday, Today, Tomorrow*, 170.

65 Shortly before her January 1967 miscarriage, *TIME* had reported, "Two years ago, after suffering a miscarriage, Actress Sophia Loren, 32, promised that next time she'd follow her doctor's orders about taking it easy. Well, it's like that now. So in the midst of making a movie called *Once Upon a Time*, Sophia canceled out of the film, suspended all other commitments and withdrew to her villa in the Alban Hills outside Rome to await the birth of her first child in May." Not even one month later, Loren had miscarried. *TIME*, 23 December 1966.

66 Sophia Loren, *In cucina con amore*, 15–23.

67 Loren, *In cucina con amore*, 40.

68 Loren, *In cucina con amore*, 28.

69 Loren, *In cucina con amore*, 133.

70 "Non mi resta che farvi gli auguri e raccomandarvi la massima attenzione, perché voglio che con le mie ricette abbiate un grande successo. E' anche questione di orgoglio personale. Vi prego, non mi fate fare brutte figure. Aprendo questo libro siate le benvenute nella mia cucina. Mangiate con me." Loren, *In cucina con amore*, 13.

71 Loren, *Yesterday, Today, Tomorrow*, 175.

72 Loren, *In cucina con amore*, 94–5.

73 "Due superpromessi sposi dell'Italia moderna." Pensotti, *Le italiane*, 154. This term, used in Pensotti's collection of interviews with Italy's biggest female stars, is an allusion to Alessandro Manzoni's iconic novel, *I promessi sposi* (1827). The novel follows Renzo and Lucia, two lovers who are long prevented from marrying and struggle to reunite.

74 Vito Teti, *Il colore del cibo*, 77.

75 Gundle, "Sophia Loren," 380.

76 "Sophia mamma felice, ben lontana da quella di Sophia rubamariti." Alessandro Gatta, *Sophia Loren*, 97.

77 In 1972, Loren gave birth to a second child, Edoardo.

78 Sophia Loren, *Women & Beauty*, 184.

79 "Forse si sentono un po' uomini." Naldi, *Corriere d'Informazione*, 7 June 1961.

80 "… l'uguaglianza tra sessi, anche in cucina, è quasi stata raggiunta." Loren, *In cucina con amore*, 10.

81 "Anzi sono proprio loro, con le loro idee inadeguate all'evolvere della società, che avrebbero più bisogno di questa, diciamo, terapeutica culinaria." Loren, *In cucina con amore*, 213.

82 "Comunque, poiché è naturale che il maggior numero dei miei lettori siano donne, a loro dico: la cucina *vi piaccia, non sia* una fastidiosa routine." Loren, *In cucina con amore*, 213. The italics are mine to highlight the subjunctive mood.

83 "Qualche pietanza esotica, scoperta e adottata nel corso dei miei tanti viaggi …" Loren, *In cucina con amore*, 13.

84 "Il braccialetto, nelle intenzioni di Sellers, dovrebbe essere il primo 'pezzo' di una nuova collezione." Sofia Loren, *Gente*, 13 April 1968.

85 "Povera Sophia, per rifarsi quei gioielli dovrà lavorare almeno un mese!" *Corriere d'Informazione*, 4 June 1960.

3. "Feels Like Home": Elevation and Containment in the Patriarchal City

1 Carole Counihan, *Around the Tuscan Table*, 97.

2 Carole Counihan, *The Anthropology of Food and the Body*, 61.

3 "Insomma – conclude Pietrangeli – il film vuol dire che se queste
   disgraziate fossero aiutate nel momento più difficile (quello del
   reinserimento nella vita normale) forse si potrebbero salvare perché
   nessuno, per quanto guasto, lo è completamente. Ma 'la gente per bene' le
   considera ormai bollate per sempre e le sospinge ad una esistenza ancor
   più degradante di quella precedentemente condotta. E poiché credo in
   questa verità, credo nel mio film." Gaetano Carancini, *Fotosei,* 29 April 1960.
   The italics are the author's.
4 Colloquium with Antonio Pietrangeli, *Bianco e Nero,* 27.
5 Mary Gibson, *Prostitution and the State in Italy, 1860–1915,* 1–2.
6 Rebecca Bertini and Bianca Cecconi, "Prostitution between Law and
   Gender."
7 Gibson, *Prostitution and the State in Italy,* 2.
8 Molly Tambor, "Prostitutes and Politicians," 142.
9 Andrea Dworkin, "Prostitution and Male Supremacy."
10 Roger Matthews, *Prostitution, Politics, and Policy,* 81.
11 Tambor, "Prostitutes and Politicians," 141.
12 Natalie Fullwood, "*Commedie al femminile,*" 92.
13 Fullwood, "*Commedie al femminile,*" 97.
14 "**Articolo 8:** Il Ministro per l'interno provvederà, promovendo la
   fondazione di speciali istituti di patronato, nonché assistendo e
   sussidiando quelli esistenti, che efficacemente corrispondano ai fini della
   presente legge, alla tutela, all'assistenza ed alla rieducazione delle donne
   uscenti, per effetto della presente legge, dalle case di prostituzione.

   "Negli istituti di patronato, come sopra previsti, potranno trovare
   ricovero ed assistenza, oltre alle donne uscite dalle case di prostituzione
   abolite nella presente legge, anche quelle altre che, pure avviate già alla
   prostituzione, intendano di ritornare ad onestà di vita.

   "**Articolo 9:** Con determinazione del Ministro per l'interno sarà
   provveduto all'assegnazione dei mezzi necessari per l'esercizio dell'attività
   degli istituti di cui nell'articolo precedente, da prelevarsi dal fondo
   stanziato nel bilancio dello Stato a norma della presente legge.

   "Alla fine di ogni anno e non oltre il 15 gennaio successivo gli istituti
   di patronato fondati a norma della presente legge, come gli altri istituti
   previsti dal precedente articolo e che godano della sovvenzione dello
   Stato, *dovranno trasmettere un rendiconto esatto della loro attività omettendo il
   nome delle persone da essi accolte.*" The italics are mine.

   Legge Merlin, 20 February 1958, no. 75: "Abolizione della
   regolamentazione della prostituzione e lotta contro lo sfruttamento della
   prostituzione altrui."
15 Matthews, *Prostitution, Politics, and Policy,* 88.
16 Emma Van Ness, "Antonio Pietrangeli, the Director of Women," 110.

17 Carole Pateman, "What's Wrong with Prostitution?", 53.

18   ERCOLI: Auguri e figli maschi … sposatevi, fatevi monache, ma
         dovete restare qui e darmi quello che avevamo patturito, un
         milione al mese.
      MARILINA: Io ti denuncio!
      ERCOLI: La licenza come ve l'ho fatta dare ve la faccio togliere. Una trat-
         toria non può essere gestita da quattro come voi … siete schedate lo
         volete capire, sì o no?

19 Van Ness, "Antonio Pietrangeli," 115.

20 Slavoj Žižek, *Enjoy Your Symptom*, 53.

21 Fullwood, "*Commedie al femminile*," 106.

22 Cf. Pier Paolo Pasolini, "I campi di concentramento" (1958).

23 Sam Rohdie, "Neo-Realism and Pasolini," 168.

24 Pier Paolo Pasolini, "Diario al registratore," *Mamma Roma: La prima
   sceneggiatura*. This excerpt was found in Pasolini, *My Cinema*, 33–4. The
   italics are mine.

25 Manuela Mariani and Patrick Barron, "Cinematic Space in Rome's
   Disabitato," 309.

26 Parliamentary Law no. 43 called for "provvedimenti per incrementare
   l'occupazione operaia, agevolendo la costruzione di case per lavoratori."
   Legge ordinaria no. 43.

27 John David Rhodes, *Stupendous, Miserable City*, 134.

28 One poignant example is in Pasolini's poem "Picasso" (1953):

   … scura
   e abbagliata l'Europa vi proietta
   i suoi interni paesaggi. E matura
   qui, se più trasparente vi si specchia,
   la luce della tempesta; i carnami
   di Buchenwald, la periferia infetta
   delle città incendiate, i cupi camions
   delle caserme dei fascismi …

   Tutte le poesie, Vol. 1, 794.

29 Pasolini's notes on the Muratori building read, "The new apartment isn't
   much different from the old one: only instead of being lost in a huge
   Liberty building, it's lost in a huge modern one, of a dark red hue, full of
   windows, brand new." Rhodes, *Stupendous, Miserable City*, 117.

30 Rhodes, *Stupendous, Miserable City*, 116–17.

31 Guy Debord, *The Society of the Spectacle*, 23.

32 Rohdie, "Neo-Realism and Pasolini," 172.

33 Martin Heidegger's "Building Dwelling Thinking" can be found in full
   in *Poetry, Language, Thought* (1971). This excerpt was found in Eleonora

Sartoni, "(*Mamma*) *Roma* between Archaic and Modern Italy," 8. The italics are Heidegger's.

34 "'A sora sposa! (*ride, ride*) Ecco i nostri fratelli!" Pasolini, *Mamma Roma: La prima sceneggiatura*, 241.

35 Maurizio Sanzio Viano, *A Certain Realism*, 88.

36 "come un manipolo di matti, di condannati a morte, come un balletto." Pasolini, *Mamma Roma: La prima sceneggiatura*, 241.

37 Pasolini, *Mamma Roma: La prima sceneggiatura*, 242–3.

38   MAMMA ROMA (*furente, felice, concludendo*): Fiore de merda, / io me so' lliberata de 'na corda, / adesso tocca a 'n'altra a fà la serva!
    (*E poi, gridando scomposta*) 'A sora sposa, senza invidia! So' llibera, so' llibera!

  Pasolini, *Mamma Roma: La prima sceneggiatura*, 244.

39 Pier Paolo Pasolini in conversation with Anna Magnani, 4 May 1962, Cecafumo, Rome. From *My Cinema*, 29.

40 Pasolini, *My Cinema*, 30.

41 Pier Paolo Pasolini, "*Mamma Roma*: ovvero dalla responsabilità individuale alla responsabilità collettiva"; Pasolini, *My Cinema*, 34.

42 "*Mamma Roma*: ovvero dalla responsabilità, 34.

43 Pasolini, *Mamma Roma: La prima sceneggiatura*, 252.

44 "Già il dialetto era per me il mezzo di un approccio più fisico ai contadini, alla terra, e nei romanzi 'romani' il dialetto popolare mi offriva lo stesso approccio concreto, e per così dire materiale. Ora, ho scoperto molto presto che l'espressione cinematografica mi offriva grazie alla sua analogia sul piano semiologico … con la realtà stessa, la possibilità di raggiungere la vita in modo più completo." Pasolini, *Il sogno del centauro*; excerpted from Rohdie, "Neo-Realism and Pasolini," 172.

45   MAMMA ROMA: Ciài fame?
    ETTORE: (*con accento burino, e usando addirittura un lessico burino*) No … stamattina m' so' magnato. (*espressione burina*)
    MAMMA ROMA: (*fingendosi arrabbiata, strizzando gli occhi*) Che hai detto? Che hai detto? (*parola burina*) Che sarebbero 'ste parolacce! Tu devi parlà come parla tu' madre, no come quei quattro bigonzi, là! Guarda che se no io ti meno, sa'!
    A Ettore, con la testa bassa, scappa un leggero sorriso.

  Pasolini, *Mamma Roma: La prima sceneggiatura*, 255.

46 Roland Barthes, "Towards a Psychosociology of Contemporary Food Consumption," 28–35.

47 Barthes, "Towards a Psychosociology," 29.

48 Sartoni, "(*Mamma*) *Roma* between Archaic and Modern Italy," 2.

49 Pasolini, *Mamma Roma: La prima sceneggiatura*, 259.
50   MAMMA ROMA: Ce sta mi' fijo.
    CARMINE: Ah! Sei contenta? E pensà, ciavevo quasi l'età sua quando me
        so' messo co' te …
    MAMMA ROMA: Se! Mi' fijo è 'n'angelo!
    CARMINE (*commuovendosi improvvisamente con agli occhi le lacrime della vecchia
        commedia*) Un regazzino, ero! Nun ciavevo ancora nemmeno un filo de
        malizia! Mi' madre me lo diceva sempre, che io ero er mejo de casa! E in-
        vece no ho fatto altro che daje dolori, a mi' madre!

    Pasolini, *Mamma Roma: La prima sceneggiatura*, 258.
51   MAMMA ROMA: Va beh, va beh … ho capito … Quanto te servirebbe …
        te lo sai io non ce l'ho i soldi …
    CARMINE: Duecento sacchi …
    MAMMA ROMA: E do' li trovo io? Lo sai che me li so' spesi tutti pe' casa,
        quelli che ci avevo …
    *Carmine la guarda un poco in silenzio, con le labbra tumide sotto i baffetti del
        destino.*
    CARMINE: Aaaah, te va de giocà? Ma allora non m'hai capito! Che te lo
        devo insegnà io, come se fa a rimedià la grana? Che, te lo sei scordato?
    MAMMA ROMA: (*senza più fiato, ma dominandosi ancora*) Ma ancora nun te
        sei saziato?
    *Carmine si stacca dalla ringhiera e comincia a discendere la rampa: parla voltan-
        dosi indietro.*
    CARMINE: (*quasi dolce, comprensivo*) Ma che sarà mai! Se ce metti un po'
        de bona fantasia, in dieci giorni, li rimedi! Nun te pare, 'a Ro'?

    Pasolini, *Mamma Roma: La prima sceneggiatura*, 259.
52 "So' belle pezze, quelli! … Trovi tutti ragazzi che studiano, che vanno a
    lavorà … quelli devono esse l'amici tua!" Pasolini, *Mamma Roma: La prima
    sceneggiatura*, 254.
53 Viano, *A Certain Realism*, 95–6; cf. Stephen Snyder, *Pier Paolo Pasolini*, 53.
54 Sartoni, "(*Mamma*) *Roma* between Archaic and Modern Italy," 11.
55   *Casa Cecafumo. Interno. Alba.*
    *Mamma Roma è alla finestra, che ha appena aperta. Segnata come una vecchia
        statua, guarda e dice a fior di labbra:*
    MAMMA ROMA: Pora creatura mia.
    *Si stacca dalla finestra, va verso l'interno della casa, nella piccola cucina. Prende
        dal fornello la coccumella, si versa il latte, ci mette il pane, comincia a man-
        giare.*
    MAMMA ROMA: Pora creatura mia. (*dopo un profondo silenzio … con
        gli occhi persi*) E' venuto ar mondo e è stato sempre solo. Solo s'è

ritrovato come un Cristo passeretto … A guardasse intorno, a aspettà chissà che, su 'sto mondo, solo …
Inghiotte il boccone di pane e latte, con gli occhi pieni di lacrime.

Pasolini, *Mamma Roma: La prima sceneggiatura*, 359.

56 *Nella cella non c'è niente. Un solo lucernario, in alto, da cui entra la luce della luna. Non c'è niente. Il pavimento, le pareti alte, il soffitto. E un letto di cemento con in mezzo un buco.*

Ettore è legato al letto. Mezzo nudo, come si trovava in infermeria, quando ha incominciato a urlare.

E' come un piccolo crocifisso, con le braccia tese, coi polsi legati: legati sono anche i piedi, e una cinghia gli stringe anche il petto.

Ettore continua a urlare: dicendo parole incomprensibili, agitandosi come un pazzo, divincolandosi disperatamente.

Pasolini, *Mamma Roma: La prima sceneggiatura*, 355.

57 Sartoni, "(*Mamma*) *Roma* between Archaic and Modern Italy," 19.

58 Sartoni, "(*Mamma*) *Roma* between Archaic and Modern Italy," 19.

59 "Stupendous, miserable city" is a line from Pasolini's 1956 poem, "Tears of the Excavator."

60 Gianni Biondillo, *Pasolini*, 76.

4. Crises and Revolutions in the Work of Pasolini

1 "E' in brusio la vita, e questi persi / in essa, la perdono serenamente, / se il cuore ne hanno pieno: a godersi / eccoli, miseri, la sera: e potente / in essi, inermi, per essi, il mito / rinasce … Ma io, con il cuore cosciente / di chi soltanto nella storia ha vita, / potrò mai più con pura passione operare / se so che *la nostra storia è finita*?" Pier Paolo Pasolini, "Le ceneri di Gramsci," in *Pasolini: Poesie e pagine ritrovate*, 118–28. The italics are mine. The English translation was provided by the "Antonio Gramsci in the World" Conference, Duke University, 19–20 April 2013; accessed 3 June 2022: gramsciintheworld.wordpress.com.

2 Cf. Jean-Paul Duflot's interview with Pasolini, in Pasolini, *Il sogno del centauro*, 27.

3 Cf. Sam Rohdie (*The Passion of Pier Paolo Pasolini*), Robert S. Gordon (*Pasolini*), and Noa Steimatsky (*Italian Locations*, 2008).

4 "Povero Stracci. Crepare … non aveva altro modo di ricordarci che anche lui era vivo."

5 Luke 23:34–7, *Good News Bible*, 1552.

6 Luke 23:48–9, *Good News Bible*, 1552–3. The italics are mine.

7 Anthony Giddens, "Time, Space, and Regionalisation," 266.

8 Vito Teti, "The Alimentary Cultures of the Mediterranean," 55.

9 See also Maurizio Sanzio Viano, *A Certain Realism*, 101.

10 Giddens, "Time, Space, and Regionalisation," 268.

11 See also Albert Elduque, "Pasolini and Third World Hunger," 374. Elduque, a Brazilian film scholar, emphasizes the repression of Stracci's personal rhythms to align with those of film production.

12 Elduque, "Pasolini and Third World Hunger," 374.

13 Teti, *Il colore del cibo*, 83.

14 This description of ricotta cheese, particularly the Roman variety, may be found in the glossary of ingredients in Oretta Zanini De Vita's *Popes, Peasants, and Shepherds*, 332.

15 Platina, *On Right Pleasure and Good Health* (circa 1465), Book 2.16, 157. As another example in support of milk's healthfulness, Papal steward Antonio Latini wrote: "Milk strengthens the brain, fattens the body, is beneficial for the consumptive, cools the urine, is highly nourishing, gives a beautiful color to the body, invigorates for coition, removes cough, clears the chest, and heals the convalescent or consumptive ..." Tommaso Astarita, *The Italian Baroque Table*, 211.

16 Pier Paolo Pasolini, "Observations on the Sequence Shot (1967)," 236–7.

17 Pier Paolo Pasolini, "Is Being Natural? (1967)," 243.

18 See also Elduque, "Pasolini and Third World Hunger," 374.

19 Rohdie, *The Passion of Pier Paolo Pasolini*, 159.

20 Elduque, "Pasolini and Third World Hunger," 375.

21 Cf. *Le regole di un'illusione. Il cinema, i film*, ed. Laura Betti and Michele Gulinucci (Rome: Fondo Pier Paolo Pasolini, 1996). This excerpt is from Pasolini, *My Cinema*, 48–50.

22 Viano, *A Certain Realism*, 102.

23 Silvia Carlorosi, "Pier Paolo Pasolini's *La ricotta*," 263.

24 "Povero Stracci. Crepare ... non aveva altro modo per *fare rivoluzione*." The italics are mine.

25 Geoffrey Nowell-Smith, "Pasolini's Originality," 16–17.

26 Rohdie, *The Passion of Pier Paolo Pasolini*, 33.

27 Viano, *A Certain Realism*, 150.

28 Pier Paolo Pasolini, *Il sogno del centauro*, 94.

29 Stefano Baschiera, "The Embodiment of the Bourgeoisie," 70–1.

30 "educatamente, civilmente: la tigre, per esempio, non dice 'Ho fame,' ma 'Ho un po' di appetito." Pier Paolo Pasolini, *L'Aigle*.

31 "che stabilisce subito un'omertà 'tra poveracci.'" Pasolini, *L'Aigle*.

32 Oswald Stack, *Pasolini on Pasolini*, 101.

33 "Aveva perduto [quel valore poetico] per due ragioni: l'impossibilità di Totò a interpretare un 'personaggio cosciente,' in 'possesso dei privilegi

culturali.' … Egli è un 'innocente': ed è come 'innocente' che può divenire poetico. L'altra ragione è la scarsità dei mezzi con cui ho girato l'episodio. Il non avere che quattro lenzuoli bianchi alle pareti, mi ha costretto a girare l'episodio appunto come un ghirigoro in bianco e nero, una specie di illustrazione di se stesso, fatta con due o tre elementi enormemente poveri: il bianco, il nero, qualche grigio (un Léger alla parete), e le facce dei protagonisti. Tutta la possibile abbondanza espressionistica è andata perduta in tanta stilizzazione." Pier Paolo Pasolini, "Confessioni tecniche," 55.

34 Claude Lévi-Strauss, *Tristes Tropiques*, 1281.

35 Stephen Snyder, *Pier Paolo Pasolini*, 79.

36 Stack, *Pasolini on Pasolini*, 101.

37 Pier Paolo Pasolini, "Ecco il mio Totò," *La Repubblica*, 3 August 1976.

38 Cf. Rémi Fournier-Lanzoni, *Comedy Italian Style*, for a detailed explanation of *l'arte di arrangiarsi* – the art of getting by – which was central to the *commedia all'italiana*.

39 Scarpellini, *Material Nation*, 167. She is referencing a 1964 survey, estimating that "6.6 million young Italians had a good 250 billion lire available, which they spent respectively on non-essentials like drinks, cigarettes (50 billion); Vespas and Lambrettas (another 50 billion); clothes, cosmetics, and hairdressers (25 billion); music (23.5 billion, of which 12 on records, 5 on record players, 6.5 on juke-box tokens); transport by motorcycle, bicycle, and car (22 billion); cinema and sports events (21 billion); books, newspapers, magazines, and comics (20.5 billion); and other things (38 billion)."

40 Scarpellini, *Material Nation*, 176.

41 G.K. Chesterton, *St. Francis of Assisi*, 102–3.

42 Chesterton, *St. Francis of Assisi*, 110–11.

43 Leo Politi, *Saint Francis and the Animals*, 3.

44 Chesterton, *St. Francis of Assisi*, 107–8.

45 Viano, *A Certain Realism*, 147.

46 "Round Table on Pasolini with Ninetto Davoli."

47 "quelli che ciànno dato quella ricotta così bona." Pier Paolo Pasolini, screenplay of *Uccellacci e uccellini*, from Pasolini, *Uccellacci e uccellini: Un film*, 118.

48 "Guardate che belle prugne, a frate Ciccillo! Annamose a ffà 'na magnata!" But the food in the pot on-screen is nondescript. Pasolini, screenplay of *Uccellacci e uccellini*, 119.

49 "P'abbuscatte er Paradiso, fijo mio!"

50 "Forse Ninetto sogna a colori. Il blu di Prussia, un po' sgualcito e liso, il morello, il sangue di bue, l'ocra, il grigio pantano … Da una parte c'è un coretto di maschietti, messi tutti in fila, e le file una sopra l'altra. Dall'altra c'è un coretto di femminucce. Il canto è angelico."

51 "Egli vede per prima cosa una lunga tavola di legno coperta da una
tovaglia linda, bianchissima, che ricade tesa sugli spigoli. E sopra, ogni
ben di Dio, ma come l'avrebbe dipinto Giotto, con grande sobrietà e quasi
grandiosità: ricotta, formaggi, pagnotte, scodelle, cocomeri …
 FRATE NINETTO: (*provandoci timidamente*) Ciò 'na fame!
 PADRE ETERNO: Mangia quanto vuoi!
*Ninetto corre al tavolo e si riempie la bocca di ricotta, poi con la bocca piena e le
labbra bianche, si guarda intorno, ridente, e vede:
Contro una purissima paretina trecentesca, un grande letto, e intorno, come
li avesse messi la Befana, un mucchio di giocattoli.*" Pasolini, screenplay of
Uccellacci e uccellini, 131–2.

52 "un primitivo, festosa e nuda." Pasolini, screenplay of *Uccellacci e
uccellini*, 132.

53 CICCILLO: Falchi, falchi, venite, ascoltate … Venite, ascoltate …
 I FALCHI: Chi siete? Che volete?
 CICCILLO: Siamo creature di Dio, vogliamo parlare con voi, creature di
  Dio.
 I FALCHI: Dio? Chi è Dio?
 CICCILLO: Il creatore delle creature.
 I FALCHI: E per quale ragione Dio ci ha creati?
 CICCILLO: Voi perché avete creato i vostri figli?
 I FALCHI: Allora ognuno di noi è Dio.
 CICCILLO: Esagerati! Ecco, non gli puoi dare un po' di considerazione
  che s'allargano subito.
 I FALCHI: E che cosa vuole da noi questo Dio?
 CICCILLO: Amore!
 I FALCHI: AMORE … AMORE!
 *Dissolvenza. Frate Ciccillo e frate Ninetto ridiscendono tutti allegri le strade
  che avevano salito pieni di apprensione e sconforto. Ninetto viene giù quasi
  ballando, come nel suo sogno in Paradiso e frate Ciccillo ha il passo deciso e
  lo sguardo fiero del giusto.*

 Pasolini, screenplay of *Uccellacci e uccellini*, 136.

54 Kathryn St. Ours, "*Uccellacci e uccellini* and the Ambiguities of Bakhtin's
Carnival," 421.

55 CICCILLO: Passeri, venite, ascoltate … Venite, ascoltate …
 I PASSERI: Chi siete? Che volete?
 CICCILLO: Siamo servi del Signore, vogliamo portarvi la buona novella.
 I PASSERI: Oh, finalmente! Era tanto che l'aspettavamo!
 CICCILLO: Questa è bella! Davvero?
 I PASSERI: Eh sì, specialmente d'inverno, quando la neve copre tutto, e
  non si vede più una briciola di cibo in tutta la campagna!

> CICCILLO: Un momento! Che razza di buona novella state aspettando, compari?
>
> I PASSERI: Beh, la buona novella che ci annunci ammassi di miglio, di grano tenero, da farci diventare tutti grassi come tordi!
>
> CICCILLO: Ahi, orbi, quanta fatica dovrò durare a portare tra voi la vera buona novella!
>
> I PASSERI: Beh, che cosa vuole da noi questa vera buona novella?
>
> CICCILLO: Il digiuno!
>
> I PASSERI: Che? Che hai detto?
>
> CICCILLO: Il digiuno! Ma non proprio il digiuno digiuno … Non vogliamo mica farvi morire di fame … insomma il sacrificio, l'amore … Oh, Signore, l'amore!
>
> I PASSERI: Amore … Amore!
>
> *Dissolvenza.*

56 Cf. Gary Chapman, *The Five Love Languages: How to Express Heartfelt Commitment to Your Mate* (1995).

57 Colleen Ryan-Scheutz, *Sex, the Self, and the Sacred*, 94.

58 Pasolini, *My Cinema*, 90. Excerpted from "Le fasi del corvo."

59 Pier Paolo Pasolini, "Le fasi del corvo," 58.

60 Snyder, *Pier Paolo Pasolini*, 75.

61 "Il filosofo ha dovuto precisarsi, poichè senza la precisione non è possibile la semplificazione (necessaria non come elemento obbligatorio, ma come affascinante norma prosodica), per un prodotto i cui destinari siano gli spettatori cinematografici, ecc. ecc." Pasolini, "Le fasi del corvo," 57.

62 Stephen Gundle, *Between Hollywood and Moscow*, 22.

63 Gundle, *Between Hollywood and Moscow*, 66.

64 Simona Bondavalli, *Fictions of Youth*, 131.

65 Gordon, *Pasolini*, 238–9.

66 Pasolini, screenplay of *Uccellacci e uccellini*, 211.

67 Ryan-Scheutz, *Sex, the Self, and the Sacred*, 95.

68 Ryan-Scheutz, *Sex, the Self, and the Sacred*, 95.

69 "Sono finito … è passata la mia ora … Le mie parole cadono nel vuoto."

70 Snyder, *Pier Paolo Pasolini*, 75.

71 "Tanto che sta a 'ffa, me pare pure matto!" Pasolini, screenplay of *Uccellacci e uccellini*, 221.

72 "Amici cari, / come sempre, / finisce così, comincia così, si chiude così, continua così! / questa storia di *Uccellacci e uccellini*."

73 "I professori vanno mangiati in salsa piccante, ma chi li digerisce diventa un po' professore anche lui!"

74 Stack, *Pasolini on Pasolini*, 106.

75 See Gramsci's *Selections from the Prison Notebooks*, 1.48 and 8.236, and his "History of the Subaltern Classes: Methodological Criteria" (1934–5).

76 "Prima di essere mangiato il corvo dice: 'I maestri sono fatti per essere
   mangiati in salsa piccante.' Devono essere mangiati e superati, ma *se il loro
   insegnamento ha un valore ci resterà dentro*." Alessandra Spadino, *Pasolini e il
   cinema "inconsumabile"*, 27. The italics are mine.

77 Pasolini, *My Cinema*, 120–2. Excerpted from *Entretiens avec PPP* (1970), ed.
   Jean Duflot.

78 Pier Paolo Pasolini, *Teorema*, 88.

79 "Che cosa hai distrutto in me?
   Hai distrutto, semplicemente,
   – con tutta la mia vita passata –
   l'idea che io ho sempre avuto di me stesso.
   Se dunque da molto tempo io avevo assunto la forma che dovevo
   assumere
   e la mia figura era, in qualche modo, perfetta,
   ora, che cosa mi rimane?
   Non vedo niente che possa reintegrarmi
   nella mia identità."
   Pasolini, *Teorema*, 91–2. I refer to Stuart Hood's English translation, 88–9.

80 Ryan-Scheutz, *Sex, the Self, and the Sacred*, 154–7.

5. *La grande abbuffata*, or the Reawakening at the End of the World

 1 Scarpellini, *Material Nation*, 178.

 2 Frank Trentmann, "Consumer Society Revisited: Affluence, Choice and
   Diversity," 20.

 3 Emanuela Scarpellini, "L'utopia del consumo totale," 38.

 4 Scarpellini, "L'utopia del consumo totale," 38. Cf. Carol Helstosky, *Garlic
   and Oil*, 143.

 5 Scarpellini, *Material Nation*, 212–13.

 6 Excerpted from Scarpellini, *Material Nation*, 219.

 7 Trentmann, "Consumer Society Revisited," 27.

 8 Trentmann, "Consumer Society Revisited," 20.

 9 Gerda Reith, *Addictive Consumption*, 120.

10 Niki Kiviat and Serena J. Rivera, eds., *(In)digestion in Literature and Film*, 2.
   In the Introduction to our volume, we reference Gilles Deleuze and Félix
   Guattari's *AntiOedipus*, 34.

11 Kiviat and Rivera, eds., *(In)digestion in Literature and Film*, 6. We cite
   Bernard McElroy's *Fiction of the Modern Grotesque* in that the literary
   grotesque functions as an examination of hostile physical worlds that
   "overwhelm the individual, denying him a place and identity" (17),
   surrounding him with violence, brutalization, and dehumanization.

12 Teti, *Il colore del cibo*, 117.

13 George Ritzer, *The McDonaldization of Society*, 14.

14 Laudan, *Cuisine & Empire*, 309.

15 Ritzer, *The McDonaldization of Society*, 32. He bases these ideas on Weber's *Economy and Society* (Totowa, NJ: Bedminster, 1921/68).

16 Ritzer, *The McDonaldization of Society*, 159.

17 Reith, *Addictive Consumption*, 110.

18 Scarpellini, *Material Nation*, 202–3.

19 Counihan, *Around the Tuscan Table*, 179–80.

20 Maurizio Grande, *La commedia all'italiana*, 151–2.

21 Angelo Miglianni, *Marco Ferreri*, 121.

22 Daniele Rugo, "Marco Ferreri," 134–5.

23 Jean-Luc Nancy, *The Sense of the World*, 3.

24   RIAMBAU: *Uno de los aspectos que más me interesa de sus películas es su capacidad para crear nuevos espacios a partir de previos espacios reales, como si fuera un puzzle.*

FERRERI: Esta es una cuestión relacionada con la pregunta de ¿dónde nace el cine? Siempre tiene que nacer de una pequeña historieta porque el cine siguen siendo las imágenes de una pequeña historieta.

RIAMBAU: *Cuando habla de 'pequeña historieta' ¿se refiere a los* fumetti?

FERRERI: No, a pequeños cuentos. Después se produce toda una relación con la imagen que cambia. Pienso que es muy importante la imagen, la estructura, cómo cambia y construye nuevas realidades. Cada historia tiene su imagen. América es una imagen. Hay toda una discursión cotidiana mía, interior, respecto de todo eso. Sin embargo, ahora resulta que lo más importante es la anécdota, el pequeño cuento. Los productores sólo quieren eso.

RIAMBAU: *Sin embargo, sus películas insisten continuamente sobre la creación de nuevas realidades, como la utilización que hizo del hueco de Les Halles para el rodaje de* Touche pas la femme blanche *(1974).*

FERRERI: El cine es cine. Es la fuerza visual. La fuerza de la imagen debe ser, por lo menos, igual a la fuerza del texto. Este, para mí, es mucho menos importante pero eso no se puede decir porque, ahora, todo el mundo pide texto.

Esteve Riambau, "Del neorrealismo a la crisis del cine," 16.

25 Cesare Zavattini, "Some Ideas on the Cinema," 54.

26 Zavattini, "Some Ideas on the Cinema," 54–5.

27 Casimiro Torreiro, "La muerte de la máscara," 68.

28 Torreiro, "La muerte de la máscara," 71.

29 Grande, *La commedia all'italiana*, 155.

30 Roberto Buffagni, ed., *Ugo Tognazzi*.

31 "… poco más que un mono atrapado en los insondables vericuetos de su propia impotencia." Torreiro, "La muerte de la máscara," 68.

32 Gabriele Rigola, *Una storia moderna*, 156.

33 Stephen Gundle, "Sophia Loren," 370.

34 Rigola, *Una storia moderna*, 160–1.

35 "Ho la cucina nel sangue. Il quale, penso, comprenderà senz'altro globuli rossi e globuli bianchi, ma nel mio caso anche una discreta percentuale di salsa di pomodoro … L'attore? A volte mi sembra di farlo per hobby. Mangiare no: io mangio per vivere." Ugo Tognazzi, *L'abbuffone*, 8. His other cookbooks include *Il rigrettario. Fatti, misfatti e menù disegnati al pennarello* (1978); *La mia cucina* (1983); and *Afrodite in cucina* (1984).

36 "Questo frigorifero è la mia cappella di famiglia. Capita che ogni tanto, di mattina, mia moglie mi sorpenda inginocchiato davanti a questo feticcio, a questo totem dell'umana avventura. Me ne sto lì, raccolto in contemplazione, in attesa d'una ispirazione per il pranzo. Questa immagine … può darvi una idea di quanto ascetico sia il mio attaccamento ai prosaici piaceri della tavola, e quindi della vita; e di come, in fondo, io sia da considerare un martire del focolare, anche se sulle braci roventi, in genere, non amo disporre la mia persona ma, sia pur con infinita cura, bracioline di vitellino da latte." Tognazzi, *L'abbuffone*, 7–9.

37 "Cene con dodici amici invitati: gli 'apostoli.'" Fabrizio Natalini, "Ugo Tognazzi," 8.

38 "La cena non ha nulla di formare: è il gusto di stare insieme, è pura convivialità." Natalini, "Ugo Tognazzi," 8.

39 "'straordinario' a 'grandissima cagata' – con biglietti inseriti in un bacile d'argento." Natalini, "Ugo Tognazzi," 8.

40 Donald Dewey, *Marcello Mastroianni*, 213.

41 Paul Guermonprez, "La Grande Bouffe, Arte."

42 Viviana Lapertosa, *Dalla fame all'abbondanza*, 139.

43 Jacqueline Reich, *Beyond the Latin Lover*, 1.

44 Dewey, *Marcello Mastroianni*, 214. There is some debate among scholars as to whether this claim is necessarily accurate. Pascal Schembri, for one, writes that *La grande abbuffata* was actually Mastroianni's last *film corale* because he felt that it was unfair that he was killed off first.

45 "Mastroianni era un uomo con un umorismo innato. Piacevolissimo nonostante la fissazione per il cibo. Passava la giornata di lavoro a pensare a dove saremmo andati a mangiare a fine riprese. La sera, dopo cena, si scolava una bottiglia di grappa intera … L'amore per la vita va di pari passo con l'amore per il cibo e con l'amore per le donne. Mario Monicelli sembra contrapporli in principio, quando sostiene che tutte sul set si innamoravano di lui ma lui non pensava che al cibo. Questo forse perché loro gli si offrivano, il cibo invece se lo doveva cercare, con attenzione,

andando magari a pescare ristorante particolari in luoghi non sempre facili da raggiungere." Schembri, *Marcello Mastroianni*, 155–6.

46 "'Voglio morire, voglio morire, è meglio farla finita,' per poi gettarsi su un piatto di pastasciutta appena fortunosamente sbarcati." Schembri, *Marcello Mastroianni*, 160–1.

47 James R. Keller, *Food, Film and Culture*, 52. For further analysis on masculine performance by way of athletics, please consult Mark Simpson's *Male Impersonators: Men Performing Masculinity* (1993).

48 Angela Bianca Saponari, *Il rifiuto dell'uomo nel cinema di Marco Ferreri*, 41.

49 Volney P. Gay, *Freud on Sublimation*, 96.

50 Gay, *Freud on Sublimation*, 98.

51 For more on Ferreri's "*gioco di annientamento*," see Lapertosa, *Dalla fame all'abbondanza*, 138.

52 Miglianni, *Marco Ferreri*, 116–17.

53 Sam Rohdie, *The Passion of Pier Paolo Pasolini*, 122. Rohdie writes, "At these banquets everything was reversed. The sacred was not found in a celestial heaven, but in terrestrial shit. Pasolini reversed the conventional order of the sacred and in so doing offered a criticism of the existing order, and of order itself, especially that of the authorities, of power. He countered power with shit and in a language often composed of it."

54 Maurizio Sanzio Viano, *A Certain Realism*, 155.

55 Stefania Parigi, "Le immagini di Marco Ferreri," 30.

56 Parigi, "Le immagini di Marco Ferreri," 27.

57 For further reading, I recommend Victoria de Grazia's *How Fascism Ruled Women* (1992).

58 Saponari, *Il rifiuto dell'uomo*, 10.

59 Rémi Fournier-Lanzoni, *Rire de plomb*, 117.

60 "Fu il momento più incontaminato e promettente del cinema. La realtà, sepolta sotto i miti, raffiorava lentamente. Il cinema cominciava la sua creazione del mondo, ecco un albero, ecco un vecchio, ecco una casa, un uomo che mangia, un uomo che dorme, un uomo che piange." Zavattini's words are found in Stefania Parigi, *Fisiologia dell'immagine*, 41–2.

61 Rugo, "Marco Ferreri," 130. The italics are mine.

62 Rugo, "Marco Ferreri," 139.

Conclusion

1 Peter Bondanella, *A History of Italian Cinema*, 201.

2 Carol Helstosky, *Garlic and Oil*, 157.

3 Helstosky, *Garlic and Oil*, 157.

4 Mira Liehm, *Passion and Defiance*, 250.

5 Mira Liehm, *Passion and Defiance*, 250. See also Bondanella, *A History of Italian Cinema*, 497.
6 Bondanella, *A History of Italian Cinema*, 498.
7 Bondanella, *A History of Italian Cinema*, 211.
8 Nick Ramsey, "Pasta Barilla Boycotted after CEO's 'Homophobic' Remarks.'"
9 Nadia Lee Cohen, "Dinner's Ready."

Bibliography and Filmography

Accialini, Fulvio, and Lucia Coluccelli. *Marco Ferreri*. Milan: Edizioni il
  Formichiere, 1979.
Albertoni, Pietro, and Felice Rossi. "Bilancio nutritivo del contadino abruzzese
  e sue condizioni fisiologiche, psichologiche ed economiche." Originally
  published in 1906 and reprinted in Commissione per lo Studio di Problemi
  dell'Alimentazione. *Studi sulla alimentazione di Pietro Albertoni e di Angelo
  Pugliese*. Naples: N. Jovene, 1937.
Anile, Alberto. *I film di Totò, 1946–1967: La maschera tradita*. Genova: Le Mani,
  1998.
Arecco, Sergio. "Il cinema e il suo doppio. Totò e la *pochade*, a prescindere."
  Cineforum 48, no. 1 (January–February 2008): 52–5.
Aristarco, Guido. *La Stampa*, 11 April 1962.
Astarita, Tommaso. *The Italian Baroque Table: Cooking and Entertaining from the
  Golden Age of Naples*. Tempe, AZ: ACMRS, 2014.
Balduini, Consuelo. *Miracoli e boom: L'Italia dal dopoguerra al boom economico
  nell'opera di Cesare Zavattini*. Reggio Emilia: Aliberti, 2013.
Barthes, Roland. "Towards a Psychosociology of Contemporary Food
  Consumption." Excerpted from *Food and Culture: A Reader*. Ed. Carole
  Counihan and Penny Van Esterik. New York: Routledge, 2008.
Baschiera, Stefano. "The Embodiment of the Bourgeoisie: Body and Social
  Class in Pasolini's *Mamma Roma* and Fassbinder's *Martha*." *Pasolini,
  Fassbinder, and Europe: Between Utopia and Nihilism*. Ed. Fabio Vighi and
  Alexis Nouss, 65–81. Newcastle upon Tyne: Cambridge Scholars Publishing,
  2010.
Benini, Stefania. *Pasolini: The Sacred Flesh*. Toronto: University of Toronto
  Press, 2015.
Bernardini, G. Rosi. *Fotosei*, 7 June 1957.
Bertini, Rebecca, and Bianca Cecconi. "Prostitution between Law and
  Gender." Paper sponsored by the Institute of European Law and Gender at

the University of Pisa, 2019–2020; accessed 25 July 2023: https://elan.jus
.unipi.it/elan-studies/publications-and-working-papers/.

Biondillo, Gianni. *Pasolini: Il corpo della città*. Milan: Unicopli, 2001.

Bìspuri, Ennio. *Totò Principe Clown. Tutti i film di Totò*. Naples: Alfredo Guida, 1997.

– *Vita di Totò*. Rome: Gremese, 2000.

Bobroff, Maria Park. "Gluttonous Pleasures: Arlequin, the Nouveau Théâtre Italien, and the Eighteenth-Century French Stage." *Food and Theatre on the World Stage*. Ed. Dorothy Chansky and Ann Folino White. New York: Routledge, 2015.

Bondanella, Peter. *A History of Italian Cinema*. New York: Continuum Publishing, 2009.

Bondavalli, Simona. *Fictions of Youth: Pier Paolo Pasolini, Adolescence, Fascisms*. Toronto: University of Toronto Press, 2015.

Bourdieu, Pierre. *Distinction: A Social Critique of the Judgement of Taste*. Cambridge, MA: Harvard University Press, 1984.

Brewer, John. "Il tempo minimo: Storia culturale e vita quotidiana." *Studi culturali*, 1/2004. Bologna: Il Mulino, 2004.

Brunetta, Gian Piero. *Cent'anni di cinema italiano, Vol. 2: Dal 1945 ai giorni nostri*. Rome: Laterza, 2010.

Buckley, Réka. "Marriage, Motherhood, and the Italian Film Stars of the 1950s." *Women in Italy, 1945–1960: An Interdisciplinary Study*. Ed. Penelope Morris. New York: Palgrave Macmillan, 2006.

Buffagni, Roberto. Ed. *Ugo Tognazzi: La supercazzola*. Milan: Mondadori, 2006.

Cammarota, Domenico. *Il cinema di Totò. La prima guida critica a tutti i film del Principe della Risata*. Rome: Fanucci, 1985.

Capatti, Alberto, and Massimo Montanari. *Italian Cuisine: A Cultural History*. New York: Columbia University Press, 2003.

Carancini, Gaetano. *Fotosei*, 29 April 1960.

Carlorosi, Silvia. "Pier Paolo Pasolini's *La ricotta*: The Power of Cinepoiesis." *Italica* 86, no. 2 (Summer 2009): 254–71.

Centorrino, Mario, ed. *Consumi sociali e sviluppo economico in Italia, 1960–1975*. Rome: Coines Edizioni, 1976.

Chandler, Frank Wadleigh. *Romances of Roguery: An Episode in the History of the Novel*. New York: Macmillan Company, 1899.

Chesterton, G.K. *St. Francis of Assisi*. Garden City, NY: Doubleday, 1931.

Chianese, Gloria. *Storia sociale della donna in Italia, 1800–1980*. Naples: Guida Editori, 1980.

Cohen, Nadia Lee. "Dinner's Ready." Commercial, released 16 October 2019; accessed 8 August 2020: https://www.youtube.com /watch?v=0fdHLN6G9Hc.

Colloquium with Antonio Pietrangeli. *Bianco e Nero*, no. 5, May 1967. Excerpted from Io la conoscevo bene *di Antonio Pietrangeli. Infelicità senza dramma*. Ed. Lino Micciché. Turin: Lindau, 1999.

Corriere d'Informazione, 22 August 1957.
– 4 June 1960.
Il Corriere Lombardo, 23 June 1957.
– 29 June 1957.
– 21 August 1957.
Counihan, Carole. *The Anthropology of Food and the Body: Gender, Meaning, and Power.* New York: Routledge, 1999.
– *Around the Tuscan Table: Food, Family, and Gender in Twentieth-Century Florence.* New York: Routledge, 2004.
La Cucina Italiana, January 1952–December 1960. Milan. Reproduced with thanks to Academia Barilla, Parma, Italy, 17 June 2024.
Curle, Howard, and Stephen Snyder, eds. *Vittorio De Sica: Contemporary Perspectives.* Toronto: University of Toronto Press, 2000.
d'Amico, Masolino. *La commedia all'italiana. Il cinema comico in Italia dal 1945 al 1975.* Milan: Arnoldo Mondadori, 1985.
D'Apice, Carmela. *L'arcipelago dei consumi: Consumi e redditi delle famiglie in Italia dal dopoguerra ad oggi.* Bari: De Donato, 1981.
Darnantier, Vieter. *La Notte*, 9 April 1957.
de Arlucea, Ana V. Perez. "Cervantes y sus personajes eran lo que comían." *El Español*, April 2016: https://www.elespanol.com/reportajes/20160422/119238275_0.html.
de Bonstetten, Charles-Victor. *The Man of the North and the Man of the South.* New York: F.W. Christern, 1864.
Debord, Guy. *The Society of the Spectacle.* New York: Zone Books, 1994.
de Grazia, Victoria. "American Supermarkets versus European Small Shops, or How Transnational Capitalism Crossed Paths with Moral Economy in Italy during the 1960s." Paper delivered in Trondheim, Norway, for the Trondheim Studies on East European Cultures & Societies, March 2002.
– *Irresistible Empire: America's Advance through Twentieth-Century Europe.* Cambridge, MA: Belknap Press/Harvard University Press, 2005.
Deleuze, Gilles, and Félix Guattari. *Anti-Oedipus.* Vol. 1 of *Capitalism and Schizophrenia* (1972). Trans. Robert Hurley, Mark Seem, and Helen R. Lane. London and New York: Continuum, 2004.
Della Casa, Stefano. "Ferreri y el neorrealismo: Historia de una extraña relación." *Antes del apocalipsis: El cine de Marco Ferreri.* Ed. Esteve Riambau. Madrid: Ediciones Cátedra, 1990.
– *Mario Mattoli.* Florence: La Nuova Italia, 1989.
De Martino, Ernesto. *Magic: A Theory from the South.* Trans. Dorothy Louise Zinn. Chicago: HAU Books, 2015.
De Santi, Gualtiero, and Manuel De Sica. *Ieri oggi domani di Vittorio De Sica: Testimonianze, interventi, sceneggiatura.* Rome: Associazione Amici di Vittorio De Sica, 2002.

De Stefano, Stefano. "Peppino attore del futuro." *Per Peppino De Filippo, attore e autore*. Ed. Pasquale Sabbatino and Giuseppina Scognamiglio. Naples: Edizioni Scientifiche Italiane, 2010.

Detassis, Piera. "'A Castelluccio non ci torno più …' Storie di donne nell'Italia di Pietrangeli." *Il cinema di Antonio Pietrangeli*. Ed. Piera Detassis et al. Venice: Marsilio, 1987.

Dewey, Donald. *Marcello Mastroianni: His Life and Art*. New York: Birch Lane Press, 1993.

Douglas, Mary. "Deciphering a Meal (1972)." *Implicit Meanings: Selected Essays in Anthropology*. London: Routledge, 2003.

Dunn, James. Letter to George C. Marshall. Rome, Italy, 17 September 1947. In Mistry, *The United States, Italy, and the Origins of Cold War*.

Dworkin, Andrea. "Prostitution and Male Supremacy." *Michigan Journal of Gender and Law* 1, no. 1 (1993); accessed 26 July 2023: https://repository.law.umich.edu/mjgl/vol1/iss1/1/

Elduque, Albert. "Pasolini and Third World Hunger: An Approach to Cinema Novo through *La ricotta*." *Journal of Italian Cinema & Media Studies* 4, no. 3 (2016): 369–85.

L'Espresso, 7 August 1960.

Faldini, Franca, and Goffredo Fofi, eds. *L'avventurosa storia del cinema italiano raccontata dai suoi protagonisti, 1960–1969*. Milan: Feltrinelli, 1981.

Fàvaro, Angelo. "'Mamma quando si parte?'… Cesira o della madre colpevole." *Atti del Convegno Internazionale (III): Alberto Moravia e La ciociara. Letteratura, storia, cinema*. Ed. Angelo Fàvaro. Avellino: Associazione Culturale Internazionale; Edizioni Sinestesie, 2015.

Fissore, Gianpaolo. "Gli italiani e il cibo sul grande schermo dal secondo dopoguerra a oggi." *Il cibo dell'altro. Movimenti migratori e culture alimentari nella Torino del Novecento*. Ed. Marcella Filippa. Rome: Edizioni Lavoro, 2003.

Fo, Dario. *Totò: Manuale dell'attor comico*. Florence: Vallecchi, 1995.

Fofi, Goffredo. "Totò e Pulcinella." *Totò: Storia di un buffone serissimo*. Ed. Goffredo Fofi and Franca Faldini. Milan: Oscar Storia [Mondadori], 2004.

Fofi, Goffredo, and Franca Faldini. *Totò, l'uomo e la maschera*. Rome: Edizioni Minimum, 2017.

Fournier-Lanzoni, Rémi. *Rire de plomb. La comédie à l'italienne des années 70*. Paris: L'Harmattan, 2017.

– *Comedy Italian Style: The Golden Age of Italian Film Comedies*. New York: Continuum, 2008.

Frosini, Fabio. "¿Qué es la 'crisis de hegemonía?' Apuntes sobre historia, revolución y visibilidad en Gramsci." *Las Torres de Lucca* 6, no. 11 (2017): 45–71.

Fullwood, Natalie. "*Commedie al femminile:* The Gendering of Space in Three Films by Antonio Pietrangeli." *Italian Studies* 65, no. 1 (2010): 85–106.

Garrick, Jacqueline. "The Humor of Trauma Survivors: Its Applications in a Therapeutic Milieu." *Trauma Treatment Techniques: Innovative Trends.* Ed. Jacqueline Garrick and Mary Beth Williams. Binghamton, NY: Haworth Maltreatment and Trauma Press, 2006.

Gatta, Alessandro. *Sophia Loren.* Rome: Gremese, 2014.

Gay, Volney P. *Freud on Sublimation: Reconsiderations.* Albany: State University of New York Press, 1992.

La Gazzetta del Mezzogiorno, 15 March 1966.

Gelsi, Salvatore. *Lo schermo in tavola. Cibo, film e generi cinematografici.* Mantua: Tre Lune, 2002.

Gente, 12 March 1964.

Gibson, Mary. *Prostitution and the State in Italy, 1860–1915.* New Brunswick, NJ: Rutgers University Press, 1986.

Giddens, Anthony. "Time, Space, and Regionalisation." *Social Relations and Spatial Structures.* Ed. Derek Gregory and John Urry. London: Macmillan, 1985.

Ginsborg, Paul. *A History of Contemporary Italy.* London: Penguin Books, 2003.

Giornale del Mattino, 7 May 1961.

Il Giorno, 11 April 1957.

– 23 June 1957.

– 11 September 1957.

– 28 September 1957.

– 24 November 1957.

– 15 December 1957.

Goethe, Johann Wolfgang von. *Italian Journey.* New York: Penguin Classics, 1971.

Good News Bible. Philadelphia: American Bible Society, 1992.

Gordon, Robert S. *Pasolini: Forms of Subjectivity.* Oxford: Clarendon Press, 1996.

Gottardi, Alessandro, et al. "Le migrazioni Sud-Nord dal dopoguerra ad oggi" (2003); accessed 1 November 2018: http://www.cpc-chiasso.ch [full document no longer available online].

Governi, Giancarlo. *Alberto Sordi: Un italiano come noi.* Milan: Milano Libri Edizioni, 1979.

Gramsci, Antonio. *Selections from the Prison Notebooks.* Ed. and trans. Quintin Hoare and Geoffrey Nowell-Smith. London: Lawrence & Wishart, 2005.

Grande, Maurizio. *La commedia all'italiana.* Ed. Orio Caldiron. Rome: Bulzoni, 2003.

– "Caricare il reale. Il volto dell'attore nel cinema di Ferreri." *Si fa per ridere … ma è una cosa seria. Aspetti del cinema comico italiano dal dopoguerra a oggi.* Ed. Sandro Bernardi. Florence: La Casa Usher, 1985.

Gribaudi, Gabriella. "Neapolitan Mothers: Three Generations of Women, from Representation to Reality." *La mamma: Interrogating a National Stereotype.* Ed. Penelope Morris and Perry Willson. New York: Palgrave Macmillan, 2018.

Guermonprez, Paul. "La Grande Bouffe, Arte: 8 choses à savoir sur ce film à scandale." *Télé Star*. 17 July 2016; accessed 12 February 2019: https://www.telestar.fr/culture/la-grande-bouffe-arte-8-choses-a-savoir-sur-ce-film-a-scandale-photos-219670.

Gundle, Stephen. *Between Hollywood and Moscow: The Italian Communists and the Challenge of Mass Culture, 1943–1991*. Durham, NC, and London: Duke University Press, 2000.

– "Sophia Loren: Italian Icon." *Historical Journal of Film, Radio, and Television* 15, no. 3 (1995): 367–85.

Hebdige, Dick. *Hiding in the Light: On Images and Things*. London: Routledge, 1989.

Heidegger, Martin. "Building Dwelling Thinking" (1951). From *Poetry, Language, Thought*. Trans. Albert Hofstadter. New York: Harper Colophon Books, 1971.

Helstosky, Carol. *Garlic and Oil: Politics and Food in Italy*. Oxford: Berg Publishers, 2004.

– *Pizza: A Global History*. London: Reaktion Books, 2008.

Hotchner, A.E. *Sophia: Living and Loving*. New York: William Morrow and Company, 1979.

Jovane, Paolo. *Corriere d'Informazione*, 11 September 1957.

Kanin, Garson. *Together Again! Stories of the Great Hollywood Teams*. Garden City, NY: Doubleday & Company, 1981.

Keller, James R. *Food, Film and Culture. A Genre Study*. Jefferson, NC: McFarland, 2006.

Kiviat, Niki, and Serena J. Rivera, eds. *(In)digestion in Literature and Film: A Transcultural Approach*. London: Routledge, 2020.

Kuisel, Richard. *Seducing the French: The Dilemma of Americanization*. Berkeley and Los Angeles: University of California Press, 1993.

Lapertosa, Viviana. *Dalla fame all'abbondanza: Gli italiani e il cibo nel cinema italiano dal dopoguerra a oggi*. Turin: Lindau, 2002.

Laudan, Rachel. *Cuisine & Empire: Cooking in World History*. Berkeley and Los Angeles: University of California Press, 2013.

Lawrence-Doyle, Georgia. "From Arlecchino to Wertmuller: Modern Italian archetypes in the *commedia all'italiana*." *Modern Italy* 22, no. 3 (2017): 275–89.

Legge Merlin, 20 February 1958, no. 75: "Abolizione della regolamentazione della prostituzione e lotta contro lo sfruttamento della prostituzione altrui"; accessed April 2018: http://www.altalex.com/documents/leggi/2013/10/24/legge-merlin.

Legge ordinaria no. 43, approved by the Chamber of Deputies and Senate of the Republic, 28 February 1949; accessed 11 January 2018: http://www.normattiva.it/uri-res/N2Ls?urn:nir:stato:legge:1949-02-28;43.

Lévi-Strauss, Claude. *Tristes Tropiques* (1955). Trans. John and Doreen Weightman. Excerpted in *The Norton Anthology of Theory and Criticism*, 2nd edition. Ed. Vincent B. Leitch et al. New York: W.W. Norton & Company, 2010.

Liehm, Mira. *Passion and Defiance: Film in Italy from 1942 to the Present.* Berkeley: University of California Press, 1984.

Lirani, Mauro. *La Settimana Incom*, 4 May 1957.

Loren, Sophia. *In cucina con amore.* Milan: Rizzoli, 2013.

– [As Sofia Loren] *Gente*, 13 April 1968.

– *Women & Beauty.* New York: William Morrow and Company, 1984.

– *Yesterday, Today, Tomorrow: My Life.* New York: Atria Books, 2014.

Marcus, Millicent. *Italian Film in the Light of Neorealism.* Princeton: Princeton University Press, 1986.

Mariani, Manuela, and Patrick Barron. "Cinematic Space in Rome's Disabitato: Between Metropolis and Terrain Vague in the Films of Fellini, Antonioni, and Pasolini." *Modernism/Modernity* 18, no. 2 (2011).

Martellini, Luigi. *Ritratto di Pasolini.* Rome: Laterza, 2006.

Matthews, Roger. *Prostitution, Politics, and Policy.* Abingdon: Routledge, 2008.

McElroy, Bernard. *Fiction of the Modern Grotesque.* London: Palgrave Macmillan, 1989.

Miglianni, Angelo. *Marco Ferreri: La distruzione dell'uomo storico.* Pisa: ETS, 1984.

Mistry, Kaeten. *The United States, Italy, and the Origins of Cold War: Waging Political Warfare, 1945–1950.* Cambridge: Cambridge University Press, 2014.

Moe, Nelson. "Naples '44 / 'Tammuriata Nera' / *Ladri di biciclette*." *Italy and America, 1943–44: Italian, American, and Italian-American Experiences of the Liberation of the Mezzogiorno.* Ed. John A. Davis. Naples: Città del Sole, 1997.

– *The View from Vesuvius: Italian Culture and the Southern Question.* Los Angeles and Berkeley: University of California Press, 2002.

Momigliano, Franco, and Alessandro Pizzorno. "Consumi in Italia." *Consumi sociali e sviluppo economico in Italia, 1960–1975.* Ed. Mario Centorrino. Rome: Coines Edizioni, 1976.

Monterde, José Enrique. "De la decadencia a la utopía." *Antes del apocalipsis: El cine de Marco Ferreri.* Ed. Esteve Riambau. Madrid: Ediciones Cátedra, 1990.

Morandini, Morando. "Il milanese in Spagna." *Matrimonio in bianco e nero: L'ape regina.* Rome: Carocci, 1963.

– *La Notte*, 18 December 1957.

Moravia, Alberto. *La ciociara.* Milan: Bompiani, 1957.

Moro, Elisabetta, and Marino Niola. *Andare per i luoghi della dieta mediterranea.* Bologna: Il Mulino, 2017.

Mottura, Glenda. "Totò: La maschera, il corpo, il linguaggio dell'assurdo." Thesis completed at L'Università degli Studi di Torino, 2001; accessed 17 September 2018 through the Bibliomediateca Mario Gromo, Turin, Italy.

Murphy, Jill. "Dark Fragments: Contrasting Corporealities in Pasolini's *La ricotta*." *Alphaville: Journal of Film and Screen Media* no. 7 (Summer 2014). ISSN: 2009-4078.

Murri, Serafino. *Pier Paolo Pasolini*. Rome: Il Castoro, 1994.

Naldi, Ugo, in conversation with Sophia Loren. *Corriere d'Informazione*, 7 June 1961.

Nancy, Jean-Luc. *The Sense of the World*. Trans. Jeffrey S. Librett. Minneapolis: University of Minnesota Press, 1997.

Nassau, William, Sr. *Journals Kept in France and Italy from 1848 to 1852, with a Sketch of the Revolution of 1848*. 2 vols. Ed. M.C. Simpson. London: Henry S. King, 1871.

Natalini, Fabrizio. "Ugo Tognazzi: l'uomo immagine della cucina italiana." *SINESTESIONLINE* no. 10 (December 2014): 7–37.

Newsweek, 23 January 1967.

Niceforo, Alfredo. *Italiani del Nord e italiani del Sud*. Turin: Fratelli Bocca, 1901.

La Notte, 10 April 1962.

Nowell-Smith, Geoffrey. "Pasolini's Originality." *Pier Paolo Pasolini*. Ed. Paul Willemen. London: British Film Institute, 1977.

Ottai, Antonella, ed. *Peppino De Filippo: Vita è arte*. Turin: Rai Eri, 2003.

Papazoglou, Konstantinos. "Humor and Trauma." *Encyclopedia of Trauma: An Interdisciplinary Guide*. Ed. Charles R. Figley. Thousand Oaks, CA: SAGE Publications, 2012.

Parigi, Stefania. *Fisiologia dell'immagine. Il pensiero di Cesare Zavattini*. Turin: Lindau, 2006.

– "Le immagini di Marco Ferreri." *Marco Ferreri: Un milanese a Roma*. Ed. Graziella Azzaro and Stefania Parigi. Rome: Tiellemedia, 2007.

Pasolini, Pier Paolo. "L'Aigle." *Vie Nuove* no. 7. Published 29 April 1965; found in the *Vie Nuove* collection, April–June 1965.

– "Le ceneri di Gramsci." *Pasolini: Poesie e pagine ritrovate*. Ed. Andrea Zanzotto and Nico Naldini. Rome: Lato Side, 1980.

– "Confessioni tecniche." *Uccellacci e uccellini: Un film di Pier Paolo Pasolini*. Ed. Giacomo Gambetti. Milan: Garzanti, 1966.

– "Ecco il mio Totò." *La Repubblica*. In conversation with Pier Paolo Pasolini. 3 August 1976.

– "Is Being Natural? (1967)." *Heretical Empiricism*. Ed. Ben Lawton and Louise K. Barnett. Trans. Louise K. Barnett. Bloomington: Indiana University Press, 1988.

– "Le fasi del corvo." *Uccellacci e uccellini: Un film*. Ed. Giacomo Gambetti. Milan: Garzanti, 1966.

– *Mamma Roma: La prima sceneggiatura*. Milan: Rizzoli, 1962.

– "*Mamma Roma*: ovvero dalla responsabilità individuale alla responsabilità collettiva." Interview with Nino Ferrero and Dora Mignano. *Filmcritica* no. 125 (September 1962): 440–50.
– *My Cinema*. Ed. Graziella Chiarcossi and Roberto Chiesi. Trans. Stephen Sartarelli et al. Bologna: Edizioni Cineteca di Bologna and Luce Cinecittà, 2012.
– "Observations on the Sequence Shot (1967)." *Heretical Empiricism*. Ed. Ben Lawton and Louise K. Barnett. Trans. Louise K. Barnett. Bloomington: Indiana University Press, 1988.
– "Picasso." *Tutte le poesie, Vol. 1.* Ed. Walter Siti. Milan: Mondadori, 2003.
– *Il sogno del centauro*. Ed. Jean Duflot. Rome: Editori Riuniti, 1983.
– *Teorema*. Milan: Garzanti, 1968.
– *Theorem*. Trans. Stuart Hood. London: Quartet Encounters, 1992.
Pateman, Carole. "What's Wrong with Prostitution?" *Women's Studies Quarterly* 27, no. 1/2 (Spring–Summer 1999): 53–64.
Patriarca, Emanuela. *Totò nel cinema di poesia di Pier Paolo Pasolini*. Florence: Firenze Atheneum, 2006.
Pellè, Loredana. *Mezzogiorno e il piano Marshall*. Manduria (Taranto): P. Lacaita, 2009.
Pensotti, Anita. *Le italiane*. Milan: Simonelli, 1999.
– *Oggi*, 22 December 1966.
Petraroli, Ornella. "Totò e Peppino come Arena e Troisi. Due esempi di coppie comiche." *Per Peppino De Filippo, attore e autore*. Ed. Pasquale Sabbatino and Giuseppina Scognamiglio. Naples: Edizioni Scientifiche Italiane, 2010.
Petri, Elio. "Volonté Totò ecc." Letter received by Franca Faldini, 11 August 1981; accessed 18 September 2018 at the Historical Archives of the Museo Nazionale del Cinema, Turin, Italy.
Platina. *On Right Pleasure and Good Health* (circa 1465). Ed. Mary Ella Milham. Tempe, AZ: Medieval & Renaissance Text Studies, 1998.
Politi, Leo. *Saint Francis and the Animals*. New York: Charles Scribner's Sons, 1959.
Poole, Gordon. "Totò's Talking Body." *Gesture* 7, no. 2 (2007): 241–53.
Prestipino, Giuliana. "Il comico popolare nel cinema: Totò e Peppino." Thesis completed at L'Università degli Studi di Torino, 2004; accessed 17 September 2018 through the Bibliomediateca Mario Gromo, Turin, Italy.
Ramsey, Nick. "Pasta Barilla Boycotted after CEO's 'Homophobic' Remarks." *MSNBC*, 26 September 2013; accessed 8 August 2020: http://www.msnbc.com/the-last-word/pasta-barilla-boycotted-after-ceos.
Ravesi, Giacomo. "Cinema, vita ed esperienza urbana." *Marco Ferreri: Un milanese a Roma*. Ed. Graziella Azzaro and Stefania Parigi. Rome: Tiellemedia, 2007.
Rees, Jonathan. *Refrigeration Nation: A History of Ice, Appliances, and Enterprise in America*. Baltimore: Johns Hopkins University Press, 2013.

"Refrigerator a Luxury in British Homes." *Times of London*. 25 September 1957; accessed via Web Archives 19 November 2024: https://www.thetimes.com /tto/archive/find/refrigerator/w:1957-08-01~1957-12-31/1.

Reich, Jacqueline. *Beyond the Latin Lover: Marcello Mastroianni, Masculinity, and Italian Cinema*. Bloomington: Indiana University Press, 2004.

Reith, Gerda. *Addictive Consumption: Capitalism, Modernity, and Excess*. London: Routledge, 2018.

Rhodes, John David. *Stupendous, Miserable City: Pasolini's Rome*. Minneapolis: University of Minnesota Press, 2007.

Riambau, Esteve. "Del neorrealismo a la crisis del cine. Una conversación con Marco Ferreri." *Antes del apocalipsis: El cine de Marco Ferreri*. Ed. Esteve Riambau. Madrid: Ediciones Cátedra, 1990.

Rigola, Gabriele. *Una storia moderna. Ugo Tognazzi: cinema, cultura e società italiana*. New York: Kaplan, 2018.

Ritzer, George. *The McDonaldization of Society: An Investigation into the Changing Character of Contemporary Social Life*. Thousand Oaks, CA: SAGE, 1996.

Roache, Madeline. "Is Capitalism or Communism Better for Women? How the Kitchen Debate Gave a New Meaning to the Cold War 'Home Front.'" *TIME*, 24 July 2019; accessed 29 July 2024: https://time.com/5630567 /kitchen-debate-women/.

Rocchio, Vincent F. "Patriarchy Has Failed Us: The Continuing Legacy of Neorealism in Contemporary Italian Film." *Quarterly Review of Film and Video* 29, no. 2 (2012): 147–62.

Rohdie, Sam. "Neo-Realism and Pasolini: The Desire for Reality." *Pasolini Old and New: Surveys and Studies*. Ed. Zygmunt Baranski. Dublin: Four Courts Press, 1999.

– *The Passion of Pier Paolo Pasolini*. Bloomington: Indiana University Press, 1995.

"Round Table on Pasolini with Ninetto Davoli." Sponsored by NYU's Casa Italiana Zerilli-Marimò, 12 December 2012; accessed via YouTube 23 April 2019: https://www.youtube.com/watch?v=_J9xBNaL0Qo.

Rugo, Daniele. "Marco Ferreri: The Task of Cinema and the End of the World." *Journal of Italian Cinema & Media Studies* 1, no. 2 (2013): 129–41.

Ryan-Scheutz, Colleen. *Sex, the Self, and the Sacred: Women in the Cinema of Pier Paolo Pasolini*. Toronto: University of Toronto Press, 2007.

Sala, Americo. *Corriere d'Informazione*, 11 April 1962.

Salvatori, Maria Paola Moroni. "Ragguaglio bibliografico sui ricettari del primo Novecento." *Storia d'Italia, Annali 13: L'alimentazione*. Turin: Einaudi, 1998.

Saponari, Angela Bianca. *Il rifiuto dell'uomo nel cinema di Marco Ferreri*. Bari: Progedit, 2008.

Sartoni, Eleonora. "*(Mamma) Roma* between Archaic and Modern Italy: Urbanisation and the Destruction of Poetical Dwelling." *Senses of Cinema* no. 77 (The Legacy of Pier Paolo Pasolini) (December 2015).

Scarpellini, Emanuela. *Food and Foodways in Italy from 1861 to the Present.* Trans. Noor Giovanni Mazhar. Houndmills, Basingstoke, Hampshire: Palgrave Macmillan, 2016.

– *Material Nation: A Consumer's History of Modern Italy.* Oxford: Oxford University Press, 2011.

– "L'utopia del consumo totale. L'evoluzione dei luoghi di consume." *Il secolo dei consumi: dinamiche sociali nell'Europa del Novecento.* Ed. Stefano Cavazza and Emanuela Scarpellini. Rome: Carocci, 2006.

Scarpetta, Eduardo. *Miseria e nobiltà* (1887). *Miseria e nobiltà e altre commedie.* Ed. Vanda Monaco. Naples: Guida, 1980.

Schain, Martin, ed. *The Marshall Plan: Fifty Years After.* New York: New York University Press, 2001.

Schembri, Pascal. *Marcello Mastroianni. Lo spessore della trasparenza.* Rome: Edizioni Sabinae, 2016.

Scuriatti, Massimiliano. *E io lo nacqui: Totò, o l'arte della commedia bassa.* Milan: Bietti, 2015.

Snyder, Stephen. "Hiding in the Light: De Sica's Work in the 1960s." *Vittorio De Sica: Contemporary Perspectives.* Ed. Howard Curle and Stephen Snyder. Toronto: University of Toronto Press, 2000.

– *Pier Paolo Pasolini.* Boston: Twayne Publishers, 1980.

Spadino, Alessandra. *Pasolini e il cinema "inconsumabile": Una prospettiva critica della modernità.* Milan: Mimesis Edizioni, 2012.

Sperber, Dan. *Rethinking Symbolism.* Trans. Alice L. Morton. Cambridge: Cambridge University Press, 1975.

Stack, Oswald. *Pasolini on Pasolini: Interviews with Oswald Stack.* Bloomington: Indiana University Press, 1969.

Stasera, 4 September 1962.

St. Ours, Kathryn. "*Uccellacci e uccellini* and the Ambiguities of Bakhtin's Carnival." *Forum Italicum* 43, no. 2 (2009): 418–32.

Sutton, David E. *Remembrance of Repasts: An Anthropology of Food and Memory.* Oxford: Berg, 2001.

Tambor, Molly. "Mothers, Workers, Citizens: Teresa Noce and the Parliamentary Politics of Motherhood." *La mamma: Interrogating a National Stereotype.* Ed. Penelope Morris and Perry Willson. New York: Palgrave Macmillan, 2018.

– "Prostitutes and Politicians: The Women's Rights Movement in the Legge Merlin Debates." *Women in Italy, 1945–1960: An Interdisciplinary Study.* Ed. Penelope Morris. New York: Palgrave Macmillan, 2005.

Teti, Vito. "The Alimentary Cultures of the Mediterranean: Tradition and Invention in the Dietary Regimes of the Italian South." *The Mediterranean*

Reconsidered: Representations, Emergences, Recompositions. Ed. Mauro Peressini and Ratiba Hadj-Moussa. Ottawa: University of Ottawa Press, 2005.

– *Il colore del cibo: Geografia, mito e realtà dell'alimentazione mediterranea.* Rome: Meltemi, 1999.

TIME, 23 December 1966.

Tognazzi, Ugo. *L'abbuffone: Storie da ridere e ricette da morire.* Milan: Rizzoli, 1974.

Torreiro, Casimiro. "La muerte de la máscara. El actor en el cine de Ferreri." *Antes del apocalipsis: El cine de Marco Ferreri.* Ed. Esteve Riambau. Madrid: Ediciones Cátedra, 1990.

Totò. *Fegato qua, fegato là, fegato fritto e baccalà.* Ed. Liliana de Curtis and Matilde Amorosi. Milan: Rizzoli, 2001.

– "Malafemmena." Song. 1951; accessed 19 November 2018: https:// lyricstranslate.com/en/malafemmena-bad-woman.html.

Trentmann, Frank. "Consumer Society Revisited: Affluence, Choice and Diversity." *Transformations of Retailing in Europe after 1945.* Ed. Ralph Jessen and Lydia Langer. Farnham: Ashgate Publishing, 2012.

Treveri Gennari, Daniela. "A Regional Charm: Italian Comedy versus Hollywood." *October* (MIT Press) 128: *Postwar Italian Cinema: New Studies* (Spring 2009): 51–68.

Valenze, Deborah. *Milk: A Local and Global History.* New Haven: Yale University Press, 2011.

Van Ness, Emma. "Antonio Pietrangeli, the Director of Women: Feminism, Film Theory, and Practice in Postwar Italy." PhD dissertation, UCLA, 2013.

Verga, Giovanni. *Cavalleria Rusticana and Other Stories.* Trans. G.H. McWilliam. London: Penguin Books, 1999 edition.

Viano, Maurizio Sanzio. *A Certain Realism: Making Use of Pasolini's Film Theory and Practice.* Berkeley: University of California Press, 1993.

Zamagni, Vera. *The Economic History of Italy, 1860–1990.* Oxford: Clarendon Press, 1993.

Zanini De Vita, Oretta. *Popes, Peasants, and Shepherds: Recipes and Lore from Rome and Lazio.* Berkeley: University of California Press, 2013.

Zavattini, Cesare. "I pesci rossi e il disonesto" (1946), in *Neorealismo ecc.* Ed. Mino Argentieri. Milan: Bompiani, 1979.

– "Some Ideas on the Cinema." *Vittorio De Sica: Contemporary Perspectives.* Ed. Howard Curle and Stephen Snyder. Toronto: University of Toronto Press, 2000.

Žižek, Slavoj. *Enjoy Your Symptom: Jacques Lacan in Hollywood and Out.* New York: Routledge, 1992.

Filmography

Brusati, Franco. Dir. *Pane e cioccolata*. Prod. Maurizio Lodi-Fe. 1974.

De Sica, Vittorio. Dir. *I bambini ci guardano*. Prod. Scalera Film. 1943.

– Dir. *La ciociara*. Prod. Compagnia Cinematografica Champion. 1960.

– Dir. *Ieri, oggi, domani*. Prod. Carlo Ponti. 1963.

– Dir. *Ladri di biciclette*. Prod. Produzioni De Sica. 1948.

– Dir. *L'oro di Napoli*. Prod. Ponti–De Laurentiis. 1954.

– Dir. *Sciuscià*. Prod. Alfa Cinematografica. 1946.

– Dir. *Umberto D*. Prod. Rizzoli. 1952.

Ferreri, Marco. Dir. *La carne*. Prod. M.M.D. 1991.

– Dir. *El cochecito*. Prod. Film 59/Paramount Pictures. 1961.

– Dir. *Dillinger è morto*. Prod. Pegaso Srl. 1969.

– Dir. *La grande abbuffata*. Prod. Marafilms. 1973.

– Dir. *Il seme dell'uomo*. Prod. Polifilm/Cineriz. 1969.

Mastrocinque, Camillo. Dir. *Totò, Peppino e … i fuorilegge*. Prod. D.D.L. 1956.

– Dir. *Totò, Peppino e … la malafemmina*. Prod. D.D.L. 1956.

Mattoli, Mario. Dir. *Miseria e nobiltà*. Prod. Lux Film. 1954.

– Dir. *Signori si nasce*. Prod. D.D.L. 1960.

Monicelli, Mario. Dir. *La mortadella*. Prod. Compagnia Cinematografica Champion. 1971.

– Dir. *I soliti ignoti*. Prod. Lux Film. 1958.

Özpetek, Ferzan. Dir. *Mine vaganti*. Prod. Domenico Procacci/Fandango. 2010.

Pasolini, Pier Paolo. Dir. *Mamma Roma*. Prod. Janus Films. 1962.

– *La ricotta* (as seen in the omnibus film *Ro.Go.Pa.G.*, dir. Jean-Luc Godard et al.). Prod. Arco Film. 1963.

– Dir. *Teorema*. Prod. Manolo Bolognini and Franco Rossellini. 1968.

– Dir. *Uccellacci e uccellini*. Prod. Alfredo Bini. 1966.

Pietrangeli, Antonio. Dir. *Adua e le compagne*. Prod. Titanus. 1960.

– Dir. *La parmigiana*. Prod. Gianni Hecht Lucari. 1963.

Risi, Dino, et al. Dir. *Paradiso per tre ore* (as seen in the omnibus film *L'amore in città*). Prod. DCN. 1953.

Rossellini, Roberto. Dir. *Germania anno zero*. Prod. Tevere Film and Salvo D'Angelo Produzione. 1948.

– Dir. *Roma città aperta*. Prod. Excelsa. 1945.

Steno. Dir. *Un americano a Roma*. Prod. Titanus/Minerva Film. 1954.

Index

Series Editors: Jayeeta (Jo) Sharma, H. Rosi Song, and Robert Davidson